May the

But not too...

All the best

Antonio

C000175069

The Working Man's Ballet

The Working Man's Ballet

Alan Hudson

Robson Books

First published in Great Britain in 1997 by Robson Books Ltd,
Bolsover House, 5–6 Clipstone Street, London W1P 8LE

Copyright © 1997 Alan Hudson

The right of Alan Hudson to be identified as author of this
work has been asserted by him in accordance with the
Copyright, Designs and Patents Act 1988

British Library Cataloguing in Publication Data
A catalogue record for this title is available from the British
Library

ISBN 1 86105 104 2

All rights reserved. No part of this publication may be
reproduced, stored in a retrieval system, or transmitted in any
form or by any means, electronic, mechanical, photocopying,
recording or otherwise, without the prior permission in writing
of the publishers.

Photoset in North Wales by Derek Doyle & Associates, Mold,
Flintshire. Printed and bound in Great Britain by Butler &
Tanner Ltd, London and Frome.

Contents

Devil in a Blue Shirt
A Foreword by Terry Venables

I coached Alan Hudson when he was twelve, during my spell at Chelsea in the early sixties. He had undoubted talent and was as good with the ball as anyone I ever saw. The first time I ever played against him was at Loftus Road in the FA Cup in 1970. I was playing for QPR, and Alan had recently broken into the Chelsea side. Chelsea went on to win the FA Cup that year. Brazil lifted the World Cup a few months later.

I considered Alan to be a little slight for the conditions and decided to get stuck into him early on. The Chelsea midfielder literally ran me off my feet. I could not believe how strong he was. I had never seen such powerful runs. That day he was truly amazing. It was an unbelievable performance by such a young player. Sir Alf Ramsey watched that game and Alan's display prompted his famous quote about his potential: 'There is no limit to what this boy can achieve.' He never spoke a truer word.

Glenn Hoddle told me there was one reason why he learned to practise and master the ball the way he did and that was because he saw Brazil and the great players of that era play on television when he was a kid. Alan deserves to rank alongside those names.

Cockney Rebel
by Dennis Waterman

Having been brought up in Putney, I'm naturally a Chelsea fan, and a season-ticket holder of the late sixties. I believe the seventies team was one of the most entertaining in Britain at that time, and that Alan was pivotal in that great team. He became an immediate hero to us Sunday League players. Good-looking, great vision and fantastic flair. I was fortunate to meet many of the team, and found that in the evening Alan had even more flair and amazing stamina. We had some seriously good times!

I've played football with him (I scored, he didn't), I've socialised with him and I've laughed a lot with him. I've moaned about how few caps he got and I've even forgiven him for going to Arsenal. Basically he was a wonderful footballer and a smashing bloke, and still is.

So from one Cockney Rebel to another, thanks for all those great times, both on and off the pitch. Cheers, mate!

The Pleasure and the Pain
by the late Matthew Harding

How can I ever begin to describe how I feel about Chelsea, the club I have loved, cherished and adored for more than thirty years? Indeed, ask any football supporter to put their feelings about their club into words and they would have trouble telling you.

I am no exception. My love affair with Chelsea began at the tender age of 8¾. I can even remember the date and the match clearly: 3 November 1962, Chelsea versus Newcastle United. They were in the old Second Division then. I can even remember where I sat: in the front row of the old North Stand, perched high above the corner flag. From that day, I was smitten. It was the start of a special relationship that has never waned. Chelsea Football Club has meant more to me than even I thought possible.

I am a fan, pure and simple. Unlike many boys, I never dreamed of playing for my club, not that I was good enough. Being a fan was good enough for me. The sense of belonging that being a supporter brings has given me joy beyond belief. I never chose to support Chelsea. I was taken there by my father and didn't have much say in the matter. But it was love at first sight and that is how it should be. That's why I did exactly the same with my own children a quarter of a century later, and like me, they are now all Chelsea die-hards.

Any player wearing Chelsea blue has been the object of my

devotion which has never faltered in thirty years. Blue was and is the colour as far as I'm concerned. As long as he wore the blue Chelsea shirt, that was all that mattered. Once a Chelsea player moved to another club and the initial sense of loss and grieving was over, I would eliminate him from my thoughts; I still do. Similarly, if a player from a rival club came to Chelsea, he would have my undying support the minute he put on the Chelsea strip. I can't really explain why – can any fan?

Chelsea players have come in and out of my life and I have in turn worshipped and adored them. From Bobby Tambling in the sixties to Ruud Gullit in the nineties, all have had my undying support and devotion. Alan Hudson is no exception.

I was there when he scored his first home goal against Sheffield Wednesday at Stamford Bridge in March 1970. It was an evening game and from my vantage point in the North Stand, I watched as he appeared to glide effortlessly towards me. The Wednesday defenders seemed to move out of his way as he strode towards the goal before sliding the ball deliciously past the keeper from just inside the penalty area. When Alan scored that goal, he did it just for me. No one was happier than I was that night, jumping up and down in my seat. I'm sure my joy matched his. But tragedy struck just five days later. Alan damaged his ankle ligaments very badly at West Bromwich Albion, a match that appropriately we lost. With the Cup Final only a fortnight away, I was distraught. The pain I felt when I heard the news must have been as great as his. I was only sixteen at the time but twenty-five years later my memories are just as vivid.

I never felt the need to meet Alan – with that Chelsea shirt on his back I already knew him. He was part of my life and that was that. But recently I have had the good fortune to meet him and it has been like greeting an old friend. It must be the blue blood that runs through his veins! The pleasure and the pain – Chelsea is both those things to me. It's hard to explain but like any great love I don't question it or ever feel tempted to stray. I just know that Chelsea and I were meant for each other.

Introduction
by Alan A Hudson

It was 3.30am, and I was as usual feeling very melancholy. I felt that at this time of the morning, just home from a night out with the boys, I should just sit down at my bar, fix myself my favourite tipple, Crown Royal and ginger ale with a slice of orange on top of a crystal glass of ice, and let Frank Sinatra take over.

It was 148 South East 48th Drive, Belle Vue, Seattle, Washington, USA. The house of my dreams. Many miles from our Chelsea prefab. Along with Sinatra, it was my inspiration. It gave me the feeling of achievement. That night I decided to write my life story, 21 June 1981, thirty years after my birth in St Stephens Hospital situated in the Fulham Road, Chelsea, just about half a mile from Stamford Bridge. As I sat listening to my all-time favourite songster, looking out over this most beautiful city, I realised that I had come many miles, seen many places, met more than enough people, and ended up in a place which I just did not want to leave. It was the place I had been looking for all my days, it was the only love I have ever had that I truly miss – apart from my family that is – and would return to.

Born Alan Anthony Hudson on the 21 June exactly thirty years earlier, I was the second son of Bill and Bub. I had the most wonderful upbringing, and put all my success down to that. The appreciation of good things. On this evening my inspiration was that of feeling that I would never see these shores again. I really felt I had found my resting place. The man upstairs had other ideas!

My eldest son, Allen Mark, was nine. I found that coming here I had so much more time with him. Anthony Patrick was soon to become an American citizen. He is now fourteen and wanted by several League clubs. They have a step-brother, Adam, who they never really had that much time to get to know – neither did I come to that!

This is what our game does to you, builds you up, knocks you down, fulfils your dreams and then gives you nightmares, just when you think that you've arrived. Frank sang he did it 'His Way', I certainly did it mine. This book will take you on a rollercoaster ride much like the hills in Seattle, very bumpy.

The Working Man's Ballet is all about a kid from the backstreets of Chelsea fulfilling his and every other kid's dream. Your first is to become a professional footballer, then to play in the first team, followed by playing in an FA Cup Final and then the ultimate, to play for your country. In eight short months I had done this, or so I thought. 'He' had other ideas once again!

This book is especially for my father Bill, without whom I really do not know what I would be writing about. Mr Tony Waddington, the man who confirmed to me that there was more to life than football, but to get it in the right order. He gave a new meaning to performing to the very best of your ability, hence the title of this book.

Thirdly, it is for Leslie May who was with me through most of this, a friend you could never replace, we were inseparable. We lost Les through terrible circumstances, I hope his mother Eileen and the rest of his family will read this and be reminded of all the great times we shared. George Benson sang 'Everybody's searching for a hero', my cousin Anthony Mason is mine. He has been a credit to our family by the way he has kept such dignity through all the nightmares of his journey through a life that many people take for granted. More than anything he has charmed people and maintained his wonderful sense of humour. I am very proud of him!

Both Bill and Tony were my motivation and my mentors. My

father brought me up to play the game properly, an art I try to carry over to all youngsters, and then passed me on to Tony to take me even further. My title is theirs, my game is theirs, and my reaching the top is theirs. The two most knowledgeable people in my football life. Their passion was that of a Sinatra song. Their love of life and humorous outlook to go with that passion was almost uncanny, two men coming together to give me the feeling that 'There is someone up there'. When they met and shook hands I just left them alone. Waddington was the only man that my father ever admired. They are both now up there together I suppose still watching over me and wondering what the next twist will be. I am prouder than I can put into words to say that not only did I have a great love for them both, but I actually played for them and earned their respect. The game and my life is lesser without them.

Best, Cruyff, Beckenbauer, Haynes, Greaves, Mackay, Baxter, Pele and the late great Bobby Moore all came from working-class backgrounds. In the seventies, greats such as Bowles, George, Osgood, Currie and Frank Worthington the same.

My first visit to Wembley was to watch Billy Digweed and Johnny Fennell play for Hounslow against Crook Town. This was the day I just knew I had to make it. My father insisted afterwards that I would go back there but not in an Amateur Cup Final. Teddy Weston, Paddy Long, Bobby West, Buddy Herbert, Harry Yewings, Charlie Mason and his brother and Anthony's father George were just some of the many very talented local lads. Later on there was Bobby Eyre, who could play in today's Premier, David Carter and Rodney Udall, both of whom could have gone to the top. Chelsea was an area where football was rife. It was second nature, it was Saturday morning, afternoon, evening, Sunday morning, afternoon and so and so. Even parties in the prefab were split into two, with Sinatra in our front room and my father holding court in the kitchen.

My uncle George must have a big mention for he has been the most consistently wonderful man in my lifetime. A man who would look after you no matter what. He has been the rock since my father moved on, and has been such a very special part of my life. It is not surprising his son is my hero!

I am told on good authority that Billy Hudson could play a bit.

He played at Wimbledon before they changed the rules. Thanks to him I could make the quantum leap not only to the stars but to play with and against them. Bill Shankly once said to me, 'I thought that I'd seen the finest ever performance from Peter Doherty, but you have just surpassed it.' Helmut Schoen remarked, 'At last England have a World Class player', and Mr Waddington once told the media that 'Alan Hudson will play for the World XI before he plays for his country'. Those words coming from three such giants in our game are my CV, and I owe it all to one William Hudson.

As always my mother takes back seat in all this football talk, or so it seems up till now. She was responsible for getting me prepared for my matches and telling my father not to get too excited. My father, you see, knew I would make it, whereas my mother dreamed about it. That was two dreams fulfilled!

My elder brother John, younger sister Julie and myself had a most fantastic upbringing. They were the happiest times of my life and so important when you have to go out into the unknown on your own. Whenever things go wrong or I feel I do not deserve such a bad break I think of my times in our prefab, and how all the other kids from all over would gather. Our prefab was my father's Lancaster Gate, the 'Cage' where we used to play our Wembley, and my mother was that woman of whom they used to say 'Behind every great man ...'

This may be the longest introduction you have ever read, but when you have just finished your own story after fifteen years, what would you expect?

My thanks go to Chris Willsmore, for brushing off the cobwebs from Seattle, Martin Knight, who has come along and been of great encouragement, my girlfriend Ann, who has been of more help than she knows. And of course Ian MacLeay, the man responsible for jogging my memory by bringing back the atmosphere of those fantastic times down the King's Road and who is someone I could not have replaced in finishing this work. We have worked together on this for the past eighteen months and hope you enjoy reading it as much as we have writing it. Last but not least Malcolm Molineux who has put this project before all others in my plight to get the best possible product to my publisher. It is not an easy thing to do, but what really is, if you want to do it well? All I can say is that I have found the experience the next best thing to playing the game, because it has brought back so many fantastic memories of those wonderful matches and times we all had.

Welcome to and enjoy *The Working Man's Ballet*.

1

Almost Blue

(With apologies to Elvis Costello,
who wrote another song about going to Chelsea)

Summer '95, the hot one. I was having a drink in the bar opposite the main gates of Stamford Bridge. It used to be called The Rising Sun, back in the days of Danny Gillen, a lifetime ago. I had just been in with Ken Bates about the book. The kids came along with their autograph books. After I'd signed them, one of the lads said that Robbie from Take That, a nice young fella from Stoke-on-Trent, was in the next bar with Baywatch Pam. The kids had the new strip on, which probably cost more than my weekly wage in that fantastic first season.

The story I am going to tell you could be a sad one. One of the main characters is dead, a couple of others have poor health. Few of us made the fortune we should have, and few of us tasted the lasting success we should have. Yet it is an uplifting story of hope, of courage and all-too-brief glory; a group of young men who lived a dream. Perhaps it was your dream, or possibly still is.

When the kids had gone, I looked for my pen, but it had left with

them. Good times! We had such good times, great times. Two
people dominated my life early on, my father Bill and my surrogate
father Tony Waddington. Both have been taken from us, and I
dedicate this book to them.

The thing that disturbs me most about the modern game is that
the youngsters do not seem to follow the sport as they did in my
day. We would spend hours trying to emulate our heroes, and
football has never needed heroes more than at this present moment.
I was lucky enough to rub shoulders with such heroes – the greatest
footballers on the planet: Pele, when I was only nineteen; Cruyff,
when I was a year younger; Best, at his best; and probably the
biggest hero this country will ever produce, Robert Chelsea Moore.
Today, the role models 'kung-fu' the fans.

I wonder how they would have stood up to the white heat of that
1970 FA Cup Final replay where there were absolutely no prisoners
and definitely no love lost. Tommy Baldwin and Terry Cooper, two
of the quietest men in football, kicking lumps out of one another as
the battle began. Tommy, a prolific goalscorer when given the
opportunity, was handed strict orders not to allow the weaving
Leeds full-back to get too far over the halfway line, if over at all.
Ron 'Chopper' Harris did not need any telling. His scything tackle
on the wing-wizard Eddie Gray in the opening minute was chilling.
That set the pattern of the match. It was the only way we could
have won it, by fighting white fire with blue fire, and the outcome
was for all to see. Someone joked that Gray was picking Chopper's
studs out of his shins well after that final whistle. He collected more
shrapnel in that game than a veteran of the Somme in World War
One!

I was born within an Ian Hutchinson long throw of Stamford
Bridge. First I lived in Elm Park Gardens, and then moved even
closer to the ground, the place I would learn my trade. 23 Upcerne
Road was our prefab. I bet most of your readers have never even
heard of a prefab, let alone been inside one. Well, this was our
Football HQ as well as our home, a penalty-kick away from the
'Cage', our wire fencing six-a-side pitch. Now Chelsea Harbour
dominates the skyline and overlooks where I once dwelt and spent
long hours dribbling, juggling, passing and working on my game.
Michael Caine, Sam Fox and Elton John, a big hero of mine, have

all owned property there; ex-Walsall chairman and racehorse-owner Terry Ramsden also. It is said that Terry lost £52 million on the horses – and I thought my old pals Stan Bowles and Don Shanks were big time! Stanley and Donald, as I like to know them, were the greatest double-act in the game. It's a shame that, like myself, they have been left 'labelled', for they should both still be in the game which is dominated by lesser mortals. Donald believes in that great old saying, 'Work Hard, Play Hard'. There is absolutely nothing wrong with that outlook in my book. The ones who have got it wrong are those goody-two-shoes who, because they don't step outside the door, believe they don't have to work as hard as we did.

I was born in June 1951 under the influence of the star sign Gemini. It is represented as the Twins, Castor and Pollux. Egyptian astrologers depicted them as a pair of ghosts, while Arabian astrologers symbolized them as peacocks. Characteristics include being quick and restless, mutable, not to be depended on. I made my debut for Chelsea in circumstances that were to be all too familiar in my career. It was a spring afternoon in 1969. Four Chelsea players were dining in Barbarella's restaurant the day before an away match at Southampton. It's still there on the Fulham Road where the road curves, opposite the off-licence, and the wine connoisseurs amongst the Chelsea crowd are known to congregate there before all home matches. Barbarella's was a typical Italian place where, years later, I would spend many long hours wining and dining with the owners and staff, who were a joy. It had that lovely atmosphere that you'd see in those wonderful gangster movies *The Godfather* and *Goodfellas*.

Someone had dropped a coin on these 'wise guys' though, and had grassed them up to our manager Dave Sexton. Twenty-four hours before a League match – Dave wouldn't have it four days before a friendly match in the Outer Hebrides! The story goes, and I did get it first-hand from one of the famous quartet, that a furious row developed and spilled out on to the pavement just outside a small hotel next door. Well, moving backwards away from Dave, no doubt trying not to let him get too close to his breath, Charlie Cooke went down as if he was trying to dodge a Paul Reaney tackle. Charlie was the most perfectly-balanced footballer I ever had the pleasure to play with, and was famous for his control. That really took the biscuit for the now-raging Chelsea boss: CC lying on the floor in front of passers-by, some of whom were probably getting their tickets for the following day. The other three – Peter Osgood, Tommy Baldwin and Johnny Boyle made up the table for lunch – were in tears. Oscar Wilde once said that we are all in the gutter but some of us are looking at the stars. Any passing Blues fan would have seen the opposite on this particular day. In what was to mirror the tragic break-up of our great Cup-winning team, Sexton axed these four rascals for the following day's match at The Dell. Enter, stage left, young Huddy.

A star is born; more like a star is torn. At that precise moment I was receiving treatment at the ground, only the other side of the pitch. If they could have moved the hotel I would have had a first-class view of this hilarious comedy. Harry Medhurst, our club trainer, was sitting having his usual cigarette when the phone rang. Strange character, Harry – Harpo Marx had more to say for himself – but a really nice man who was very popular with the lads and an easy target for our club mickey-takers. He used to make odd noises and shook his head when replying to you, especially if it was something of real importance like 'How is he doing today, Harry?' He would shake his head a few times and make a couple of his little noises before looking at the player concerned to get some kind of assistance with the question.

One of our funny men was John Dempsey, who we called 'Biz'. Demps was a real nuisance in the dressing-room and gave poor old Harry the complete run-around. If he saw half a chance, he was in like Jimmy Greaves on a stray ball in the eighteen-yard box. His timing was superb and he had that wonderful ability to make you forget any problems you had, not that we had many in those days. 'Biz' would don Harry's white medical coat, just like the doctors wear, and walk around the treatment room examining the injured. He would go down Harry's pack of fags and have a broom in one hand sweeping the floor while giving the player his verdict as to whether he would be fit for the following Saturday. Ninety-nine times out of a hundred the result was 'Sorry son, your leg's got to come off ', or 'No chance son, just take it easy for a few days. Have a cup of tea while us lot are all out getting flogged by Stiff Neck.'

That was our manager's nickname. In those later, sad days, Demps was worth his weight in gold, always the same, never changing his brilliant outlook – and never underestimate this fella when it comes to playing. While on the subject of John Dempsey, I must not forget to tell you about his funniest moment in the game, and it could only have happened to him. He was playing in an international for Eire in Norway and as usual was giving their centre-forward his full range of tricks; absolutely anything to put him off his game, and he was so good at it, especially when he told them one of his ridiculous jokes. The ball went out of play and he got tapped on the shoulder. As he turned around to react, this little old lady hit him over the head with her umbrella! When he told us on his return to the Bridge, we were in hysterics; but if only we'd been there to witness it.

The phone call was from a very distressed Dave Sexton, asking about my fitness. Harry grunted a few times before looking at me, first putting his thumb up and then down. I did not have a clue what was going on by now. After putting down the handset, Harry went for his cigarette packet and this is when I knew something was amiss. Harry looked worried – you see, he idolised Ossie – and just sat back drawing in.

'What's up, H?' I said.

'If you are fit, you play at The Dell tomorrow.' I nearly fell off the treatment table.

Well, the rest is history and I made my first-team debut. It turned out to be nowhere near as exciting as the events twenty-four hours earlier outside Barbarella's – unless you were a Saints fan. We were hammered 5–0. Welcome to the big-time, Al. Demps, one of my heroes from when I used to stand behind the goal at Craven Cottage week in, week out, was to make his debut too in this calamity. Two Fulham supporters on the end of a 5–0 hiding, that's rare! Little did we both know, we were about to embark on the most exciting period in Chelsea's history, albeit so short.

Chelsea had a habit of washing their dirty linen in public. Tommy Docherty sent eight first-team players home from Blackpool, including Terry Venables and George Graham, just before a vital League match at Burnley. My brother John was in that squad and nearly got his debut the same way as his younger brother; wouldn't that have been something? Even more amazing was that the scoreline wasn't much different. At least I could say we only got beat five; the boys lost six that day. From then on, the tabloids had a field day with the playboy image of the club. When I found out the circumstances for my sudden call-up I just had to laugh, although I knew I was on a hiding to nothing. I knew I would not stay in the side at that time, for Charlie was at the top of his game. The laugh was nearly on me, though, as I recall thinking that the débâcle would end my career before it got off the ground. The papers were full of 'Chelsea stars axed after lunch-time booze-up' stories, but my favourite was the one headlined 'Local boy makes good'. At least I had got much further than so many of the rest of our local Chelsea talent, something I could never understand considering the quality of the neighbourhood boys I mentioned in my introduction. The picture next to the newspaper article showed me with a French crew-cut, quite different from the image that was to follow the following season. I honestly believe that Chelsea will never produce a local-born hero like Alan Anthony Hudson again – not that they produced me, I had my teacher at home and then at school. I can never see the fashionable backwaters of Chelsea producing a youngster good enough to go as far as I did in the game.

When I go to the Bridge now, I walk past houses that cost as much to buy as Kevin Keegan's strikers, just across from the prefab. That part of London has seen enormous social changes since I broke into the team. When Chelsea played Millwall in the Cup not so long ago, disturbances were reported in the press. They told of 'local inhabitants cowering inside their book-lined mansions while gangs of bomber-jacketed hooligans terrorized the local streets'. Correct up to a point, only bomber-jackets went out of vogue about the time I jacked it in. Now all the yobs wear Schott rainwear and Ralph Lauren golf jackets.

My early days at the Bridge were spent around a couple of players who have gone on to become real giants in management, George Graham and former England coach Terry Venables. Chelsea fans used to moan that while these two were harvesting trophies across the other side of town, the Stamford Bridge cupboard was totally bare under the management of such luminaries as Bobby Campbell,

Ian Porterfield and my old team-mate Johnny Hollins. Not to forget that they even had to stand for the likes of Geoff Hurst, who tried to bring the West Ham 'Academy' to the Bridge. I'm sorry, Hursty, not even Mooro could have done that! When Geoff first took over the reins at the Bridge, he was warned by my great friend Micky Droy (now what would he be worth today, if Pallister and Adams are the best we have to offer?), that he should leave things as they were and not try to introduce his 'claret and blue' tricks on our patch. After he'd looked down on Mickey – yeah, Hursty would truly believe he could look down on Micky – the big fella said to him, 'I'll tell you what I'll do, Hursty. I'll be at the front office when you get the sack, because you'll be going well before me.' Micky kept his promise. I almost signed to come back to the Bridge after talks with that charming man Danny Blanchflower, but he was sacked on the eve of me putting pen to paper. What a shame that was. Enter Geoff Hurst, exit Alan Hudson. Hurst disappointed me with his first phone call, so I told him how he could put the contract to better use.

El Tel and Gorgeous George had relatively short spells at Chelsea, but both were tremendously popular and impressive in a side that could have gone on to break the northern hold. I truly believe Chelsea had the nucleus of doing a Liverpool, especially adding the youth of Osgood and Hudson along with the wizardry of Cooke. What a squad that would have been! Nowadays it would be unbuyable. But both Terry and George went on to fall out with the Doc. Terry's battles now seem as if they were a warm-up or a sparring match before going in with Alan Sugar. They paralleled mine and Ossie's with Dave Sexton. What goes around comes around. Not quite a circle though, more like a spiral, a continuous curve. I would love to have come into that Chelsea side and especially to have played alongside Terry Venables. He was a player I watched and studied, a player I took a lot out of and put into me. His total confidence was his key, and it showed. I was a tremendous fan of Venners; in fact my dream midfield then would have been Hudson, Haynes and Venables. Haynes could do what he wanted, while Terry could organise and I could have done their running. It would have been my pleasure.

George Graham was a real piece of work. I always thought the nickname Gorgeous was very appropriate; a class man on and off the field and a proven man too. Who can doubt such credentials? The nickname came from a famous American wrestler of the same name whom Ali, another star turn, had modelled himself on. Just as well Muhammad Ali wasn't in town when George and Tel were strutting their stuff in the early sixties. All the current Leeds boss's faults became his virtues and I admire him for that, for he had seen it and done it on both sides of the fence and passed the best side on to his players, the *winning* side. I have nothing but time for GG and always get a good feeling when I see him. He's quick with that smile that once knocked the girls over, and he was a vastly underrated footballer, another class act. I am pleased to see him come back and head the pack again; after all, at least when he was winning things he gave you the impression he was enjoying it, whereas up at Old Trafford they're so glum and full of their own self-importance. I'll take Gunner George, thank you. It was fantastic the way he stood by Paul Merson in the early part of the Arsenal player's troubled days. I wish our manager at Chelsea had taken a leaf out of George's book in the handling of his players. Merson, a self-confessed alcoholic, would have had Dave Sexton hanging off the nearest bridge.

The other side of Venners was the archetypal London John. Would you buy a used car from him? Sgt Bilko meets Budgie! That TV character he created with Gordon Williams, 'Hazell', was his alter ego. I often wondered why he stopped writing, it caught the mood of London so well. Terry once paid me the highest compliment by saying I was a better player than him. I will not argue with the ex-England coach! But I don't think he knows how influential he was in my becoming so. Tommy Docherty has gone on record as saying that it was when he saw my potential starting to blossom that he began planning to move El Tel from Chelsea. I cannot believe that entirely, for Tommy brought down Charlie Cooke and it seemed to me that CC was the one to take over from Chelsea's midfield general. However, it is a lovely thing coming from Tommy, for if anyone knows a player it is certainly the Doc, who I believe never got the credit he deserved for producing three great managers (Eddie McCreadie being the other). Sexton got rid of me with the same thing in mind, if what he says is gospel. He kicked me out – yes, literally – to make way for the up and coming Ray Wilkins. It backfired on Dave though, because Chelsea were relegated, Dave got the old tin-tac and I went on to help take Stoke City into Europe with a run in which we lost only two of our last twenty-five matches. We went from third from bottom to fifth place in the Championship.

My first game back at the Bridge for Stoke saw us needing to win to qualify for Europe. I got the only goal of the match and never felt so good about a goal in my whole life. I was cast out of Chelsea like in one of Richard Attenborough's movie scripts (even Dickie himself spread rumours that yours truly was an alcoholic – glad he never told Tony Waddington). 'Butch' Wilkins came in and fulfilled all the promise. He was a good player, but put alongside Charlie and myself, I ask you? To think I had only just turned twenty-three with all my best years in front of me. Ludicrous. How could a board of directors give the manager their blessing to sell Peter Osgood and Alan Hudson and then sack him? Ray has now followed all the other good boys into management and, not surprisingly to me, has immediately followed Sexton in the relegation stakes and is now between posts. Take a look at his backroom staff at Loftus Road and you do not really see winners, do you? John Hollins made a hash of the Chelsea managerial hot-seat; Billy Bonds, I hear, spent more time bird-watching than on the training ground; and Frank Sibley has been number two to everybody except Frank Sinatra. Long live Queen's Park Rangers, all they would need now is for Rodney Marsh to join them to make it a full-house. Marsh was no help to Gerry Francis in his hour of need at QPR. He can now boast of dragging two very famous clubs down. He left Tampa Bay Rowdies in a hurry before coming back over here to escape from the embarrassment.

Like Venners, Butch Wilkins exudes the corporate image demanded by the FA as pre-requisite for the post of running the national team. He also is as sharply dressed as George or Terry, but he hasn't got that strength that goes with it or that special presence and charisma of Terry. The assistants in Armani must break into the broadest smile when any of these walks into their store, much like the scene from *Pretty Woman* when Richard Gere does his number on the kitting-out of Julia Roberts. Tel learned how to cultivate the media many moons ago; he had a good teacher in the Doc, and to a lesser extent 'Big Mal'.

A line in *The Godfather* always sticks with me, as Marlon Brando tells a young Al Pacino, 'Keep your friends close, but your enemies even closer.' Terry learned this very important lesson well (I wonder if he saw that movie as many times as I have?). His public persona is superb. To the press he is always marvellous copy, ready with a quip and a smile. Managers like Graham Taylor were not so media-friendly and very naive, finally paying the ultimate price; Taylor not only losing his job but being dragged through that horrid cabbage-patch, or in his case turnip-patch.

I have always believed that Chelsea suffered at the hands of the media because Ken Bates ruffled so many of their feathers. Twenty-odd years ago chairmen never talked to the press. The Chelsea fans were always portrayed as something out of an Oliver Stone movie. This was in stark contrast to fans of other clubs that also had a dangerous, albeit small, hooligan element in their following. If Chelsea had been involved in the Heysel tragedy, I wonder what the outcry and punishment would have been?

The most exquisite time of Venables's life, in my view, was when he was captain of Chelsea and barely out of his teens. No team in the history of the game ever caught the mood of the times as Chelsea did in the period from the early 1960s through to the break-up of the side ten years later. It started in the Swinging Sixties. The trendy King's Road with its baronial rock stars and air of decadence threw out vibes that were to change society. Anything and everything seemed possible; a strong feeling that something quite unique could happen. The tremendous bond between the fans and the team was forged then. When it all went sour, Chelsea lost many followers who never went back. They still had great affection for the team and what it had and should have done, but not the club. None of them started supporting other teams. They had just had enough. Venables, it seems, had it sussed. He always maintained that the biggest potential in London was at Chelsea. The cliché 'sleeping giant' is trotted out every so often. I just wonder how it would have worked out if first Tommy 'The Tyke' Docherty and then Dave 'Stiff Neck' Sexton had seen it differently. The best of both men's Chelsea teams would have scooped prizes, of that I'm totally convinced. Can you picture a team of Bonetti, Harris, McCreadie, Hinton, Webb or Dempsey, Cooke, Hudson, Osgood, Hutchinson, Venables and Graham? Don't forget, George Best wanted to come down to us. I often think to myself that in a perfect world, instead of my leaving for Stoke City we should have swapped Dave Sexton for Tony Waddington. Tony loved talent like the names I just mentioned, and would have tried to keep us all together until we were as old as Sir Stanley Matthews was when he brought him back to Stoke City. Another of Venners's dreams was of a London team playing in a huge stadium with all the power of a one-city team.

In the future it is not hard to visualise a global League emerging. Already Japan are developing (could that be the reason Terry took his England team all the way to the Far East to prepare for Euro 96? I cannot think of any other). Soon the Gulf will follow, just like all the other small countries who have caught us up and in many cases overtaken us. Look at our first match in Euro 96; thirty years ago the Swiss were part-timers, yet in that opening match it looked the other way around. Venables knows this to be true. The future of English football lies in the hope that a Fowler, a Scholes or a Redknapp will burst through to dominate our game. I would truly love to play a part in helping this kind of exciting talent get us back on the right road. I know I will never have the opportunity, but I have the self-belief to do as good a job as anyone has done yet. I know I would certainly improve on the Graham Taylors of this world!

Docherty's part in the explosion at Chelsea, which is still an influence in the game, should never be overlooked. The combination of him and Sexton would have been as great as any in sport, but as individuals they were flawed. I would truly have loved to play under Dave Sexton as a coach, for I liked him in that role; he was comfortable and he was confident. To me it seemed that he disliked managing, just like Don Howe, who was fantastic for me at Arsenal as the everyday man on the training ground. But put him or Dave in the office and they were like 'Jaws' out of water. All those personality clashes, blown-up egos and 'one of us must lose' syndromes seemed a far cry from the 'Cage', where we could just go and express ourselves without a manager causing a problem out of nothing. Alan Ball once said while playing for Arsenal that they did not need a manager, just someone to keep them fit and let them go out and play. It's the wisest thing he's ever said, and he's proved you don't need a manager once again in the season just gone!

You have no doubt grabbed the fact that I was a Fulham supporter as a young lad. My hero was Johnny Haynes, and still is as a matter of fact. I saw JH a couple of times recently at different dinner functions and he still exudes that magic. When Chelsea were blazing, Haynesy was Leo Sayer, a 'One-Man Band', surrounded by Tommy Trinder's cast at the London Palladium. When Tommy went on stage he should have taken Jimmy Hill with him. I'm sure they would have been a match for Morecambe and Wise, and I know which one would not have been Eric. A few years ago I applied for the Fulham manager's job. My schoolboy's dream would have been fulfilled, but the reply from the chairman was that he would prefer someone like Dave Bassett. Fulham have even embarrassed Johnny Haynes. How can a man like Hill have been on the same field as JH, yet refuse a meeting with yours truly then employ the man who left Matt Le Tissier out of the team at Southampton, and continue to make or try to make fools of their loyal supporters? When I received the call from the late Bobby Keetch, co-creator of the wonderful *'Football Football'* eating establishment, saying that Hill would not even consider me, I was not surprised but disappointed for all those loyal Fulham fans, including my chum Billy Boyce who is still there through thick and thin, having to watch the chairman sit on *Match of the Day* spouting irrelevant nonsense.

I can recall so vividly how Hill, on his BBC laugh-in, ignored one of my greatest ever performances for Mr Waddington, at Newcastle. At that time I was playing some of the best football I have ever played. I really was on top of my game and our team were doing great. I came home that Saturday evening to find I had not even been mentioned by Fulham's ex-star. As luck would have it, one of the all-time greats (so my father told me), none other than the legendary Len Shackleton, gave me maximum points out of ten the following day. Who should be on the telly, I ask you? I was to get seven such scores that season, which is still a record. Not bad for an alcoholic! What's changed, Alan Hudson had left the building.

Gerry Francis is another of today's 'big name' people I have had cause to be disappointed with. As my England room-mate, Gerry demonstrated qualities he now preaches against as manager of Tottenham. If his current players had the same attitude as he did then, he would be walking in the same direction as his predecessor. He was another Kevin Costner-like figure, preaching all the good things in the game and yet forgetting about the day he walked out on the afternoon of my England debut against West Germany.

That's nice, I thought. Thanks, Gerry. He just upped and went home, obviously wishing me all the best! It's no wonder Gerry, who talks about the fair play and teamwork he was taught by Sexton, works without a contract, free to walk away from any situation that does not agree with him. Francis, like Keegan and Revie, walked away from England. It didn't bother me; he did me a favour, because I knew I was on my own. What did hurt me later was that Revie made him captain. Imagine the uproar if it had been yours truly who did a runner!

It's amazing, really, how they all seem to stick together. Gerry, while he was actually in our room, did nothing but moan about all the bad players in our squad. It was as if he wanted to cause some kind of interruption. I, as usual, said nothing. Not about our team-mates. Can you imagine the Tottenham manager hearing this from his players now? I do not think so. Gerry was born only a bus ride away from me. I call him Gerry through respect of Stan (Bowles, that is), both from working-class backgrounds. Earlier my international career had stalled because I refused to tour with the Under-23 squad. Stan the Man had the same problem. He once walked out when Ron Greenwood was in charge of the national side. To this day, Stan is a loyal follower of Gerry. If only people were as loyal to Stan himself.

Bowles and Hudson were always labelled as being rebels, yet here was Francis, in a fit of pique, walking out on his country and colleagues. When I woke before that big match against our old enemy, Gerry had gone. There is one thing about the great events not only in football, but in life: you stick together! Gerry didn't see it that way. I had never had that problem with any other footballer before, until my run-in with Bruce Rioch in Seattle some years later.

I had been rejected by Fulham once before, when I was twelve. My dad took me there to get a trial. I have learned since, that is now I'm the age my father was then, that that is not a good ploy. I was not at this time interested in managing them, although if I had known then what I know now I might have put in for the job with Boycey. I was very slight then and was rejected; why do Fulham keep doing this to me and my family? My world was shattered, a feeling that I was to encounter a few more times in my football career. My father, once again, rebuilt my confidence. He never pushed me, never bullied me, never pretended to me. He just told it as it was. He was adamant that I had more ability and a better footballing brain than my contemporaries, but I would not realise this until I had developed and grown just like the other kids who towered above me, or so it seemed. I started to go evening training at Stamford Bridge every Tuesday and Thursday. Whenever I see Venners now we chuckle about it, for that was the first time we came into contact. One of Tommy Docherty's revolutionary ideas was to have the established players in his squad, in fact all of them, take the youngsters in the evenings. Not only was this so valuable for the kids and good for team morale, it meant that Tommy had everybody where he wanted them. What better place to have your players on a Thursday evening? Very clever, Tom! That's just one of the reasons why I make Tommy Docherty one of the absolute best managers in my lifetime – and when I tell him so, he blushes! Because he knows I'm right. Can you imagine the impact these evenings had on an impressionable youngster; rubbing shoulders with Terry Venables, George Graham, Eddie McCreadie (still my favourite of all) and all the others?

I obviously do not forget Tommy Harmer – 'The Charmer', for you Spurs fans – showing these three how to chip the ball on to the crossbar, with all the kids' eyes popping out. Footballers can seem so remote, not only to the fans but to the young up and coming kids like us. Was it only the Doc who could do it? I wonder now what pub they went down to afterwards, with or without Tommy. Maybe this is why Chelsea in those days had so many brilliant young prospects. Many of them went on to be household names and shaped the future of the modern game.

I still thought that my size was against me. My father nurtured me, and trials followed for West London and then London Boys. I thought I had blown my chance at one particular trial but my old man told me to 'forget it'. The whole thing seemed so frightening – why should any kid be put in front of such idiots? – but once again I was assured I would be OK. I often wonder what happened to so many of those young boys; maybe they should have used my old man as their guide and mentor. I could see no way then of breaking through in front of them, but persistence overshadows everything in life, even talent. It is, in my view, the most valuable resource we have.

Alan Ball was very special to me as a player, one of my heroes in fact. I first fell for him at Craven Cottage when he got a hat-trick in a 3–3 draw. Dave Metchick got our hat-trick, but never went on to be as superb as Bally as a player. Last time I saw Dave was in the Fulham Road in a little local of ours. He should have been a film star with his James Dean looks. He was just too short for acting and playing, and I say that with love, Dave. That night, you and Bally stole the show. People forget how great a player Bally actually was. They saw him as just a runner, a worker, a wholehearted player. He was not! He was that and more, probably the greatest one-touch player we will ever see. He always talked about the huge debt he owed to his father, who taught him that football was not just a game but a way of life. Ball had such fire, energy and tenacity! Even if he was having a dodgy game – and I didn't see him have many of those – he never gave up chasing and running. It was the way I liked to approach the game. We should have played together at Arsenal, we were so much alike in our approach. People who tried to kick us, we loved. We knew we could wear them down. I knew my fitness would get the better of them in the last twenty minutes of any match. I would take them all over the field on a cross-country run until I saw them flagging, and then in the closing stages, having burnt them out, I would try to use that extra time and space to damage their team.

Up until his recent departure from Maine Road, Alan Ball was the only Premiership manager who had a World Cup winners' medal. Why has he never lived up to it as a manager? I believe his strengths as a player are his weaknesses as a manager. It was just as well he was not around when the *Titanic* went down, I'm sure he would have been aboard. Matt Le Tissier was one player who saved yet another boat of his from sinking, by single-handedly keeping Bally in the Premier League at Southampton. But Bally left him behind for a bigger club and forgot to take him with him. Le Tiss, a 'Maverick' in my book, kept the Saints up that season with a catalogue of classic goals, the one against Blackburn being the best. He made a mockery of the old cliché that one man doesn't make a team. I have long been campaigning for Le Tissier's inclusion in the England team, and it seems Glenn Hoddle and myself both disagreed with Venables's judgement on this rare, magical talent.

The Summer of '69; Bryan Adams wrote a song about it. This is when Tommy Baldwin's drinking exploits earned him the nickname 'Sponge'. I for one like it, for you can see it for so many reasons. Tommy is a man's man. He will run for you, fight for you and score for you. Tommy is a gem. The fans always thought his nickname came from soaking up all the punishment, but the truth was ...

The Southampton débâcle on my debut still haunted me, but my father told me to remain patient. He made plausible the idea of my becoming a first-team player. By now I was in the Combination side at the start of that momentous season. I thought that if I got into the first team and could play up to what I thought was good enough, I could stay in the side. My dream was to captain Chelsea like Venables. I had captained every team I had played for so far: Park Walk Primary with Mr Robertson; Kingsley Secondary and West London Schoolboys with Mr Tranter; Chelsea Boys Club Under-14s with Mr Hudson; Chelsea Youth Team with Mr Blunstone; and now I wanted the first-team armband with Mr Dave Sexton. It wasn't that simple – if only I had known what was in store. I would watch Charlie Cooke, bought by Tommy Doc to replace Venables, in training at every opportunity. When he had the ball, if he was in the mood, it was almost an impossibility to get it off him. Yet he seemed so unimpressed with his own God-given talent. Soon it was to be my job to make sure he got as much of the ball as humanly possible.

The sweet smell of success seemed a long way away as the season started badly for Chelsea. It had been a long, dry, hot summer, rather like the one when this book was conceived. The hard-baked grounds were anathema to a player like Charlie Cooke. He actually could play on any surface, especially the ones I hate, like icy surfaces, where he would be like a ballet dancer. Chelsea's first match was away to Liverpool. Good to have an easy one to start with! On a blazing hot day we were beaten 4–1. Hutch headed Chelsea's goal and I recall Holly getting run ragged at full-back by Peter Thompson, who terrorised most defenders. What great left-wingers they had in that era. I did not play in that one. Anfield was a nightmare for me, but I always loved playing up there. In that match, Tommy Smith was kicking lumps out of Os. Hutch, Ossie's minder, was not happy. He articulated his unhappiness to Smithy and they changed partners. While changing, Os told Smithy what Hutch had said about his skin complaint! Chelsea were well beaten, but a few scores were settled. Smith hated Londoners, it seemed. Or did he just kick everyone? He never forgave Charlie George for scoring that magnificent goal against him in the FA Cup Final that clinched the double for the Gunners.

Two nights after the Liverpool defeat, Chelsea travelled across to West Ham. Again the team was ravaged by injuries. Hinton, suave Marv, played in the number eight shirt, and Bobby 'Jumbo' Tambling, towards the end of his glorious Chelsea career, was to play one of his last games. The World Cup duo of Hurst and Peters got the goals on another sweltering night. Hutch's header then won our first two points of that season against Ipswich at home. I was playing down at Bristol for the Combination side; Birchenall was my inside-forward partner. Two more draws left Chelsea sixteenth in the table with five matches gone. On 27 August, Chelsea were away to Tottenham Hotspur in a midweek fixture. I reported to Stamford Bridge for what I thought was going to be 'Just Another Day', as Paul McCartney would later sing. A training session with the reserves, and then on to White Hart Lane to watch the first team. But at four o'clock, Ron Harris came over to me and gave me my four complimentary tickets. That was when I first knew I was back in the big time.

At the hotel at 6pm Dave Sexton ran through his team-talk as per usual, giving each player his role. He told me, 'You will be picking up Mullery.' I regard that as the moment when I was launched into big-time football. White Hart Lane was to become a very special and magical ground for me. The Alan Hudson debut matches were also to be a bit special, always. Marking Mullery – if you could call it marking, picking up was more accurate – was a great thrill for me. I had watched him week in, week out at Fulham, along with all my other heroes, including Georgie Cohen, the World Cup winning right-back. Lovely fella, George is. Mullers – now the manager at Barnet – used to have a Capital Radio talk show. He took more pot-shots than a sniper in Bosnia. Horrified by the bungs, coke and fixes of the nineties, he was sanctimonious in the extreme. Mullery was the first player to be sent off playing for his country. Playing at Tottenham was an added thrill for me, as my Dad used to take me at every opportunity to watch the likes of Greaves, White, Smith, Gilzean and the one and only Dave Mackay. A few weeks later I was to face the great man, at that time playing for Derby County. He pushed me away on our dog track at the Bridge as I was collecting the ball to take a throw-in. In his broad Scottish accent he muttered, 'Give me that', and, wiping the ball on his shirt as only he did, said that I shouldn't even be on the same field as him. Another illusion shattered! Confidence is everything in life. People like Mackay would try to shake it, whereas someone like Bobby Moore would increase it with his manner. My father, and then Tony Waddington at Stoke, made me aware that I could control my response to events even if I could not always control events themselves.

On my way to White Hart Lane I was shaking; just with sheer excitement, not fear. My only real worry was that the night should not turn out like my only other match at Southampton. Thinking about it now, that was the happiest time of my life. The prefab was always full of people, it was cheerful and happy and life was sweet. I wore Osgood's famous number nine shirt that night. He wore seven and Charlie had Nobby Houseman's eleven. Cooke took an early knock and was replaced by Stewart Houston – 'Sammy' is now manager at QPR after deputizing for George Graham and Bruce Rioch at Arsenal. The crowd was 47,395. It was like entering a gladiators' arena for me. I can still recall the opening moments of the game. It seemed so quick, though compared to today's game it must have been like a stroll down the old King's Road. I looked up at the terrace where I used to watch the matches perched on my father's shoulders. He had followed my career from the 'Cage' in Upcerne Road to White Hart Lane. It must have been a very proud moment for him as he watched the match sitting alongside Tommy Harmer. He had watched me play in literally hundreds of schoolboy, junior and youth games.

David Webb, playing at right-back, put us ahead. That was his first goal of the season. Who could have guessed then just how vital his last one would be? He scored so many important goals for Chelsea. The steep learning-curve of Chelsea, playing and managing, is now helping him in his time at Brentford. Stan Bowles is helping him out a couple of days a week, and Webby has mentioned to me that he would like me to join the ex-QPR superstar. Why were so many talents like Stan's not used more? By virtue of their vast skill and knowledge, players like Stan must have had more to pass on than so many other lesser mortals. I call them the '*Reservoir Dogs*' – a huge lake of talent waiting to be passed on, yet treated like rabid dogs by the establishment that strangles the game.

Eleven minutes from time, Jimmy Pearce thundered a shot past Peter Bonetti from about thirty-five yards, no mean feat. Jimmy Greaves missed a chance near the end, but we deserved to share the spoils. After the match, though, I was brought down to earth by Dave Sexton for giving away the equaliser. He blamed me for giving a square throw-in about the halfway line. It was intercepted and gave Spurs the possession from which they eventually equalized. It was my first taste of being singled out because I was the youngest. I did not realise you could not throw it in on the halfway line in the big time.

The next day I went shopping down the King's Road with my best mate at the club, Tony Frewin. Frew was a tall, rangy centre-half who should have gone all the way in the game. Born in Ilford, he later moved to Stevenage, the Noke in fact, from where he commuted every day. More often than not he would end up staying at the prefab to save his strength and his fares. Like most young men of our age we took a healthy interest in the opposite sex, and Tony had the film star good looks and of course put them to good use! Dave Sexton had us pegged as troublemakers right from the start. That's why I think he outed my pal. Frew drifted out of the game after a spell in South Africa. He was far superior to so many centre-halves I was to go on to play both with and against. The last I heard, he was running his very successful business. As my good friend Paul McCormack would say, 'Good luck to him.'

I bought a suit from The Squire Shop. It was owned by a guy called John Simons who still has a shop in Covent Garden. Tony and I used to go to his shop, which used to belong to a butcher. It had an amazing Tudor interior. In those days John was selling a three-piece French look with wide lapels on the jacket and high waistcoat. I figured I had to look smart, as I had no intention of going back to the 'Stiffs', Combination football! I stayed in the team for the next match, a 1–1 draw with Crystal Palace. Os scored the equalizer from a long diagonal ball delivered by Eddie McCreadie. We kept playing Palace that season, it seemed. At Christmas we crushed them 5–1 at Selhurst Park, Os helping himself to four of them.

In the autumn I forced myself into the side. I began to pick up the pace of the game, and it was quickly becoming easy for me. I had more time and space than I could ever have dreamed about. We drew our next match against Wolves in the pouring rain. Derek Dougan, a legend in the game, was their star. We were cruising, 2–0 up with a few minutes left, when he popped up to lay on two goals. The Wolves match always sticks in my mind for several reasons. I remember getting a dead-leg, as we kids called it, and 'The Doog' coming across to pick me up. Then I recall limping to my brother John's wedding reception. He married the lovely Pauline Thomas from Victoria and had two children: Billy, who is the face off my old man, and Claire, who's a ringer for her mum. I remember the wedding for the reason that the guests seemed more interested in what had gone on at Stamford Bridge that afternoon. Victoria is the home of Chelsea supporters.

Next it was Leeds United in the League Cup. Injury kept me out of the first match at Elland Road but we fought out a draw and brought them back to the Bridge. Playing our best football so far that season, we beat them 2–0 after a tactical change at half-time.

Sexton had me playing against the powerful Paul Madeley in midfield. It was then that I realized I had to strengthen myself up and really reach peak fitness. After switching to the right wing, I was able to boost my confidence by nutmegging my all-time favourite Leeds player, Terry Cooper. I had a feeling after that night that it was my time.

2

The Hudson Bay Company is Formed

'When a true genius appears in the world, you may know him by this sign, that the dunces are all in confederacy against him.'
Jonathan Swift

By Christmas 1969 I was established in the team and looking forward to a Cup run. After beating Leeds (in that replay) in the League Cup we had unluckily gone out at Carlisle after Peter Bonetti had been dazed by a coin thrown from the terraces and Carlisle scored in the confusion. Ossie reckoned Catty was still looking for the penny! Imagine that happening today, especially if a Chelsea fan had chucked such an object. This was my best performance so far. On a beautiful pitch, we played football close to what I was used to in the 'Cage'. I returned to Carlisle years later and played one of my finest matches ever.

I really felt now that I was becoming an important part of the team, I mean a real part, not just another player. My performances were improving with every ninety minutes and I was becoming a player who could do more than the next man. That was the way I saw it then, and still do today: I was not happy with my game if I was not the best player on the field. That was my goal, my aim in every single match, and I carried that through to the end until I realised I could no longer achieve that. I prided myself on consistency. I recall some years later in Boston, USA, sitting in our hotel bar with the former Fulham and Norwich full-back John Ryan, at that time my team-mate at Seattle Sounders. Picking up his drink, he said, 'Can I tell you something, Huddy? Playing at full-back I can see everything that goes on, the whole picture, and in our four matches on the road (*this one in Boston being the last of them*), unbelievably you have not lost us possession once.' I drank a toast to that, as one does, and thanked him for the compliment. Those four matches, coming in the space of eight days, had been against the likes of the great Peruvian Cubillas, New York's Chinaglia and Bogicevic and the one and only Franz Beckenbauer. John followed that by saying he had never seen such consistency and controlled football. I treasure compliments like that, but only when they come from people who can play the game – and Ryan could.

The lads in the Chelsea team were now accepting me and encouraging me to play my own game, my natural game. Players like Eddie Mac and Marvin Hinton were showing me respect, and that was good enough for me. I knew that Ossie and Hutch would hold the ball up when I played it through. The best exponent of that in the modern game is now in Chelsea blue: Mark Hughes. Although Mark is not in Ossie's shirt or in his class when it comes to all-around ability, that's taking absolutely nothing away from the ex-Manchester United striker. There were not many who were in Osgood's class. Like Hutchinson, he could 'hurt defenders' and make space for his team-mates.

One of my assets was my ability at corner-kicks: I even scored a couple. I could float them, hang them, curl them or drive them. It was best to hang them with the likes of Osgood, Hutchinson, Webb and Dempsey piling into the six-yard box, and I had the best view of all. Chelsea had more air-power than a squadron of B-52s. It was easy to pick these people out. Hutch once scored at Highbury from one I drove hard across the flag. From where I stood, he got to the ball so early it seemed he was above the bar – crossbar, that is – with Bob Wilson on his heels wondering what he should do. The answer, when Hutch is like that, is nothing, Bob!

My career could have been over before it started. Between the ages of ten and fifteen, I would suffer a terrible pain in my left knee at the slightest touch. In my first year as an apprentice, Harry Medhurst sent me for an X-ray and examination by the club specialist. I was to see a few of those in the coming years. The initial scans were negative but later they revealed that two bones in my knee were not 'fusing' properly as I grew. The condition was known as (wait for it) Osgood Slater's disease. The condition had no relation to Peter, and I never found out who the Slater was in this deal. I was told that I must have complete rest from that time up until the age of twenty-one. That was five years away, so you can imagine my early frustration. Nothing changes!

That was the start of the 1967–68 season (the summer of love, hippies and all the rest) and I spent eight months sweeping the dressing-rooms, cleaning the boots and the big marble home-team bath – in fact, doing every chore that Harry and his very likeable son Norman Medhurst could think of. This was harder than any cross-country run or set of doggies, I can promise you! The only consolation was that Tommy Docherty would take me as skip-boy for our first-team away matches, although this meant I had to miss Fulham's home ones. I would help set the kit out and change the players' studs as they warmed up for what to me was really big-time. This was my first taste and I was just praying my knee would knit together as quickly as possible so I could have some of it. I loved the atmosphere of those away games, for no matter where Chelsea played they would always have a large away following. This added to the excitement. My knee improved, and my determination to overcome this set-back and make up for lost time stiffened my resolve to make the first team. Before the end of the season I played a few matches. One of them was a testimonial for Mike Keen, the QPR skipper. His son played at West Ham, Wolves and Stoke City. Dave Sexton saw me play that evening, and he must have seen enough in me to sign me as a professional that July. Frank Blunstone, in his day a flying left-winger, was our coach. Along with Tommy Harmer they gave me great encouragement, always pushing me, as if I needed that after the last few months. Tommy the 'Charmer', one of the last of a dying breed, the great ball-playing, juggling inside-forward, would always drum into me how important that 'first touch' was. He had a glittering career at Tottenham before the Doc snapped him up to give some much needed experience and knowledge to his young 'Diamonds', as he called them. Harmer was one of the most skilful and naturally talented players I have had the pleasure to see, let alone work with. He was just as much at home juggling with an orange or a tennis ball as he was with a football. A TV documentary on Maradona showed him juggling with a golf ball. See! The real greats never stopped practising their touch, such was their love of the game and the simple arts connected with it. Tommy taught me that without your touch you were nothing but average. Needless to say I worked hard on that, but I didn't need Tommy to tell me. I already had the finest teacher.

I wanted to be both a taker and maker of goals. To finish like Greaves and pass like Haynes – that was my goal. Doubtless in the football-speak of the nineties, I would be known as the midfield player who operates 'in the hole'. The old-fashioned term of the Harmer era, inside-forward, suited me better. I watched Suarez, a player I was once likened to, and Rivera, two players from outside England whom I always tried to emulate in our 'Cage'. Then there was the magic of Ferenc Puskas; what genius! I was privileged to meet the great man a few years ago at the opening of Wolverhampton Wanderers' superb new stadium.

When I broke on to the scene, coaches like Revie and his ilk were already dreaming up ploys to curb the style of the more talented players. I think the whole root of my conflicts with the system was that I could play and most of the people who coached and managed could not. It seemed as if they were jealous of my talent, and could never get to grips with it. People from West Ham like Malcolm Allison, John Bond, Dave Sexton himself, and later on in the USA another nearly man, Bobby Howe. I always think of that great boxer John Conteh, who, had he been a footballer, would surely have played for Chelsea. Once, a reporter lamenting his politically incorrect career told him how much greater he could have been but for 'women and drink'.

'The only reason I did anything,' John told him, 'was for women and drink.'

Different motives drive different people. Dave Sexton could never grasp that. People who do not drink themselves fail to understand that in some cases it enhances performance by giving confidence and insight. In the case of the group of players I mixed with at Chelsea, the social side forged that deep bond, team spirit and camaraderie that was us. Dave had a very quiet personality. He was in a state of perpetual inner exile, very edgy. Looking back, I can see it was not personal but just a lack of communication. I use this book as an olive branch to him. 'If only' ... the two biggest words in the universe.

Being a Gemini, I always place great store on my first impressions. The first time I was introduced to him was by Tommy Docherty, then managing Chelsea whilst Dave was first-team coach. It was on a Tuesday evening and we were training behind the goal at the 'Shed' end. Sexton was to replace Docherty when the volatile Scot was sacked, a break-up of a great partnership in my view. The playing career of Dave Sexton was always shrouded in mystery to me. To this day I have never come across anyone who saw him play. He was part of that West Ham 'Academy' mafia I spoke of earlier, along with Chief Godfather Malcolm Allison who played for the Hammers before his career was cut short by TB. John Bond played in the same side, and they formed a mutual admiration society called the 'Academy'. I was to have a run-in some years later with Bondy in Seattle, where he tried to do a Rodney Marsh and poke his nose into somebody else's club, where it was not wanted and most definitely not needed. Sexton was part of the coterie, and they all obtained the overblown reputation that they were experts on the game, part of the myth that 'If you haven't played at West Ham, then you can't know anything about the game.' Come off it, chaps! When reminded of this years later by our coach Bobby Howe in Seattle, I had no choice but to question this utter rubbish. On more than one occasion Howe whispered this to young naive Americans. To say he picked on the wrong one in a downtown bar one evening is an understatement. He really believed that these men from Upton Park came from another planet. I disagreed strongly and a brief scuffle ensued. We decided to sort out the argument on the training pitch the following day. Guess who didn't show? So much for the 'Academy'.

West Ham United had three World Cup winners in Moore, Peters and Hurst. Rather like Chelsea, though, at any given time they had a bewildering mixture of brilliance and mediocrity. Both clubs were, and still are, under-achievers with a fanatical following that deserves far more than the lean years their average play gave them. In the sixties and well into the seventies, the 'Academy' had a huge influence over the game. I found it very narcissistic. Allison's partnership with the late great Joe Mercer was one of the most exciting pairings in football management. Only Brian Clough and Peter Taylor matched it and went beyond it. They all fell out, though; like Tina and Ike, Lennon and McCartney, Charles and Di, Chelsea and me. Quite often the sum is greater than the parts. Allison and Clough never rediscovered the glory they had with their partners; rather like Liverpool, who dominated for so long but whose players were found to be lacking individuality.

Recently I was in Terry Venables's drinking den, Scribes. I met Craig Johnston, now very successful in television. Craig, a very likeable fella, made a special point of coming over to shake hands. He told me that he had won five Championship medals, a European Cup winners' medal and a host of other honours, but considered me to be a real player. Just a little story to show the esteem in which the seventies Chelsea side was held. Not like Terry McDermott, who mouthed at me at Stamford Bridge, after his and Keegan's side had lost yet another London match, to 'put my medals on the table'. That does not cut any ice with me; anyway, we did not have a twelfth man dressed in black at the Bridge, and we all know what that means. We never played on all day until we finally got an equalizer. We were the original Chelsea boys. Webb, Osgood, Cooke, Baldwin, McCreadie, Garland, Hutch and myself. We were princes of the King's Road. The search has been on for the new Chelsea boys ever since, like the crock of gold at the end of the rainbow. Fruitless, of course. It was serendipity.

Dave Sexton failed to control the potential of the situation. In those days, the players were just one step away from being fans on the terraces. Now, there are not even terraces. We were earning good money, but not to the extent that it caused the gulf between players and fans that I find today. In my day we drank in pubs, not nightclubs. Well, only occasionally. Our main watering-hole after hours was The Cromwellian. This became our office after 11pm. Our afternoon hideaway was The Townhouse, which is now a recording studio. The upstairs bar was ours. The players involved mainly were myself – obviously, being the local bar finder – Micky Droy, Tommy, Ossie and whoever was in town that night. We would be in competition with my great pals, then and now: TD, a tipper driver in those days; Leslie May, whom you have heard all about; Bobby Eyres, he was the dancer; and big JF, or Fennell as the Chelsea players knew him. They would have loved to be in our squad, and this was the nearest they ever came to it. Harry 'Heart' was our bartender and the best I've seen anywhere in the world. A tiny little gay fellow, did you guess, with a glass which would take a bottle of Campari at a time, and a delightful man who could quip with the very best. When Harry started, you stood back next to the fireplace and watched him tear people apart. I remember one evening when John Hollins's wife Linda had let him out and he was on his best form. A very funny man Holly was, when in such spirit. But I can assure you he did not heed the warning of 'Don't mess with Heart'. After aiming some kind of funny at the very busy bartender, he was quickly put in his place by the retort, 'Is that really you or are you standing in a hole?' I fell out with Holly, sadly. I'll tell you why later. The Crom has gone now and with it our beloved Heart, last seen in an off-licence in Bow after a spell in a bar in Brighton. One of several gay friends we met along the way, he still holds a special place in my heart. Good times! Recently the tabloids were full of stories about players swilling champers at £150 a bottle. At today's prices not many fans can afford to go to the matches, let alone socialize. Remember, Moet and Chandon was £5 a bottle in the Crom.

I literally could not wait for games to come around. I also could not wait to meet Maysie, Eyrsie and Frew after matches and do the King's Road. The Markham Arms was always our last stop before the Crom. Fun, it was called then. Perhaps you remember the word? The media lament the waste of talent of my generation of players. The point was, we had a lot of talent to waste. Perhaps we were seen in terms of presence rather than achievement. The

Chelsea team of 1970 crystallized the era. What does Blackburn sum up today? A glorified First Division side beefed up by a multi-millionaire's whim? Roy of the Rovers stuff? From scraping in to the play-offs a few years ago to playing in the European Cup! With Blackburn, Manchester United and Leeds all being totally outclassed in Europe in recent seasons, it makes it very difficult to foresee where the next serious challenge will come from. It will definitely not be from Newcastle, even though they have spent the crown jewels in trying to qualify for the competition. Money cannot buy you success, as Kevin Keegan has shown us, but what it can do is get you massive publicity. His signing of Asprilla was nothing short of ludicrous. Not since Allison messed up with Marsh, and Ramsey with his substitution in Mexico, can I recall such an X-rated horror movie.

Chelsea's run-up to success in that watershed year of 1970 started with a home Cup tie against Birmingham City on the first Saturday in a bitter January. As both sides wore blue, we had to change our strip. I still do not understand why, as we were the home team. We wore yellow shirts and blue shorts. I always liked those colours, which were lucky for us. The following season, Arsenal wore them as their second colours and won both the Cup and League. Everton, who won the title that season, also wore that colour combination. Birmingham wore an all-white strip on this particular day. Leeds had sported those colours for some years, a direct copy of the strip worn by Real Madrid. In the Birmingham line-up were two ex-Chelsea men, Albert 'Ruby' Murray, as the crowd called him (to us he was 'Satch'), and Tony Hateley, Mark's father. A guy called Trevor Hockey played too. He looked a lot like Dave Lee Travis, the disc jockey. Trevor died of heart trouble not so long ago. The tension was running high between the two sets of fans. A Chelsea fan had been chucked under a bus a few years before, and I always recalled trouble at St Andrews. It would be tempting to add that little has changed. Just ask Millwall!

The first half was tight and the pace frenetic, but right on half-time we obtained the vital breakthrough. I found space out wide on the right and got to the by-line, something we seldom see today, and crossed for Peter Osgood to score the first of his Cup goals that season. That settled us down, and the second half was comfortable. Thirteen minutes from the end, a little passing move out on the left between myself and the two Peters, Houseman and Osgood, was finished in typical style by Ian Hutchinson from close range. Hutch scored his second and our third in the last minute, from a Hollins cross. We were on our way. To celebrate, I bought a new jacket from Take Six, Prince of Wales check. I had loved clothes for as long as I could remember, and you can imagine what it was like when I became friendly with Peter 'Jason King' Wyngarde. All the rascals I knew in the neighbourhood dressed well, with the smartest of the lot being Brian Harrison. Immaculate is the word. Not like their counterparts today.

In the fourth round we were drawn at home again, this time to Burnley. They have fallen on hard times in recent years and are now managed by my lovely little mate, ex-Everton and Stoke City star Adrian 'Inchy' Heath. But in those days they always gave Chelsea a run for our money.

We scored twice in two minutes to set up what appeared to be a comfortable victory. Hollins got the first, and I set up Ossie for number two. It was one of the best bits of play in the whole Cup run, maybe the entire season. I bounced a throw-in on my thigh, flicked it over one defender's head and in the same movement just lobbed a curling cross to the far stick. I knew Peter would be there. I could always anticipate his runs, sense his presence. At times it was as if we were telepathic. He converted the chance nonchalantly as usual. Pictures of the goal show the big man in the back of the Burnley net with the goalkeeper stranded at the near post. With ten minutes left and Chelsea cruising, Burnley gambled, pushing Martin Dobson up front from a defensive position. Dobson was a neat player who would have been even more appreciated in today's game. He was a player who could operate anywhere, with lots of stamina, and he had that ability to win any aerial tussle, which is needed in midfield today. He scored twice in the dying minutes to force a replay and take us out of London for the first and only time in that Cup run.

Three nights later, we wore the yellow and blue at Turf Moor. The stage had been well set for a night of electric tension and the gates were locked ages before the kick-off. Thousands were turned away. Chelsea took a huge contingent, who gave fanatical support.

When the deck was stacked against the Blues, we could always count on the support of those marvellous fans. We needed it that night because we were totally overrun in the first half. If Dobson had been their ace on the Saturday, Ralph Coates was their star turn now. He had had a very quiet game at the Bridge, but certainly made up for it here. Coates joined Tottenham soon after, but was never able to recapture this kind of form. He always reminded me of Danny De Vito. Coates's best game for Spurs was against us in the League Cup semi-final the following season. He found it hard to win over those Spurs fans, perhaps the most demanding in football. Even Terry Venables as a player felt their wrath. They had no love for Chelsea players at Tottenham. In more recent times, the likes of Gordon Durie and Jason Cundy have suffered at their hands, Durie only recapturing his form when he returned home to Glasgow Rangers.

Coates shot Burnley ahead with a crisp, low drive from the edge of the box ten minutes from the break. The tackling was fierce, and there were more fouls than passes in the first twenty minutes. Ron Harris and Eddie McCreadie were working overtime on Coates and both found themselves in the referee's book. The flying Burnley winger kept changing flanks, but as the game wore on the panic he was causing was slowly contained. In the second half, Coates began to run out of steam, slowed by some of Ron and Eddie's tackling. We gradually eased back into the game. Now it was Peter Houseman who was giving *their* full-back the runaround, and I was getting loose from that tough little man-marker Brian 'Bhudda' O'Neil, a player who later went on to that great 'drinking team' at Southampton. Time ticked by. We were ourselves tired by now, but the Chelsea fans who had travelled up from London lifted us. Eighteen minutes from time Nobby won the ball from O'Neil, ran about 30 yards and rifled in a low shot from just outside the box. A rare Houseman goal, but a great one. I can see him now, as he stood there punching the sky. Looking back with a watery eye of memory, that was probably the most important goal in the competition for us, and the late Peter's finest moment in Chelsea colours. He was one of the best-balanced players I ever saw, and, like a true winger, could beat full-backs on the inside and out, and often did both. He seemed to lack a little pace, but made up for it with his very educated left foot and brain. Houseman was Sexton's personification of what a footballer should be. He was not one of our school as regards socialising. God rest his soul! The crowd saw him as Bill Wyman to Osgood's Jagger. I will not include Keith Richards in this analogy.

The irony of it was that Peter and his lovely wife Sally were killed in a car crash. If any other of the Chelsea forwards had met with a similar fate, it would have compounded the legend that sprang up about us and curiously still seems to be spreading. River Phoenix was born that year. If any Chelsea player had died at a similar age, the legend, like that of Monroe, Dean and Presley, would have been complete. Houseman made such a massive contribution to the winning of the Cup that year; he seemed to be up for every game. It was as if he knew what the future had in store. Let me just say that Nobby Houseman – I really do not know how he came by that name – was a diamond, always had a smile and could not have been more genuine. His family must have been very proud of him. In writing this book, looking back and talking to people from Oxford, Peter's last club, I was not surprised at the unbelievable affection they held for Peter.

Towards the end of normal time, we poured down on the Burnley goal. Hutch nearly brought down the crossbar after I had slipped him one through, but the game went the distance. Three minutes into extra-time, Tommy Baldwin, deputizing for Os, headed us in front from Nobby's cut-back cross. I told you he could get goals given the opportunity. We were now swamping them. The killer instinct came out of us for the first time that night; detached and clinical. Charlie Cooke missed a good chance to wrap it up before Houseman capped his finest performance with a third goal in the last minute. The Chelsea fans must have shouted themselves hoarse, and at the end they went wild with excitement. They didn't care tuppence how they got back to London. For Houseman it was his first-ever double for the club, and it was never needed more. Poor old Peter! I still cannot believe he is gone.

Our victory at Burnley made everyone in the game sit up and take notice. Earlier Chelsea sides might have crumbled under such intense early pressure. That night at Turf Moor we showed a combination of the will to win and resilience that was to weld us into a very tough unit. The ability to endure is the hallmark of all winning teams. The fifth round draw took us back to Selhurst Park early in February. It had been a cold and very wet winter, and the Palace pitch resembled the Southwell all-weather racetrack. Charlie Cooke missed the game and Tommy Baldwin switched from Ossie's nine to the number seven shirt. My friendship with Tommy was by then developing, and I can happily say we are great friends now. Chelsea were still in the running for the Championship but we were really fired up for the Cup, especially after the two previous semi-final disappointments under the Doc. I was beginning to get a lot of press, the media seizing on the King's Road connection and the long-hair, trendy-clothes image. This was a heady cocktail for Fleet Street. Osgood's four-goal spree on his last visit to Selhurst was featured in all the nationals. The family dog was called Ossie, and I was pictured with him in my arms outside the prefab (the dog, that is).

The dog actually caused a slight domestic problem in the Hudson prefab. My brother John was a huge Osgood fan and wanted to christen this little poodle after our centre-forward. For some strange reason I wanted to name him after Rodney Marsh; how glad I am they didn't listen to me. The crowd for the Palace match was 48,000 (or twelve Wimbledon average home gates today). The gate receipts were a record £22,000; hardly the Brinks Mat job today, but solid money then, when I was on £75 a week. Palace's top player was Steve Kember, who was later to figure in my life considerably. He was out injured that day.

Peter Osgood was about as popular at Selhurst Park as Cantona is now. It was poetic justice that he put us ahead from a Houseman corner almost on half-time. Palace complained that it had been the result of a foul, but the goal stood. They booed Ossie for the rest of the game, but he loved that. I do not recall him resorting to kung-fu that day. Early in the second half, Palace equalized. A boy called Hoy scored it; he had done the same thing at Chelsea earlier in the season. Palace threw everything forward, and we were under the collar for a short period of time. Suddenly we broke out of defence with a couple of devastating strikes to put the game out of their reach. John Dempsey got the crucial goal, meeting a towering centre from Holly to beat the Palace keeper John Jackson all ends up. It was

Demps's first Cup goal for Chelsea. Dave Sexton never really knew
what a character he was getting when he signed him from Fulham. I
cannot understand why, really, because Dave was his coach there
too.

In those days the atmosphere at the club was fantastic, with
absolutely no hint of the trouble that was to come – but we were
winning matches, weren't we! John Dempsey's humour became
even more important as times got harder, and his wit helped break
the building tension. I do not know how Demps got on with Bobby
Robson at Fulham. Not really one for a smile, is he? Robson was
just starting out in his managerial career, which was to take him to
the very top. He missed one player though, when my father tipped
him off about a young lad playing at Burton Albion called Ian
Hutchinson. Fulham's loss was Chelsea's tremendous gain. It was
on the underground coming home from an Arsenal match at
Highbury that my father approached Robson in his own particular
way. I could see immediately that the ex-England boss thought he
was talking to just another keen Fulham supporter. Little did he
know, it was a very costly assumption. To be honest, perhaps
Robson was right – who wanted to sign a lad in a leather jacket who
rode round on a motorbike, with a name like Ian Hutchinson?

Osgood was being watched by Sir Alf Ramsey, who was looking
for players to take to Mexico to defend the World Cup. That must
have been the first time he'd seen me play, although I'd been quite
outstanding earlier in the season when we whipped his old team
Ipswich 4–1 in East Anglia, where he was living. Osgood should
have scored immediately after Demps put us back in front. A
goalmouth mêlée ended with him hitting the post after firing
through a crowd of players. Jackson could only stand and watch;
Ossie was becoming a nightmare to poor old Jacko! The crowd were
in full swing now, and another free-kick by Webby saw Dempsey
head into the path of Houseman, who crashed in another
left-footer. In his first title fight with Sonny Liston, the boxer then
known as Cassius Marcellus Clay would yawn to show his contempt
for his opponent. The ability to score almost at will was a similar act
of arrogance. My theory about the apparent inconsistency of the
club was that we were more vulnerable against lesser teams,
because we considered them to be beneath us and not so much

effort was put in to obtain a result. But isn't that human nature? I read about carbon molecules which could have the bejesus beaten out of them and yet bounce back. Chelsea were like that in those days, such was the spirit in the side. Hutchinson grabbed a fourth, but the game was already over and Palace played out the rest of the game as if they were on Prozac, devastated by the savagery and speed of the Stamford Bridge onslaught. Bert Head's team were wrecked, and we were game for anybody now.

The draw kept us in London once again; away to QPR, then a Second Division team (just as they are now, really). Birmingham had fielded two ex-Chelsea players in the earlier round, and Rangers had three: former England centre-forward Barry Bridges, Ronnie Harris's brother Allan, and one Terry Venables, who had finished his unhappy time at Tottenham. Rodney Marsh – who you must have gathered by now is not on my Christmas card list – also played, as did Venners's alter ego Hazell! Playing at right-back was Dave Clement, who sadly committed suicide. The tragic story goes that he was told he had cancer and decided to finish it all, but they later found that he had been misdiagnosed. Terrible thing, nice fella, and a very useful player at the Rs for many years; a great club man. The match was a real grudge affair, which suited us just fine. Chelsea fans outnumbered QPR's as usual, even though they were the home side. A few weeks before this sixth round tie, a coaching course had been run at our Mitcham training ground. Amongst the FA coaches was the Rangers goalkeeper Mick Kelly, and everybody passed this particular course except two players, Osgood and Webb. Oh, how they were looking forward to this one. One of the heroes of Euro 96 was the superb David Seaman, and I was interested to read Bob Wilson's comments on how Seaman nearly walked out of the England set-up over a certain goalkeeping coach, because he didn't do extra training. Mick Kelly is and has been that England coach for some time now. What a tragedy it would have been if Seaman had been forced out by such people.

Rangers tore into us and almost drew first blood through a Bridges snap shot, but that blood got spilt all over them as the Blues (still in the yellow-and-blue ensemble) scored twice in the opening moments. The first goal was breathtaking. With seven minutes gone, David Webb won the ball deep in his own half and pelted through the Loftus Road mud-heap, exchanging diagonal passes first with Cooke then Hollins. Near the Rangers goal, he took Hollins's pass and swept it high into Kelly's net. Then, within sixty seconds, Cooke put Osgood through to thunder one past the FA coach. Rangers' record crowd of 33,000 – it seemed we were breaking all ground records now – gasped when McCreadie brought down his old team-mate Bridges, who was always a handful with that electric burst of speed. We disputed the penalty and Peter Bonetti saved Venners's first attempt. The referee, Kevin Howley, adjudged Catty to have moved and this time the ex-Chelsea skipper coolly slotted home. Venables was one of the all-time great penalty-takers. He was as cool as if he was facing down Sugar in court. His boot-lace had come undone and he had to cut off some of it. I always thought his range of skills was limited, but free-kicks and other dead-ball moves were his speciality. He was a great scavenger of ideas, always picking things up from those around him, asking questions and listening to anything and everything, then piecing them together; a great football mind.

Rangers asked questions of our defence. A backheader from Vic Mobley worried Bonetti, and another header from Bridges grazed the angle of the bar and post. Osgood was booked for a foul on Clement and the Rangers fans howled – Os was already waiting on an appearance before the FA for three bookings (good job Kelly was not on that committee too). Right on half-time, though, he slammed home his second to restore our two-goal lead. Sometimes you need a slice of luck, especially on a Cup run, and we got it here when a John Hollins shot was saved by Kelly but was allowed to bounce from his chest – and there was the big man, ready to pounce on any little mistake this particular keeper made: 3–1. At that time, there was no greater finisher in football. Kerry Dixon was the nearest striker in contemporary times at Chelsea to compare with the 'Wizard of Os'. Ironically, Dixon's career stalled under the management of one John Hollins.

In the second half, Rangers pushed forward trying to save the game. In previous weeks we had squandered two-goal leads against Burnley and Derby County. In the latter game I scored my first League goal, volleying a thirty-yarder over the top of Les Green. He was the shortest goalkeeper in the country, though I am not saying the two things are connected.

I was having my best game of the season so far, as Terry said in his foreword. It was my first appearance at Loftus Road since I played in the Mike Keen testimonial. Venables spent most of the game trying to get to grips with me, and it was a great feeling. OK, it might have been different if they had taken the lead, but I still feel we had too much all-round strength and ability in our side. Funny! Only a couple of years before, I had been drooling over Terry's skills when I was just a rookie at Chelsea. Only recently I was telling both George Graham and Don Howe that I felt that the Chelsea team before this one, now ripping QPR apart, were more talented than us and better equipped. I remember their incredible Cup performance knocking Liverpool out 2–1 up at Anfield, which was quite remarkable. Then once again I sit back and dream that 'if only' Doc had stayed and kept Terry, who went on to win the Cup with Spurs in his first season, against Chelsea by the way! He should have kept George, who went on to win the Double with Arsenal, and bought Charlie and so on and so on. The outcome would surely have been a second League Championship for the club, with more to come. Well, I can dream like anyone else!

With Rangers attacking so much, they were open to the quick break. Cooke was involved with most things that were happening now. When we had our passing game together it was a joy. On the hour I put Houseman away. He centred low across the goal, Gillard only partially cleared it and there was Ossie again.. He instantly collected the ball, did one of his little shimmies which sent so many defenders the wrong way, and comprehensively beat Kelly with a low drive into the corner to complete his hat-trick. The script could not have been written much better. The Chelsea fans were now going nuts and smelling the Twin Towers. Kelly lay face down in the mud. The game was now beyond Rangers' reach. I ran to congratulate Os, who was in the back of the net picking the ball out. He glanced down at the Rangers keeper, the FA man who had failed him only weeks earlier at Mitcham. How ironic that Webby was the other player on Kelly's list. 'Stick to coaching,' snarled Osgood and volleyed the ball back into the net.

Still a prescient critic of that coaching doctrine, Os, together with myself, scuffled with Kelly some twenty-six years later. Chelsea had just crushed Middlesbrough 5–0 with a display reminiscent of our halcyon days. No story typifies better the freewheeling spirit of a talent like Osgood or the constraints put on it by a system regimented by the likes of Kelly. The sad thing was that the Kellys of the world to some extent won. They always do! In the same year that Osgood was scoring wonder goals, and plenty of them, another genius, John Lennon, said of the demise of the Beatles: 'The same bastards are in control; the same people are running everything; it's the same. They hyped the kids and the generations. The dream is over.'

QPR fought to the bitter end. Their Cup dream was over, while ours was very much coming true. Near the end, Barry Bridges pulled a deserved goal back, for old times' sake; he had worked tirelessly to overcome his old team. A great feature of this match was the duel between Ron Harris and Rodney Marsh. Before the match they called it Osgood versus Marsh, the 'Clown Prince' of Loftus Road versus the 'Wizard' of Stamford Bridge. One thing was for sure: they never had a Ronnie Harris, so Ossie had a head start. The cold truth of the matter was that Chopper had Marsh tucked up nicely in his pocket while Ossie ran riot. Peter Osgood proved to me that day that he was in a different league, and who better to do it in front of than Alf Ramsey. Ossie had just booked his ticket to Mexico, Marsh was going nowhere. After the match, Sir Alf said of me: 'There is no limit to what this boy can achieve.' He was wrong. There were limits put on the parameters of my career by the confederacy.

3

Tears in Heaven

*'Here we all are, sitting on a Rainbow' Lazy Sunday Afternoon –
Small Faces, from the CD* Ogden's Nut Flake *– Steve Marriott
and Ronnie Lane*

Spring 1970. River Phoenix was born. Jack Walker (the one in *Coronation Street*) died. Raymond Douglas Davies (born on the same day as me) changed the lyrics of his song, 'Lola' (Coca-Cola became Cherry Cola), to avoid a BBC ban. The semi-final draw was made and we were drawn against Watford. We were immediately installed as Cup favourites. Leeds United were pitched against Manchester United. That one was to go the distance as both sides were locked in a titanic struggle to go to Wembley.

The 'Dream Final' everybody wanted was Chelsea against George Best and Co, just as the FA Cup Final clash in recent years between Chelsea and Manchester United caught the imagination. How amazing it is that two such fantastic players as Johnny Haynes and George himself never walked out of that tunnel for the match all kids dream of. They did everything else, but I bet they would have swapped anything for an FA Cup Final appearance. I

45

was the only player in our side who wanted to play Leeds, though. I wanted to cross swords once again with Giles and Bremner. I fancied our chances of winning, because of our supremacy in midfield. Cooke and Hudson against Giles and Bremner was a mouth-watering prospect. Bremner was awarded the Football Writers' Player of the Year award a couple of weeks later, just pipping yours truly. If I could have won that, the Cup and on top of that forced myself into Ramsey's Mexico squad, it would have been the most amazing first season by a young lad ever.

Our League form was still impressive and we were riding so high that we still had an outside chance of the Championship. Maybe the Double in my first season as well, the mind boggles! I scored my second League goal at Coventry City as we crushed them 3–0. The goal followed a run from just outside my own box, carrying the ball and selling a couple of dummies before sliding it under Bill Glazier. Whenever I visit that ground, even now they still say it's the best goal they've ever seen up there. Ossie said, though, that it was second best to a similar goal he scored at Turf Moor. He told me that running back to the halfway line! Ossie was not one to be outdone, but I think I did him this time.

The spirit at the club was now sky-high, both on and off the field. At that time there was no hint of rows with Sexton; they seemed to start when we went into Europe. We were winning games and sweeping all before us. Those were the days, my friend, I thought they'd never end! Dave Sexton would never come out on any jaunts to the King's Road pubs and restaurants, nor even sit down with us on tour when invited! He would limit his time to the training ground. He lived in Brighton and would commute back and forth like an accountant to his wife and three kiddies. He had his favourites, though. I remember him taking the Harris brothers to see the Cooper–Ali fight at Highbury. Some would tell you that Ali's jab to 'Enery's eye was the best ever seen at that ground, but my old pal Charlie George disagrees.

My local was the Markham Arms, as you guessed, halfway down the King's Road between Sloane Square and the World's End. Now it is the Abbey National, and bearing in mind all the dosh we passed over the counter that is not surprising. In the eighties it became famous on the gay scene, but not in our day. In fact, the complete opposite was true. Tommy Baldwin made the Trafalgar his 'office', and a lot of the chaps liked the 'Bird's Nest'. It was actually the Six Bells and was one of the most famous pubs in London, situated almost opposite the fire station near Beaufort Street, home of George Best. I think Bowie lived there for a while too. I used to see John Lennon's Mini-Cooper 'S' with black wheels and black windows cruising around the area. Os liked the Bird's Nest. The bouncers were Chelsea boys and they played the best records. Nearer the ground we would use the Imperial or the Lord Palmerston, which was a pub owned by the boxing family, the Mancinis. My favourite, though, was the Adelaide where I would spend many hours in hysterics with my uncle George and Frew. I don't want you to get the wrong impression here, I did find time to go training! Two pubs near the ground were strongholds of the groups of young sporting men who followed Chelsea everywhere. They were the Black Bull and the Ifield Tavern. Sometimes the pubs were targets for rival fans. I recall the Ifield was 'redecorated' by some northern fans visiting London for the day. Can't think what they argued about ...

The Markham became the most popular for several reasons, and one was because of Alexandres. This was owned by an Italian-Maltese gentleman called Camillo, who was to become very close to my whole family and almost all of Chelsea Football Club. What a piece of work he was! He could get Pepe to serve you up David Webb's underpants and convince you that you were eating rack of lamb with truffle potatoes. You see, Webby was their pin-up; Manuel, Camillo's right-hand man, would scream, 'Oh David, you're so butch.' Camillo was an immaculate dresser, always in beautifully-designed handmade suits from Savile Row (Anderson and Shepherd, who made suits for Fred Astaire and the Duke of Windsor).

Great people, the Malts! I first met them through my brother John, who was now cleaning their windows. John could have been a great player. He could have been a contender, if only he had taken as much notice of my father as I did. Two years my elder, he was on Chelsea's books but fell foul of Tommy Docherty. He was deluded into thinking he would sign as a professional, but was badly let down by the management. A move to our beloved Fulham was aborted by scurrilous rumours about a drink problem. Now you are probably amazed to think a member of the Hudson/Mason family could be accused of such a thing. John was not TT, but he was not Charlie Cooke, Tommy Baldwin and Richard Harris rolled into one, as Vic Buckingham was led to believe. 'Tricky Vicky' was then the manager at Craven Cottage and he got a phone-call from someone at Stamford Bridge. No names, no pack-drill, but my father ended up chasing Tommy Docherty around the desk in his office. That was the world of football for you! My career was plagued by innuendo and downright lies. It still is, in fact. The obstacles that I have encountered even publishing this book could fill another one. What interesting people we would be if all the stories made up about us were true!

John drifted into the Southern League, going from Guildford to Bexley. He lost his appetite for the game through his experiences at the Bridge. Really he should have played alongside me, he certainly had great ability. A familiar enough story! How many times have you heard a famous player say that a relative, school pal or junior was just as good as them but never made it? Some just had the determination to overcome all the hurdles and break through; others just got the breaks. Ray Wilkins said that his younger brother Steven was as good as him. At one time there were three Wilkins brothers on Chelsea's books. Graham, the full-back, was the third. He had a somewhat chequered career at the Bridge. Steven never made it to the first team, plagued by weight problems (tell me about it!). It was Ray who pressed on to carve out a marvellous career, playing for some of the greatest sides in Europe. His father George (like mine) was a huge influence on him. Wilkins senior played in the same Brentford side as Gerry Francis's father. I wonder if one day Butch will manage Spurs?

Camillo was another father figure to me, or mother if you like! He used to look after me personally. Both Ossie and myself would have the royal table, when Webby wasn't trying to slip in with one of his high-rollers or film-star pals, like Michael Crawford. More often than not, on the next table would be some of the leading actresses of the time. Jane Seymour – what a lovely girl she was – and Jackie Bissett, quite stunning, were just two. Tennis players would come over when in town for Wimbledon, and my namesake Rock Hudson would have an afternoon rendezvous with one of our waiters, Miquela, I believe. This little screamer would just tell us, 'Oh boys, what a lovely man he is,' and lick his lips. David Webb would be in there almost every day for lunch, especially on a Friday before a match when he would order his specially cooked (or not cooked) steak tartare, raw fillet-steak. Well, Camillo and Manuel were very impressed, and Miquela would squeal in his gay Italian, over and over, 'Oh David, you're so very butch, my dear.' He was even more excited than Manuel. Good job he never saw him play!

Os and I were the two young princes – Hutch wasn't on the scene quite yet – afloat in the libertine Chelsea life in the debris of the sixties hitting the seventies. Osgood wanted to obtain some of the King's Road style, but being a country boy at heart, he was unclear how to go about this. I always figured that Peter thought he had to prove himself in London first. It did not mean anything to me. It was already my town. I was brought up years before with the likes of Joey Baines, who would introduce me to Blaises at the very early age of fifteen and a half (thanks, Joe!). I did not have to prove anything to anybody then or now, on or off the field. People said I burnt out quickly because I became too close to the environment that encouraged it. I refute that. I was part of the scene already. There was a book out called *The Joy Luck Club* in those days – that was us. We played with joy. We had spirit that had the joy of living and we also rode, and to a lesser extent made, our own luck.

The media portrayed me as someone who liked a drink, partying with a louche crowd. Players like Keegan were always more their cup of tea. He had the iron will to succeed. He aspired to live in a huge house and get mobbed in the streets – I call it 'Noel Edmonds syndrome' – and after a while people forgot their limitations as players. Recently I clashed with the ex-Newcastle boss after his team scraped a draw in an FA Cup tie at the Bridge. Chelsea, inspired by Gullit, were to win a famous victory in the replay. Osgood was in a different class from KK, yet only won a handful of international caps. The boy from Windsor was an outstanding finisher. I used to watch Jimmy Greaves, Ossie's idol, at Tottenham when my father took me and John to White Hart Lane, the first match being the 13–2 defeat of Crewe Alexandra. I noted that Greavsie could hit the ball from any angle, any position, even if he was falling down, which was almost never. That is the difference between them and some of the players today who cost a Lottery win. They need to line everything up like teeing off at golf. With the game even more frenetic today, there is simply not the time. I can still see Os pinging away a shot even as he tumbled to the turf. Remember him beating the great Gordon Banks in the League Cup Final? That was a perfect example of what I mean!

I was with Os when he bought his first suit in Take Six. I recall him trying it on and asking me how he looked in it. I nodded approvingly. He would brush off the lapels and pull down the sleeves that were always too short. A few months later he was telling me about this great shop he knew in the King's Road called Take Six. You could not beat the clothes off-the-peg in there, he enthused. Good old Os!

Twenty-five years on and he is still trying to score points off me. His only criticism of my game was my tackling; he said I couldn't tackle a good Alexandres steak pissiola. He had this quasi-ruthless streak in his game. This, I felt, was a legacy of his shattered leg, broken by a tackle from professional Scouse Emlyn Hughes. Emlyn – don't mention his name to Tommy Smith – was at Blackpool then, and Chelsea had started that season (1966–67) magnificently and were unbeaten. The horrific break put Os out for the rest of the season and Chelsea fell away. There was a school of thought that maintained that Os was never the same player after that incident, losing a bit of pace and, after the agony of the break, always 'looking' for a tackle. Graham Roberts made the memorable quote about 'getting your retaliation in first', and Os always looked after himself after his injury. All I know is, that season he was like a tank in the penalty box, scoring stupendous goals and creating havoc whenever the ball was delivered into the opponents' area.

John Hollins was voted Player of the Year for Chelsea then, just pipping Os. I was third, most promising newcomer (ironic how I was runner-up in the Football Writers' poll). Our play then was being refined. It was more staccato than the sustained effervescence of the Venables/Graham era. They were nicknamed the 'Catch us if you Can' team by the media (and I must say it suited them), after the Dave Clark Five record. I was becoming more of the midfield general, assuming greater responsibility and ready at any time to move forward. The only regret I had was that Sexton would want Holly to take free-kicks and penalties in front of me. I should have been more like Venables and pushed him out of the way, but then Terry was his senior. Things were now moving fast for me. I was called to the Under-23 squad to play Scotland at Roker Park. Os was there too. It was my first visit to this great ground (my second was a heart-breaking Cup defeat with Stoke City, and my third my only ever sending-off). Was it a surprise this match was abandoned through snow after about half an hour? Many people ask what was my luckiest ground; I answer White Hart Lane. My unluckiest? You got it!

My recollection of the semi-final was of the change of routine which almost cost us the game and would have provided one of the biggest upsets in the history of the FA Cup. It happened on the Friday before the match. Any footballer will tell you that the preparation before a vital game is all about ritual, routine, habit and sticking to the same formula. Some years later at Arsenal, Malcolm Macdonald changed what had been our Thursday drinking venue before every Cup tie, and the outcome was a defeat at the hands of Ipswich. Every Thursday from round three we had frequented the Townhouse, but we didn't before the Final. Good luck practices. Very superstitious, as blind Stevie sang! Chelsea were one of the most superstitious teams of all time. I could fill up this chapter with a list of them all. They involved clothing, mainly. I know Dave Sexton wore the same blue jacket all through our Cup run, with a button missing if I remember rightly. I think he still wears it. Joking apart, Dave was a very elegant dresser. I know before a game I would not put my shorts on until the very last moment of leaving the dressing-room, and Ronnie Harris would not speak to anyone, a habit shared by Peter Storey who I would later play with at Arsenal. The first time I was in the dressing-room with 'Snouter' Storey, I could not help thinking this was déjà-vu. The sinister build-up was uncanny. The staring into space, as if they were going into the unknown, and the withdrawn symptoms. I roomed with Peter at Highbury on my very first day at Arsenal and found him an angel, a little different from when he marked me!

Friday was normally reserved for our car park five-a-side – a warm up for the Saturday, it was supposed to be. It took place in the forecourt just inside the main gate. It's all gone now, with the redevelopment of the new ground still going on. In those days, a crowd would gather to watch the training session. More often than not, it would be a better game than the following day – and more dangerous than the one played on the pitch! The leather would get dished out, and tackles would go in that would make Vinnie Jones reach for his ray-bans. A lot of players would end up being clattered into the tin fence next to the turnstiles.

Tensions ran high in these games when, towards the end of my days at Chelsea, cliques and rows divided the team. Players who thought they should have been in the side at the expense of others would tackle those involved with a little more passion. There were many flare-ups and scuffles, including the odd right-hander. The most famous and obvious example was Tommy Baldwin, who would go into the manager's office quite regularly to ask why he wasn't in the team. Well, not happy with the outcome, and after a Thursday night in the Trafalgar, 'Sponge' would proceed to clatter 'Stiff Neck' into the boards. Dave took it well, almost knowingly, and would see it coming, but what he didn't see was the follow-up from Johnny Boyle, who would get him on the rebound off the boards. I often wondered why Dave bothered on a Friday, for he would always finish up rubbing his knees and no doubt, behind locked medical doors, have the ice packs on. This illustrates what I said earlier about the coach and manager's job not going together. To pick a team on Friday, leaving people out and then walking into a fiercely contested five-a-side was a recipe for disaster. Dave came up with the idea of the teams being called the Goodies and the Baddies. It's a wonder we could field a Goodies side. We even had our team photos taken and displayed. It was serious stuff.

Another notorious fracas involved Ron Harris and Keith Weller. The ex-Millwall and Tottenham star, another Cockney Rebel, left Chelsea on the Monday, after the practice-day incident. Weller was a tough cookie, but Ron jump-tackling on that surface was tantamount to meeting Mike Tyson in a phone box. Rumours were rife at the time. Stamford Bridge in those days was a hot-bed of gossip and intrigue. Weller was a real ladies' man, he always reminded me a little of Tony Curtis, though Os said he looked nothing like him! Curtis at that particular time was starring in *The*

Persuaders with Roger Moore, another Alexandres goer. Weller made George Graham look like Larry Grayson in the crumpet stakes. The fans loved him. They called him 'Sammy' after the character in a Charles Dickens novel. Sammy had a short Chelsea career, lasting just over a year. In his first weeks, he scored ten goals in as many games, most of them away from home and from the right-wing position. He was then carpeted by Sexton for not picking the left-back up enough. By curbing his natural predatory instincts, he blunted his game. It always reminds me of when a girl meets a boy, they get married and then she tries her damnedest to change him. That's why I could not understand Dave at times: why did he buy him in the first place? Weller joined Leicester City and a contingent of ex-London lads, including several ex-Chelsea players: pretty boy Alan Birchenall, who used to sing regularly with Joe Cocker in his early Sheffield United days; Stevie Kember, Webby (a little later) and Chris Garland. Chris is now fighting the same serious illness as Ray Kennedy, and is showing the same brave qualities he showed in a Chelsea shirt. I am still very close to Chrissy, he's one of life's gems. Always up to something or other and always with that innocent smile. I don't know where he got that from, for CG was another who fitted perfectly into our King's Road line-up. Chris tells me of the unrest and aggravation of all these London Johns and their clashes with the locals. Also at the club at that time were Lennie Glover from Charlton and ex-Arsenal 'wonderkid' Jon Sammuels. Peter Shilton was there too, and it was said that Weller once had a fight with him in the showers at half-time. I don't know what they were doing in there at half-time, but it was another reason I recall Sammy with affection.

The Friday before the semi-final, instead of having our fun and games in the car park, Dave Sexton opted to take us to a sauna bath, quite a big difference. I had given him the idea, I'm sure, by telling him about my trips to my favourite baths in Jermyn Street. I used to frequent the one at the back of St James's Square by the cheese shop, Paxton and Whitfield. Besty used to live just around the corner from there in a flat by Fortnums. He shared it with a former Miss World, Mary Stavin. I feel sorry for George sometimes. How he had fallen on hard times, living in a luxury flat in the middle of the West End with the most beautiful girl on the planet! How he wasted his life! How he wasted his time! 'Was he really happy?' I ask myself. He surely must miss those scything Ronnie Harris tackles and the pouring rain of Manchester! I restricted my visits to the sauna if it was too near a match. I felt wasted by dehydration. Dave Sexton took the Chelsea squad to the sauna in High Street Kensington. It is a book store now. Nearby is the club Scribes, run by Venables. The club is very close to where one of Terry's England squad had problems getting a cab one evening.

The Watford game started explosively. Once again the pitch was a quagmire; sand and porridge. White Hart Lane that day made the pitch at Loftus Road look like the first day at Royal Ascot. I raced away, interchanging passes with Peter Houseman down the left. It won us a corner; almost instantly I floated it on to Dempsey's head. He steered it down to the near post, just the spot where David Webb got our first goal in my first match at White Hart Lane, which now seemed an eternity ago. Webby came flying in like an Inter-City, only more reliable, and we were a goal up. This must have been one of the quickest semi-final goals ever. The Chelsea fans went berserk, behind the goal that was becoming lucky for me. Shortly afterwards, Watford equalized. A loose ball from Eddie was picked up by Garbett, who moved forward before shooting from an apparently optimistic range. The next time I met up with the Watford midfield player was in New York, when he was playing for the Cosmos against our Seattle Sounders. I think he topped his shot, but in any event it spun like a table-tennis ball, leaving poor old Catty with no chance. We were stunned. Teams had come back at us before in the Cup run, but Watford, early on, showed amazing tenacity. Tom Whalley played for them that day; I understand he is at Arsenal now. His brother was the coach when Johnny Hollins was in the chair at Chelsea some years ago. I am sure the Chelsea fans can recall some of the things he did there.

Watford's star turn that day was little Stewart Scullion, a lively, tricky winger, whom Eddie McCreadie had to show a little more time and respect to after half-time. Shortly after their equalizer, Scullion put their other winger Owen away with a great pass. Owen side-stepped Webb's lunging tackle (a portent of Wembley and Eddie Gray) and crossed from the by-line. For a split-second it looked as though it might evade Peter's hands and fall for the waiting striker Barry Endean, a reprise of the move that had put Liverpool out in the previous round, but Bonetti, as usual, made a great catch. Stung by this, we poured forward into the Watford box. We could prise them apart easily, but the packed penalty area gave us no room to create our usual openings. It was up to Charlie and me to try to keep possession and drag them out so we could get in behind them. I smacked in a shot, but their goalkeeper Walker dropped smartly on to it. Webb burst through the middle to set up a chance that Houseman hit powerfully over the bar. Os hacked one of their centre-backs from behind and the Watford fans bayed as he escaped yet another booking. Shortly afterwards, the big man hurled himself through the air, inches from Charlie's teasing cross. Just on half-time, Houseman broke through after a Watford corner. He feinted into an empty space and blazed in a fierce shot. He should have scored but Walker made yet another fine save. Peter knew he should have put us in front. I looked across at him, but the Battersea-born winger shook his head and smiled that smile of his, the one I got to know much better later on. Later he was to make up for the miss.

In the dressing-room at half-time, we all looked at each other. We were all, or so it seemed, shattered. The lethargy hung over us all, it filled the room. I couldn't stop thinking of the sauna, hoping that it hadn't taken it out of us. You think of anything, however silly, at such times, so I was to find out. For the only time in that Cup run did I see a little fatigue setting in, or was it just the worry on the boys' faces? The sixteenth-century Japanese swordsmen had a saying: 'No matter what state your mind is in, make the cut.'

In the second half, Chelsea played in bursts the kind of football we knew in our hearts that only we could play. The only comparable display was against Bruges when we won the other Cup a year later. We poured all over Watford from the very first whistle of the restart. Cooke sent over a towering cross from the right, almost in slow motion. I stood watching Hutch rise like an eagle and almost hang in the air. Like all great headers of the ball, he had that gift. The ball flew off his forehead like a steam hammer. Walker threw himself like a maniac, and scrambled it clear. The Watford defence had seemed composed before the break. Now their brave, energetic chasing became increasingly anxious. I was everywhere, sensing the game was turning. On the hour, we scored. Hutch rolled the ball to me; I had a platoon of defenders in tow, but turned away from them. I found Peter Houseman alone on the left, he sent in one of his cut-back crosses and Os jumped to head the ball into the net. Hutch was up there too, and, on the line, hammered the ball back in. It was not necessary. Os was in the goal, swinging from the net like a giant sardine caught in a trawler's net. He had maintained his record of scoring in every game: one of only eight players to score in every round of one Cup run.

The dam was bursting and, like at Palace, we could sense blood. Our game was so strong! Like all great sides, we could punish mistakes and make the cut. In the first half, the switching of the Watford wingers had unbalanced Webb and McCreadie, but this time it was our turn as Charlie and Houseman worked the interchanging double act. In the right-wing position, Peter beat three men and planted a left-foot drive into the net. Perhaps the equalizer at Burnley was the most vital, but Peter considered this to be his best ever Chelsea goal.

Hutchinson was firing everybody up. He could hurt people and make room for others to play. Defences knew they were doomed when they came across Hutch at his best. It was as if the Light Brigade, having survived everything the enemy could chuck at them in their suicidal charge, had looked up to see a Soviet main battle tank bearing down on them, the turret rotating.

Within two minutes, the game was beyond Watford's reach and Wembley was beckoning. I had a hand in the build-up to Houseman's goal and figured in the fourth. Osgood fed me, I passed to Hutchinson, and he scored with a stunning shot. He changed direction to fool the Watford defence and lashed a left-footed drive high into the net. The goal was vintage Hurst, circa 1966. The power, swivel and confidence. Who knows what sort of player Hutch would have developed into had injuries not wrecked his career?

Ten minutes from the end we scored our fifth goal, the fourth in a devastating spell. The Watford midfield had crumbled and I was spotting gaps all over the field. They had brought on a fresh player to stiffen the defence, but it was too late to stem the flow. I surged forward again and shook off one, two, three challenges, nutmegging one in the process. Hutch appeared at the edge of the Watford box. He set up an exchange of passes with Houseman. The interchanging move ended with the winger sidefooting past Walker from the channel at the near post. It could have been a routine in the car park practice game we should have played the day before. The tigers had had enough of the slaughter and we dropped a gear. Bonetti made a marvellous save from a Watford free-kick. Seconds from the end, Os netted again but it was disallowed. Six would have been something else! I do not recall a semi-final since that had such a display of attacking football.

The next day Peter Houseman and myself guested on *The Big Match* with Brian Moore. I wore a Squire Shop suit and a brown shirt. The tie was a psychedelic blend of colours, laughable today but snazzy at the time. The world was my lobster, as Dennis Waterman's employer used to say.

Three home games followed in quick succession and we won them all to keep ourselves in the Championship hunt. In the first game, a last-minute winner from Charlie Cooke, a vicious volley which beat Gordon Banks all ends up, gave us the points against Stoke. Tony Waddington may have been making notes about me that night. On the Saturday, 61,479 saw Ian Hutchinson score both goals as we beat Manchester United 2–1. The gates were closed 40 minutes before the kick-off. Best was their most impressive player. At that time the sickening pressure he was under was starting to take its toll. His performance made a mockery of the school of thought that a troubled player was a bad player. This game came two days before the second of United's three Cup battles with Leeds. A last-minute header from Bremner finally settled it.

Best once wrote to me telling me I was the finest player in the land. It was like Lennon telling McCartney he could write songs! I followed his career with great interest. Another Gemini! Who did not follow George's life and loves? The world must have seemed a pretty strange place for the past 30 years if your name was George Best. The semi-final defeat of United signalled the final break-up of their great sixties side that had won the European Cup. Later, I suppose, the defeats at Orient and at the hands of Stoke did the same for Chelsea.

The third of our home games saw us beat Sheffield Wednesday

3–1. Sinclair shot the Yorkshiremen ahead but Hutch and Ossie, with our first penalty of the season, put us in front. In the second half I scored our third goal, my first at the Bridge. Always something special about a Hudson goal! As I rolled it past Peter Grummitt in the Wednesday goal, the Chelsea crowd gave me a wonderful ovation. I always thought I owed them a special goal at home, Matthew Harding's favourite goal! Soon afterwards Ron Harris went down injured. As he lay there some wag in the crowd shouted out for a welder: 'We need him for Wembley.' Just for a second it flickered across my mind how terrible it would be to miss the Cup Final through injury ...

On the following Saturday, we went to Everton for a vital game. Merseyside was never a happy hunting ground for Chelsea. Ron had torn his left hamstring and was doubtful for Wembley. Eddie McCreadie was also out injured and we went to Goodison with Webb and an Irish lad imaginatively called Paddy Mulligan as full-backs. Mulligan had more sprout than Dave Allen on speed. Sexton was uncomfortable around him. Paddy would crack a joke and we would all go into fits. Dave would be puzzled at most of it and would just shrug and walk away.

Everton tore into us from the kick-off. Howard Kendall scored within fifteen seconds and it got worse! Kendall, unlike some of the others in that Everton side, has made a success of management. Tommy Hughes was playing in place of Bonetti, who had ankle trouble. Soon afterwards Ball scored a second; unlike Howard he has been a disaster in management. Another brilliant player who was less successful as a manager was in the Everton midfield that day: Colin Harvey. He should have won a lot more caps. Ball, Kendall and Harvey at their peak were possibly the greatest midfield trio in a golden age of midfield players. Joe Royle banged in two more goals (Joe has proved to be as good a manager as he was a player), then Alan Whittle (never a manager) made it 5–0. The Chelsea defence were taking more punishment than a client of Miss Whiplash. 60,000 Scousers roared on Everton. We scored two late goals through Dempsey and Osgood. This restored our pride a little bit, but with the wheels coming off the Leeds challenge, Everton effectively took the League title that day. We found out afterwards that Webby and Dempsey had been caught coming into our

Everton hotel at 2.30 am on the Saturday, my first experience of players drinking on a Friday night. Not the best preparation to face Joe Royle on this form.

The following Monday afternoon – it was Easter – we were away to West Bromwich Albion. Despite the drubbing at Everton I was feeling very bullish about the big game at Wembley. I was always confident we could outgun Leeds in midfield. And the higher my profile was at Wembley, the more chance I had of making the England party that would defend the World Cup in Mexico. Little did I know that my short-term objectives were to turn to dust. From then on, my life was never to be the same.

4

The Winner Takes It All

'Na Na, Na Na Na Na, Hey Hey' – Chelsea Shed Boys'

A chant by the Chelsea fans at Old Trafford, April 1970. Adapted from a popular song of the day, first recorded by the group Steam, covered in the eighties by Bananarama.

At West Brom, I went for a harmless-looking ball with nobody near me. Asa Hartford, that great little Scottish midfielder, was the closest; he could probably tell you what happened better than I. The next thing I knew, I was on the floor in the kind of pain I would not wish on my greatest enemy. Well, maybe one person! (I think you've got that?) I had always had a tendency to go over on my ankles, but this time it was major. I was not to recover from this one ever; only slight improvement came when I arrived to play in Seattle on the even surface of the Astroturf, which gave me that cushion – it was like a dream to be able to train and run around in a match with no fear of going down a hole. My confidence returned through this, and so did my fitness. There were matches later at Stoke City where Tony would get the fire brigade in for me the night before the match so I could play.

We were an hour into the match and trailing 3–1. Hutch had just pulled a goal back for us, and in doing so he had injured his hip, heading in a rebound from Ossie's ricochet shot. Bobby Tambling, who came on as substitute for me, was also hurt late in this extraordinary match. Not one of Chelsea's better afternoons! Words could not describe how I felt when I realised the extent of my injury. I was in excruciating pain. My ankle felt as if it had been half-severed inside. Nowadays, surgery is done arthroscopically and you get back much sooner. More importantly, you recover. I never did! We were in the times of just sticking you in plaster and giving you a pair of crutches. This just seemed to glue the whole joint up and the stiffness was such that I had to spend hours on the training ground smashing my foot against the wall with the ball in between. Years of fatigue ground it into gristle and what resembled a Big Mac. It was only in the USA, where there were no humps and bumps on bad pitches, that I could play without the fear of tweaking it. The psychological damage was even more lasting. I felt like a kid who had been given a brand new bike for Christmas, and then lost the use of his legs.

Once I read about phantom pain and how a patient could suffer from a bad injury even if it healed 100 per cent, such was the trauma induced. Today, I admire the likes of Paul Bracewell, another of Waddington's finds, and a young kid at Manchester City called Paul Lake who fought against all the odds to stay in our game. I was sorry to learn that he lost his battle. To this day, I do not believe how well I did with such an injury. People would not see the other side of the coin, when I would be at home sitting for hours with my foot in buckets of hot and cold water, then ice and hot water bottles, then hours up in the bathroom just sitting there, showering the foot and just praying. Do not get me wrong, I never once felt sorry for myself, in fact quite the opposite: I became more determined the second time. After all, I could still have had that Osgood something-or-other disease. I was hospitalised for intensive treatment, although I thought Dave did that to keep me from trying to go dancing on it. Only joking, Dave! I was injected regularly, which became a really bad habit.

I even had to be 'cortisoned' for my Seattle debut. Funnily

enough, that was the first time I played in a match that used what is now the new UEFA rule of the Golden Goal. I'm glad they did, as Tulsa Roughnecks got the winner just as the jab was wearing off ... now that is pain! I didn't care who got the winner that evening, so it just shows how bad I was feeling. In my hospital bed I was brought the special menu from Alexandres' great rivals, Franco's. Franco was just about on the corner of the lights leading down from Earls Court to Chelsea. He and Camillo were big buddies, and I was to be given the best in the house, usually his special minestrone and fillet steak. Unlike Webby, I had mine cooked.

There followed hours with Harry Medhurst, trying to get myself fit for that big Wembley showdown. Well-wishers bombarded the prefab and the phone never stopped for hourly updates on my progress, or in this case, lack of it. One day a little Irish lady wrote to me from her home near Victoria Station. She was a well-known faith healer in the area and her two little boys (both Chelsea mad) asked her to try to cure me. She offered to use her powers to get me fit. The letter was so convincing that I felt I had absolutely nothing to lose. She stroked my ankle and I felt a definite improvement. Or was I kidding myself? Fresh hope came when Peter Houseman told me of a spiritualist he had great faith in. I went to Wimbledon to see him, but all he forecast was that I would not score in the Final. This was true. The new England manager, Glenn Hoddle, is a great believer in acupuncture. The latter stages of his glittering career were plagued by a knee injury, and he became very interested in spiritual healing. I went to a little Chinaman in Wembley who used me as a dart-board. That was no good either. Then it was off to Sir William Tucker in Harley Street for wax treatment, another dead end. On to David Montgomery in Sloane Square, the same. I was to use David regularly after that, because not only did he know a little bit but he would always like to pop next door to the Duke of Wellington on his lunch-break. He had some great stories of when he treated the England cricket team on tour. That was good therapy and took my mind off the injury. Much better than laying on the treatment table watching Harry light one up.

In the prefab we even tried asking the cards. Leslie May, Bobby Eyres, my mum and I would get the glass in the middle of the kitchen table and put the pack of cards around the outside. 'Is there anybody there?' my mum would say, and then the glass would move and Eyrsie would burst out laughing. Bobby could never take anything seriously. That really was the last straw. We had tried everything to get me to that Final and failed. So I took my seat on the famous Wembley bench. A vortex of legend and myth swirls around those games. I wore my favourite suede overcoat I had bought from Take Six. It was a cold but bright day. It was to be the first drawn Final at Wembley. Was this a lifeline?

Jack Charlton headed Leeds into the lead. The goal was a joke. Over the years, Chelsea have given away enough bad goals to write another book about, but this one took the biscuit. Both Eddie and Ronnie were well known in our club for not having an eyesight between them. That explains it! The ball going between them and trickling gently over the line. If that was one of the softest goals ever seen at Wembley, the one that followed was to be the equalizer in more ways than one. Probably never reached the back of the net. The pitch was even worse than those at Palace, QPR and White Hart Lane, if that was at all possible. A few weeks before the game, some genius had decided to hold the Horse Of The Year Show there – Harvey Smith and all that crowd riding Mr Softee or some such animal. This game would not have room for a Mr Softee! Stanley Bowles would moan about how it was always on television yet nobody ever bet on the nags involved. These particular equestrians had spoilt the pitch to such an extent that, had I miraculously played, I would not have lasted the match out (through my ankle, that is, not my fitness). The surface was partly to blame for both Ronnie and Eddie's 'dummy' on the goal-line. Eddie skied his foot over the ball, and Ronnie, almost behind him, got his feet in a tangle and the ball rolled agonisingly over the line. Dave Sexton used to get very upset when we gave a goal away, which meant he got upset very often. On this occasion he buried his head in his hands in disbelief!

Four minutes from the break, Peter Houseman did what he did so often in this Cup run; he scored the vital goal. To the Leeds fans it must have been a sickener, as bad in its way as Charlton's goal. Peter was twenty-five yards out. He flashed in a low drive that Gary Sprake somehow allowed to slip under his massive frame. I can honestly say that if it had been a defender he could have controlled it, flicked it up, volleyed it back to Peter and asked him to try again.

The shot was what we used to say was 'No pass backs, please'. It came out of the blue and was just the lift we needed. They show that goal now and again in promos for one of the *Sky Gold* retro soccer shows. The clip shows Nobby, arm aloft, saluting his goal as his team-mates mob him. That's how it will always be remembered, and a marvellous thing to take to heaven.

In the second half, Leeds dominated in terms of possession. I only saw Bonetti play better in one other game, and that was the replay – or maybe it was just the importance of these two matches. No team could afford to lose, especially us, for we would never have heard the end of those 'southern softies' taunts and all that crap from the Leeds camp. The 'Cat' stopped everything Leeds threw at him, as Eddie Gray weaved his magic web around our David. Webby got so 'burnt' he should have used sun-block. It was never his fault in my eyes, for Webby was not a good right-back. He was an excellent middle-man, where he had players on either side of him to pick up the pieces from his kamikaze tackles. He dived in far too early, far too much. He was easy pickings for a man of Gray's brilliant close-control. The Leeds winger had a left foot just short of that of the one and only 'slim' Jim Baxter. David stuck to his task just as you would have expected, and he had the last laugh, showing the kind of grit and determination that was to carry us through. That was one thing we did have over Leeds.

Chelsea hung on until seven minutes from time, when Clarke headed against our post and Mick Jones drove the rebound past the magnificent Bonetti and into the corner of the net. A great strike from a very underrated player. Every Chelsea heart in the ground sank. The goal was scored at the Leeds end, and they celebrated it right up until we struck back, or so it seemed. I remember seeing John Hollins's face as he got up from the ground. He must have tumbled when Jones unleashed his right-footed shot. Holly looked exhausted. It now looked all over and I was looking for the nearest exit, the famous tunnel. There was no way I would have stayed for the final whistle and watched this Leeds team pick up the Cup and shove it in our faces. The year's dream was now ending in a nightmare of defeat against our staunchest rivals.

Students of the history of Chelsea Football Club will tell you that their past is littered with games they tossed away when they should have won convincingly, and games they 'stole' when they should have lost. We were witnessing yet another of these games. Hutch headed us level with a superb diving header that had become his trademark. A ball into the near post, a flying boot, this time Jack Charlton's, and the ball nestled in the corner of the net. Hutch did not know the meaning of fear. I often wondered, was he brave or mad? I went on to play with Denis Smith at Stoke, who was identical. The more boots there were flying, the more they were at home. Give me that ball to my feet any time!

Ian's goal was like the injections I was having, only this one worked! We were now, I felt, the only winners whatever happened, such were our tremendous fighting and battling qualities. In extra-time Charlie Cooke started to come into his own. He was warming up for the replay! This was the time I should have been there, to get it, keep it and let Charlie have it. When he fancied it he was unstoppable, especially when it counted. Hutch was the hero of the hour, though. Just what would he have been worth today? He was priceless. I can only sum him up in one way, and that is that he was a midfield player's dream. No matter how much skill and ability you have, there are times in a match when you just have no time and no options. With Hutch, he was always your get-out. He would make a bad pass into a great one. That summed him up for me; irreplaceable!

Extra-time was an anti-climax, more of an endurance test for everyone, all the emotions having been hung out to dry in those first, frantic ninety minutes. I actually saw hardened Chelsea skinboys crying their eyes out, disbelieving almost that we had dragged a result from the jaws of certain defeat.

They lived to fight another day. Robert De Niro was in a classic film about boxing, *Raging Bull*, based on the life of Jake La Motta. I went through my La Motta phase, even owning a nightclub. It was not in Miami though, but Stoke-on-Trent. A business partner wanted to call it the 'Carousel Club' after the infamous club owned by Jack Ruby. I don't think too many people would have got the joke though. In one scene, La Motta takes a dreadful beating from Sugar Ray Robinson, pound-for-pound one of the greatest fighters that ever lived. At the end of the fight, Robinson wins but La Motta is on his feet, thus preserving his record of never having been knocked down. As Sugar Ray collects his accolades from the crowd, La Motta, barely able to walk, mouths to the victor, 'Didn't go down, Ray. You didn't get me down.' That was Chelsea then. They had spirit. Even if they were on the receiving end of a beating, they never chucked in the towel. 'Didn't go down, Revie.'

Gray won the Man of the Match award, but Bonetti was the star performer. He had kept us in the Cup. At the end of the game both teams did the lap of honour together. First time ever! Feelings ran high between the sides and some of the feuds ran for years to come. Vendettas, more like! Racism as we know it had not crept into the game at that time. There were few coloured players around. The 'racism' was between north and south, London and the rest of the country. The funny thing was, though, that after the game the players would laugh and joke with one another. We were all on pretty decent money for 1970, and sponsorship was just creeping in, but the money was nothing like the monopoly figures of the nineties. I doubt if you would have such camaraderie among the teams today, money being the pollutant that it is.

As we walked across the pitch towards the tunnel, Dave Sexton put his arm around my shoulder and told me that we would now win the replay with me back in the team, and that I must go straight back into hospital for even more intensive treatment. Just for a short while I felt as if we had just won the semi-final again; I held out vague hopes. I returned to hospital for a week of treatment. It was just starting to dawn on me what I was missing out on. Both my father and I were concerned about the long term. We didn't know how right we were! After going outside the club for treatment, which I obviously had to pay for, I was reprimanded. This angered me. Surely if the object was to get me fit, it was in the best interests of everybody involved. I could never see their rather limited view on this. I felt the treatment I was getting was inadequate and not intensive enough. I thought then, and know now, that the plaster job was wrong. My mobility was non-existent. I always used to think the split at the club came at the time of the downward turn in their fortunes. Writing this and looking back, perhaps the seeds of discontent, of loss, of some crack in the façade, were being sown even then. In any event, I never did get to play against Leeds. I wonder how the game would have turned out had I played.

Sometimes I try to figure it out, but it always turns out differently. You see, the most frustrating thing is that those type of experiences come along only once in someone's lifetime. With all the renewed interest in seventies football and the culture involved, the BBC ran a series called *Alive and Kicking*. Nearly all of one episode concerned the Leeds–Chelsea battles. Strange how they rewrote history to exclude me from the programme, when I probably had the strongest image in the game at the time, save for Best. The fact that I missed that Final through injury was hardly touched upon, yet had Leeds been deprived of, say, either Bremner or Giles, I wonder what excuses would have been made.

In the intervening eighteen days between Wembley and Old Trafford, Leeds had lost to Celtic in the European Cup, so all that was left for them was the FA Cup. One of the upmarket Sunday papers interviewed me in hospital. One of the questions was, did I think Leeds were like Sisyphus? He had pushed three boulders to the top of three mountains and watched as they all rolled back into the Valley. Did I think Chelsea, even without my talents, could leave Leeds with nothing? I told them that Chelsea would take the Cup, and as for Sisyphus, I did not recall him playing for Charlton! When I woke up on the morning of 29 April 1970, I felt like a failed suicide. I had missed the Final, and after making Sir Alf 's forty for Mexico I had not made the final twenty-two. I was totally choked, for this was a double blow in such a short space of time. The only consolation I had, if you can call it consolation, was that I would not have been fit for that either. It wasn't until that magnificent match against the Germans that I realised just what I was missing out on. At that time I was imagining Sir Alf bringing me on at 2–0 up to replace Bobby Charlton. My first taste of the great Franz Beckenbauer, but I had to wait!

If I had played my part in that most magnificent Cup win, then gone on to play on the greatest stage of all, in what proved to be the most sensational World Cup of all, who knows what would have happened to my career? All over one split-second at The Hawthorns, and it was not even a Tommy Smith or Norman Hunter tackle! Ramsey's prediction was chillingly accurate – the feeling of unfulfilment was to haunt my life. What made matters worse was bumping into Ken Jones, that tremendous writer, at

Chelsea's Cup Final with Manchester United in 1994. 'Did you ever know that you would have played in Mexico, had you not done your ankle?' he whispered. I could have been physically sick there and then. I walked from Wembley as if the place was a complete and utter bock to me. Thanks Ken, but no thanks! I switched on the radio and the song playing was 'Na Na Hey Hey Hey'. The Shed used to sing it as a marching song. It lifted me and I joined the pilgrimage to Old Trafford. It was a lovely spring day, chilly but sunny. Chelsea fans laid siege to Manchester, blue and white everywhere you looked. It was played midweek and meant at least one day off work for the travelling fans. Of course, people had jobs then. I always remember the sky that night: a beautiful sunset, as I was to see years later as I walked the beaches of America.

The game started slowly. Ronnie had been switched to mark Gray. Webby wore the number six shirt, and Tommy Baldwin my beloved eight. Ronnie took care of Gray early on, letting him know that he had had his birthday and now it was 'game on'. A completely different ball game, the kind that Ron relished and Gray obviously did not as the Scot scarcely figured in the proceedings! After about twenty minutes, Leeds opened up a huge frontal assault on the Chelsea defence. A great tackle from Dempsey stopped Clarke – he knew him from their days together at Fulham – as he raced on to a Lorimer through-ball. Clarke was their best player that night. He had always worried Chelsea fans ever since those Craven Cottage days. Lorimer was in fine form too. He hit one of his specials just wide. Lorimer had a tremendous goal disallowed in a semi-final defeat at our hands (one of many grudges between the two sets of players) and never forgave Chelsea. He had the hardest shot that I ever saw. One Sunday, I was watching Leeds play Manchester United on television and saw one of his drives knock Alex Stepney over the line. (It was not a goal, by the way; the rebound shot about thirty yards up in the air.)

Giles missed from close in; then Mick Jones flicked the side-netting after Gray had finally escaped from Chopper. McCreadie then cleared off the line, with Bonetti stranded by another Lorimer attempt. Then Jones crashed into Bonetti as he went for a long cross from Paul Madeley. Peter hurt his knee and was down for ages. Jones was a tough, old-fashioned centre-forward. He would have made

Fash and his elbows seem like Ronnie Corbett if he played today. Jones, when he was playing and not 'slam-dunking' goalies, had a great touch, and displayed it when putting Leeds in front nine minutes from half-time. Clarke set it up, cutting across three challenges in midfield and hitting a great long ball into the path of his partner in crime. He streaked past Dempsey and eluded Hollins and McCreadie as they tried to sandwich him. The Leeds number nine unleashed his second bullet of the contest, a screecher that had Bonetti limping in vain as it crashed into the top corner. A great goal! There are some fans, though, a quarter of a century later, who maintain that if 'The Cat' had not been done by the same player, he would not only have reached it but clung on to it like only he could. I cannot say, such was the power and accuracy of the shot from Mick Jones on the run.

At half-time we trailed 1–0. Behind for the third time in two matches. What a mountain to climb against such a team on an occasion like this. However, we had done it twice, so why not again? Things looked bleak once again in this battle, as Bonetti resumed for the second half, heavily bandaged. I doubt if even Stan the Man would have bet on us at this stage. But slowly we began to open up our game, with Charlie getting more into it. We had been caught time and time again in the meshes of over-complicated passing. It was as if the team were trying to make up for my absence by playing a more involved style. With the clock ticking on, the game flowed more. The tackling was vicious. The Chelsea defence seemed to summon up some sort of demon. Up front, Hutch was incredible, dishing out leather to every white shirt that came into his path. He hated Leeds with a passion and it really showed on this particular evening! He started winding Ossie up to run at Leeds. I still cannot bear to watch the game on tape. Too painful! My overriding memory, though, is of Hutch mimicking Bremner with hand gestures as the Leeds midfield maestro protested to the referee about a Chelsea challenge. My chum Joe Royle talked about the 'Dogs of War' in his midfield when Everton won the Cup against Manchester United. I think the term had originated a lot earlier in football, as the 'Dogs of War' in the Chelsea team caused havoc in the closing stages of that match.

With twenty-five minutes left, Hutch was booked. Hollins and

Cooke were playing beautifully, moving the ball in all directions. The geometry of the play was out of this world, full of different angles and patterns. The tide flowed back. The Chelsea fans had been wonderful throughout, but the feeling of renaissance on the pitch relayed itself to the packed masses of blue and white on the Stretford End. It was a feeling that almost disorientated everybody in the ground. I never experienced that again in any other match I watched. I am sure Chelsea fans lucky enough to have been there will tell you it was one of the most emotional things that ever happened to them, certainly in the context of football.

Jack Charlton, it is said, kept a little black book with the names of players he wanted to settle a score with. Legend has it that two of those names were Peter Osgood and Ian Hutchinson, both so stunning that night. Speaking of books, while I was at Arsenal 'Chippy' Brady once told me that Eddie McCreadie and I figured in a similar book owned by Johnny Giles. Giles certainly had some comments to make about me in a Radio 5 special once, but I do not know if they came from his book.

With less than ten minutes of normal time left, Leeds forced a corner. Prior to that they had been virtually overrun by the Chelsea midfield, the hard-running Cooke in particular. Charlton edged up for the corner. It was a sight spectators had seen hundreds of times. The tactics were simple: impede the goalkeeper by whatever means necessary and create a scrimmage in the six-yard box. Get a knock-down, create panic and scramble a goal or force a penalty. A similar tactic was employed by Big Jack when he played for England. On this April evening in the Cup Final replay, the story had a different ending. As the 'Giraffe' went to impede, jostle or harry, he received a huge kick in the arse from Hutch. Jack's flashpoint was zero, his temper made Robert Maxwell seem like Michael Aspel. Losing it, he stormed off down the field, looking to gain retribution.

In the meantime, Chelsea pulled away from the desperate crisis in their own penalty area. Hollins, oiling the wheels as always, fed Os near the halfway line. Nowadays they would call it making a run and some squiggly line would illustrate the movement. Os ran to the right before switching back to Hutch. He went off in a different direction. Charlton followed. The trap was sprung. Raymond

Chandler wrote: 'There is no trap so deadly as the one you set yourself.' Charlton should have known. He left a gap in the middle of the field that you could have driven a 49 bus through. Hutch played the ball inside to Cooke, and the Scot served up a chip that Nick Faldo could have won the Masters golf with. The right foot Cooke had was God-given. The pass curved in a parabola. Osgood was still running from the halfway line. I never saw him move so fast, before or after. He took off like Concorde. He arched his back, looking as if he was flying. He met the ball at full tilt. Harvey was in the Leeds goal that night. He was an international keeper and got his hands up fast, but a brick wall would not have stopped that ball.

Roddy Doyle, who wrote a Booker Prize-winning novel, described that moment as the most poetic of his life: Charlie's chip and Os's finish. One of those funnymen who present the *Fantasy Football* TV show compared Gavin Peacock's more recent FA Cup goal against Wolves as a possible equal. I don't think so!

In the remaining minutes, Chelsea should have won it. A mate of mine who watched the game from the Stretford End described the surge when Os scored as unreal. Nobody was hurt, but a force was unleashed. 'And now you're gonna believe us,' the crowd chanted, and Chelsea went for the Leeds jugular. The game went the distance. Leeds were spent. Another eerie chant started: 'Chelsea, Chelsea, CHELSEA!' Over and over and over, like a dirge. It was a death-knell for Leeds. Another story that went the rounds of the Fulham Road bars was that when Os scored, he ran to Charlton, slapped his cheek and called him a Roger Hunt. He must have felt like one, because right on the mid-point of extra-time Hutch bombed in a long throw. The ball brushed Charlton's head and fell to Webb, up on a raid. Dave did not head it cleanly. It hit the side of his face and went in. For the first time Chelsea were in front and they stayed there. Now it was the turn of the Yorkshiremen to climb the mountain.

Five minutes from time, Osgood went off. He had kept his record of scoring in every round of the Cup. He had run himself to a standstill. Marvin 'Lou' Hinton came on as sub. He was the iceman, as cool as lemon ice-cream on a summer's afternoon. In desperation, Leeds pushed Bremner up front. Chelsea finished strongly. Like the samurai swordsmen, they had made the cut when it mattered. Their sword was broken but they had slain the monster.

BBC2 had shot a documentary on Leeds over the previous weeks in this, their nightmare season. Real 'fly on the wall' stuff. As Chelsea went up to collect the Cup, Charlton stormed off the field, the only player in the history of the competition not to go up and collect his loser's medal, such was his anger and disgust at Chelsea's triumph. I heard that he kicked the dressing-room door off its hinges. He caught a cab outside the ground, leaving in tears, unable to bear the sound of Chelsea voices singing their victory songs in the bath in the adjacent dressing-room. Charlton and Revie never forgot the humiliation they suffered at the hands of Chelsea that night. Revie did all he could to thwart the international careers of Os and myself. Charlton went on to worldwide fame and acclaim as a manager, employing the type of tactics used against Chelsea in that epic encounter.

Perhaps somewhere down the line we lost our way. We took the Cup, though, and made everyone believe in us, and did so by scoring what was probably a record number of goals in an FA Cup run. Like La Motta, we 'never went down'.

I could not wait to get out of Manchester. I caught a train and went back to London. I went clubbing. The town was throbbing but I did not feel any better.

5

Eurotrash

'Here is the perfect politician who is also the perfect gentleman,' I said to myself as he entered the room ... So much perfection argues rottenness somewhere.' Beatrice Webb on Oswald Moseley

'I would just like to say that if anybody had football in mind as a career, they would love to be blessed with the skills of Alan Hudson. He was a superb tactician and it would seem a tragic piece of misjudgement that limited him to play for his country on just two occasions.' Desmond Lynam

I was already making enemies in the game, usually those that were in a position to do my career the maximum amount of damage. One of my bitterest was Jimmy Hill. He never liked me from the time I upstaged him at the Player of the Year Awards, a few days before the Cup Final at Wembley. Billy Bremner won the award, beating me by one vote. Not bad for a young player in his first full season. I thought I had done enough to have won it.

It was no secret that Hill was not one of the most gifted players to earn his living in the game. It always seems strange that someone with no discernible flair or talent ended up in such a powerful position. It was a great pity that Desmond Lynam did not have more say during my playing days. The BBC treated me as if I had typhoid. All the suits are there, preaching the party line, outraged at the very thought of bribery, drug-taking or excess of any kind. Of course, in all their years in the game it never happened and was never even contemplated. All the participants lack insight. This is not to make me sound like the wounded genius, but why not have Best to talk about Merson or Cantona? Who betrayed football? It is all nine to five. So dreary really!

Dave Sexton was once grilled by Hill after Chelsea had lost at Liverpool. Hill was critical of a short-passing game we had employed against the Scousers. Dave was very subdued and nodded in agreement to most of it. Imagine Hill telling Shankly or Clough how to manage! Even Ferguson or Roy Evans today! It angered me that he could talk like that. I never had any respect for Hill.

A few days after the Cup victory, Chelsea bought Keith Weller from Millwall, an excellent signing. I went to Spain for a holiday with my best mate Leslie May. I bought a suit for £300 from a tailor called Majors in Fulham. He was one of the greatest tailors in London (no relation to the Prime Minister, another great Chelsea fan). Ronnie Corbett was a regular at Majors. He always had problems with his trousers, for some reason. Later, in my Stoke days, I took Geoff Hurst along. It was too upmarket for Os, but Peter Shilton was a customer also. Spain was a riot. Beaver España, I think they market it as now.

My weight soared, as I was unable to train properly because of my duff ankle. I always needed to train that much more, because of my lifestyle. That was part of the pact that I made with myself. I thought that Les and I could go away and really celebrate my first season, and that when I returned for pre-season I could work the weight off easily. I found it almost impossible, mainly because I was depressed about my injury. Thinking 'Haven't I had enough bad luck already in my first season in the game?', I still had a lot to learn about setbacks. Missing the Final still haunted me. I watched the victory parade from the Stanley Arms, now the Magpie and Stump. I was having a private party with family and friends because I could not bear to be on the open-top bus. There were scars on my soul.

The summer slipped by, played out to the backdrop of the World Cup. Brazil won for a record third time, taking the Jules Rimet Trophy outright. I watched as many games as I could, usually in the bars on holiday. The Chelsea boys suffered in Mexico. Osgood was virtually ignored by Ramsey. I recall Jeff Astle missing a chance against Brazil that even Hill could have converted (maybe not) while Osgood, at the peak of his form, sat on the bench. That was when I first realised you had to be more than the best player to get into the side, but I could not understand it. Peter Bonetti had a worse time. His heroics in the Cup Final were soon forgotten as his performance against West Germany in England's exit was slaughtered. The fact that the England defence was about as mobile as a snooker table was amazingly overlooked. Was it because he was a 'Blue'? Had I played in Mexico and been fit enough to perform to the best of my abilities, I would probably have been one of the hottest properties in the world. God knows where my career would have gone. At that time, though, Chelsea were the greatest club in the world to me, and all I could think about was playing for them again. Such faith! In the press, my father expressed concern that I might never play again. The swelling worried him. This was caused by the plaster more than the injury.

When I reported back for pre-season training, Dave Sexton threw a wobbly when he saw how my weight had ballooned up. This was my 'Elvis' period. Sexton kept an even closer eye on me. The court spies were Ron Suart and Dario Gradi, who is now doing such a magnificent job at Crewe, but at Chelsea he was disliked after he suggested that Marvin Hinton couldn't play. This came not long after Dario marked Allan Clarke in a Cup tie playing for Sutton United. Clarkey got four or five, I lost count.

I was like a bulimic in those days, gorging myself on the good times and then drinking away the depression, so sickened was I by the way I was being treated, and so frustrated at not being able to get my fitness back. As I gained experience I learned to cope, but I guess things were happening too quickly for me. I played my first, gruelling forty-five minutes against Ajax in Amsterdam one Sunday late in July. I thought I would start my comeback with an easy game! Johan Cruyff scored for the Dutchmen, who roasted Chelsea in the first half. Cruyff was a superb player. It really was the golden age of football. Everywhere you looked there were star names and superb skill. I stayed out of trouble in that game and we equalized late on. I was pleased with my passing and control, and did not get drunk at Amsterdam Airport. (At this stage in my story, this remark does not appear very relevant. Later on in the book, I will relate to you an amusing tale about Brian Clough which will make it more obvious.)

Everton came to Stamford Bridge for the Charity Shield (in those days it was not held at Wembley) and beat us 2–1. Alan Ball was Man of the Match in his white, cut-away boots. It was so hot we could have been playing in Mexico, and I really felt the pace. Keith Weller came into the side, replacing Tommy Baldwin in the number seven shirt. It was the start of an uncertain time for 'Sponge', who was forever challenging Dave Sexton about his future in the first team. Charlie Cooke was out of the side also. Rather than discuss the problems, Dave would just crawl into himself. This annoyed Tom, and the meeting would end with the Chelsea manager kicking him out of his office as the exchange became heated. Tommy would run around in training wound-up tighter than a Petticoat Lane snide Rolex. Eventually, Tom was restored to the team when Ian Hutchinson broke his leg. It was the start of the catalogue of injuries that were to wreck Ian's career and almost cripple him in later life. Whenever I hear about the film *The Lion King*, I think of Hutch. He truly was a lion. He could set the whole team afire. Players like Cooke and myself could only do so much. Hutchinson could ignite Chelsea into another dimension. In his long career, Bill Shankly scattered praise of the opposition very thin. Once Liverpool had been thrashed 5–1 by a Cruyff-inspired Ajax. At the end of the débâcle he remarked that Liverpool 'could not play against defensive teams'. The biggest compliment of my career was paid by him. The only other time I recall him praising a non-Liverpool player was when he called Hutchinson 'a very brave man, very brave'.

I was struggling for fitness in the early season games. The grounds were harder than a bank manager's heart, and the warm temperatures did not help any. My personal life was hitting the tabloids; my secret engagement leaked out. The trial of one Charles Manson started; I followed his career as closely as Besty's. I began to get to know how George must have felt. Keith Weller was an instant hit. He opened his Chelsea account with a deuce, as Chelsea drew 2–2 with West Ham in a terrific game at Upton Park. I took both free-kicks that Ossie headed down into his path.

In September, we travelled out to Greece for the first of our games in the European Cup Winners' Cup. The crowd from Alexandres wanted to go with us. Their first away match had been the replay at Burnley, and after that excitement they could not get enough. Funny how the fix of football gets to people! As we flew out for the game, I wore a matching floral shirt and tie. I bought them in a shop called Quincy's near the antique market in the King's Road. All the team had long hair then, especially Webb and myself. Other teams were finding us interestingly dissolute, particularly the northerners. We used to turn up with our long hair and flash suits and they used to make comments about us, most of them unprintable. Yet next time we played them, they would be wearing (or, more to the point, attempting to wear) poor copies. This really cracked me up. To these people, the appalling clothes they wore were a link to the world which they thought they really ought to inhabit.

The pitch in Greece was awful, dusty and with more holes in it than Wembley, even after the horses. Perhaps they had held the Greek equivalent on it? The game was dirty. Chelsea kept their heads despite a lot of provocation. The Greeks had some other endearing tricks, like spitting and swearing – well, I can only guess that's what it was! But after Leeds, these lads were choirboys. I think Ron called them something like that. We were awarded a penalty after Paddy was cut down. The Greeks made a production of it and it took ages for the kick to be taken, as they kept booting the ball off the spot. Eventually, Os took it and missed. That great Chelsea side were awarded so few penalties that missing it was a rarity. Then Dempsey was sent off. Early in the second half, the home side scored, but Os made amends for the penalty miss by volleying us level near the end, his first in a record-breaking personal tournament for him. Nothing ever phased him or damaged his unshakeable confidence.

We celebrated on the way home. High spirits! Young lads returning from abroad. 'Lager louts', I suppose they call them now, but it was just excitement. We were full of it, and why not? Sexton seemed put out. He had a face like a kite, grim and tense. I should have read it at the time. Pity was, I did not. I should have paid him more attention than I did, or perhaps he should have paid me more attention. Waddington would have. He would have sat with us and split a bottle. Had he thought we were out of order, he would have pulled us up on it and told us why. More important, I would have listened. Cooped up on the plane, Dave Sexton was even more ill at ease.

The rumour factories were working overtime. One of the stories that was going the rounds was that I was so overweight that when they took the official team smudge at the start of the season they had to superimpose my head over a team-mate's body! That was untrue. In fact, they actually put another player's head over my gut, instead of the usual insert. Not very flattering. Mind you, there were a lot of bodies that I wanted to impose myself on at the time. Most of them were Nordic, female, leggy, black-clad and ligging around the King's Road. One night I saw Judy Geeson in Alexandres. She used to live next to the gates of Stamford Bridge. Her career, like mine, was just taking off at the time, but Jayne Seymour was the real stunner of them all.

We butchered Salonika in the return match; we hadn't forgotten our treatment over there. Such was the benefit of playing away first in Europe. Two blockbusting shots from Hollins set us up in the first half-hour. Hutch weighed in with two and Marvin Hinton added another with a real sweeper's goal, breaking from deep. This was when Dave Sexton probably got the idea to move Lou into midfield. This Euro lark looked easy. A few days before the Salonika second leg, I became involved in one of the most controversial events in the history of the game. This time I was entirely innocent!

We were a Peter Osgood goal up against Ipswich at Stamford Bridge. The Suffolk side were managed by Bobby Robson, Dave Sexton's best friend in the game since their days together at Fulham. In the sixty-sixth minute, I put in a low drive from about 20 yards. A lad called Best (no relation) was in goal and the shot hit the side-netting and spun back on to the pitch. The referee, Roy Capey of Crewe, gave a goal! The game was held up for two minutes while Ipswich appealed. Mr Capey consulted his linesman and still gave a goal to Chelsea. Allan Clarke's brother, Frank, pulled a goal back, but my shot (I hesitate to use the word goal) won the points for Chelsea. My old Stoke team-mate Jimmy Robertson played for Ipswich that day, but we never mentioned the incident at the Victoria Ground in later years. Many thousands of words were written and spoken about the incident. 'Chelsea's Phantom Winner' was one headline, along with 'The Goal that Never Was'. A BBC replay confirmed that it was not a goal. At the risk of repeating myself, there was never anything straightforward about an Alan Hudson goal!

Lacking the jurisprudence of today, Ipswich did not take the matter to court. Possibly one of the reasons that Robson eventually got the England job and rose to such a position of power in the game was because he never upset the status quo or made trouble. Imagine the hoo-hah today! The OJ Simpson trial would look like pretty small beer alongside this. A team of high-powered *LA Law*-type lawyers employed by the likes of Sugar or Bates would probably have tried to have the whole League programme replayed. I would possibly have received a custodial sentence. I would have been charged with perverting the course of justice and, at the very least, bringing the game into disrepute. I would have had to take a drug test and an Aids test. I would not even have had Elizabeth Hurley to comfort me. I suspect that the animal-rights crowd would have found a slant on it. Best would probably have been arrested too. This was long before 'bungs' and betting entered our lives. This was the season that Arsenal won the Double, only the second team this century to do it. A feature of their success was that if a decision went against them (or, more to the point, they disapproved of it) they would protest en masse. Don Howe, the sharpest brain in the game, had worked out that if the arguing got a little heated and there were so many players involved, nobody could get singled out for individual punishment. On the same basis, if it was to 'go off ' between players then the whole team would jump in. 'Handbags out,' Charlie George would say. On TV once, I witnessed a huge bundle on the field between Arsenal and our chums from Elland Road. A mild disagreement, I am sure, but it ended up with more right-handers and headbutts than the Hammersmith Palais at closing time. No one walked, though, or else they all did – and when did that ever happen?

Chelsea were to suffer as a result of this mass protestation in a vital Cup replay at Highbury a few years later. Things had gone sour for us by then, and what happened was just another nail in the coffin of my career at the club. Funny how when things go well for a side they get all the breaks and good fortune, and then almost as quickly things can turn against them! When Man United clinched the Double against Chelsea, everything went for them. The next season, the Cantona affair, injuries and loss of form all hit them. In football, nobody is safe from the fickle fortunes of fate. *'Don't say a prayer for me now, Save it till the morning after.'* When I was in the States I heard that song everywhere I went one summer.

Howe reminded me of Germany's greatest general, Erwin Johannes Eugen Rommel. Both were the masters of battlefields, always relishing the challenges with the technical knowledge that was indispensable. When Howe was at Wimbledon, winning the Cup, he employed a similar tactic – not that Fash, Vinnie and Dennis Wise needed a lot of coaching in having a row. In one of his first games at Chelsea, Wise was sent off at Selhurst Park for fighting with Andy Gray (the Palace one, not the Sky one). Wise had gone in expecting his Chelsea team-mates to join in. They just stood back and young Den walked. If the Ipswich 'goal' decision had gone against one of Howe's teams, they would still be on the pitch today.

Robson did not forget the incident, though. Some time later, one Christmas, we hosted Ipswich again. Bonetti was sick and John Phillips was out injured. We sent for our third-choice keeper, a young fellow called Steve Sherwood, brother of the Olympic hurdler. A pleasant, competent lad, he ended up at Watford and had a long career in the game. He was spending Christmas with his folks and got an SOS to get to Chelsea before the 2.30 deadline, when the team sheets went in. Sexton went to see his ex-Fulham mate Robson and explained the goalkeeping problem. He asked if we could put the sheets in late, thus allowing Sherwood more time. Robson acquiesced, provided the lad was in time for the kick-off. At 2.45 Webb was wearing Bonetti's green jersey, still waiting for Steve. He was facing a barrage of comments from the lads, but put on a brave face – this showed Webb's fantastic attitude and commitment to the side. In our previous League game at Coventry Bonetti had been injured, by a dog of all things running on to the pitch (no, not one of Ronnie Harris's greyhounds!). Webb had gone in goal for an hour and had done very well. He did not expect to stay there for the next game, though.

Sherwood arrived with minutes to go, driven by scout Jack Noble. Fog had delayed their journey. Webby threw Sherwood his jumper and reached for his beloved number five shirt. As we prepared to troop out, Sexton came in looking as happy as Hitler in the bunker. Robson had insisted that the team must play as per the 2.30 line-up, with D Webb in green. There is no such thing as friendship or sentiment in football. Robson did not get to manage the England team and some of the tastiest sides in Europe by being a 'nice guy'. This one rebounded on him, though. We were so charged up by his action that we would have beaten anyone that day. We were never known for our defensive prowess, but we put up a human wall around Webb. I always recall him kneeling in a spoof praying-session by the goalpost before the kick-off. He only had one real save to make, early on from Mickey Hill. He threw himself at his feet and knocked the ball over the bar. Second-half goals from Kember and Chris Garland gave us a win. Both of them were kosher.

Robson eventually got one over on me when Ipswich beat Arsenal in the Cup Final. But we lost that match as opposed to them winning it, so bad was our performance. I was never his type of player. Only towards the end of his spell as England manager did he give Gascoigne a fair run in the side, and he only introduced him in Italy's World Cup when plan one was not working. Gascoigne's giant talent marks him as about the only English-born (apart from Hoddle) player of recent times to be truly world-class. The well of sympathy instantly conceded to a genius is soon dried up by the tabloids. When you are as publicity-worthy as Gazza, the authorities think that they are doing their job by hounding you. Having said that, I actually have no sympathy for the Glasgow Rangers clown. As I said earlier, you learn how to handle situations with experience, but it seems he just gets more childish. What a complete and utter waste of talent. I truly cannot believe someone as shrewd and canny as Terry Venables has not tried to sort him out. In fact, it's the opposite – he seems to encourage his stupidity. There was talk of Gazza coming to Chelsea. What with the Bates/Harding headlines, they would have to have a special tabloid solely for Chelsea. Imagine Wise and Gazza going out for the evening. Black cabs would take the evening off!

Our next game in Europe was against CSKA Sofia of Bulgaria. They were a fine side. They reminded me a lot of the Spanish side who put Chelsea out in the semi-finals of the Cup Winners' Cup the next time they were in it. CSKA had never lost on their own pitch to European opponents. They had a player called Jekov who was the top scorer in Europe one season. The first leg was away. We always liked that, as I explained earlier. I recall how cold it was out there. It was the end of October and still mild at home. Hutchinson was out by then and Weller was on the right. Tommy Baldwin was in the side and scored our goal from close range after another of Weller's tremendous near-post curling crosses. Keith had the art of hitting that ball at top speed – a very talented player who would have become a great asset. Charlie Cooke missed the game. His form was patchy, with marital problems debilitating his game, not to mention the demon drink.

In the second half, CSKA threw everything except their ancient floodlights at us. The defence held firm. Ron was doing his usual captain's bit, covering his mates, cajoling, always driving on. Hinton, playing because of Dempsey's ban, excelled against teams like the Bulgarians. Never a strong tackler, like myself, he preferred to win the ball by interceptions and timing. 'Nicking the ball', my father called it. Some people talk of Marvin being too short. Neither Colin Todd nor Dave Mackay were very tall, but they played with their brains and Lou Hinton was the same. The only problem he had was that he should have gone and kicked the manager's door in a little like Tommy did! People rave about Hansen, but Hinton was as cool and as classy a player. Some people are club players and some born internationals. Bobby Moore was a great example of this, and Hinton should have been another. He was a World Cup player, not a League Cup player.

You could not do much against the likes of Ron Davies, Joe Royle, Peter Osgood and the Hutchinsons of this world. In recent times, Gary Lineker said that he avoided heading the ball because he was worried about possible brain-damage in later life. I look at Gary, nicely suited, on the box selling his crisps and think how unscathed he is. Of course, there is no truth in this theory, no real shred of proof, but then I look at old Jack Charlton who must have headed the ball a million times ...

In any event, we held out and became the first team to beat them on their own ground in a European competition. Flying high in the friendly sky on the way home, the first major split between Sexton and a certain player happened. It left a sour taste in all our mouths, and for the first time it brought out into the open something that had been simmering awhile. Sexton tore into Osgood. Perhaps he saw things in our personalities that he found repulsive. Sometimes he loved us like younger brothers; other times he hated us. Someone told me once that to hate something with such spite, a part of you must love it too. Osgood had been booked in the game along with Webb. Everything Os did on the pitch was calculated. Like a seasoned gunfighter, he was always trying to gain an edge on his opponent (for example, winding up Charlton) and shave the odds in his favour. It was this calculation, plus his hair-trigger temper, which made him so dangerous. The situation with Sexton exploded, so much so that the Chelsea manager 'offered' Os out behind one of the stands upon the team's return to London.

Who would have won? Hard to say. Os was younger, and a big lad. Sexton came from a family of boxers. His nickname 'Stiff Neck' had come about because of his stance. I see Eubank today, posturing on TV, and see similarities. I could never reconcile the mixture of Dave's boxing heritage and his religious background. The two seemed in conflict with one another. Perhaps this was the crux of the problem. Osgood was called the 'King of Stamford Bridge' by his adoring fans. Anyone who ever stood in the Shed would have heard the famous carol adapted to suit Osgood's title. Sexton committed regicide. The first blow was struck then. Os never backed down, like *Raging Bull* again. Years later, as their pub crashed in a sea of debts, Os gave Hutch a black eye in a dispute. They made up, and still look after one another's backs as they used to on the field. The pressures off the field and the adjustment to facing up to not playing could be as great as any problems when you were still in the game. Wealth and glory throw a gentle hug around some players. Lineker embraced them and never abused them. Like teenage sweethearts, wealth and fame loved him back and it became a lasting romance. For the mavericks, though, it was different.

The fight never took place. It was hushed up. If the tabloids had found out then, I do not know what would have happened. Tommy Docherty always used to say that when he was Chelsea manager, the problem was that Stamford Bridge was so open to the media. No secrets could be hidden. That is probably why Chelsea always figured so prominently in the headlines. I found that out a couple of times in the 1995–96 season after a couple of disagreements in the Chelsea tunnel were blown out of all proportion by the tabloid press. When I tried to explain to Ken Bates that it was nothing, he would not have any of it. I always thought that there were two sides to any story. Not it seems, with Chelsea's supremo!

The in-flight bust-up became a microcosm of the whole soap opera that was to unfold like a soccer *Brookside*. By the end of that momentous year of 1970, we were third in the table behind Leeds and the eventual champions, Arsenal. In the autumn, we had gone out of the League Cup to Manchester United. For once, we lost at Old Trafford. Best scored the winner, a truly wondrous goal. They showed it for years at the start of *Grandstand*, or perhaps it was *Sportsnight*. The Irish genius latched on to a loose ball midway in our half. He ducked and dived past Ron Harris before Ronnie got him with one across his hip. But Best's main asset was his unbelievable balance. He half went to go down – players didn't do that in our day – and somehow kept his feet, his head, his composure and his nerve, coolly gliding past Bonetti and stroking the ball past Marvin Hinton, who I'm sure was standing drooling over what he had just witnessed. Sheer and utter genius! I watched that match from the pub opposite the front gates and rose to my feet as if he had scored it in a blue shirt. Ron was left sprawling in the Old Trafford mud, a sight I was only ever to see once. Best had not only beaten him once but went back to do it a second time, a dangerous act when your opponent was Chopper Harris. Few people ever got around him or McCreadie once, but more often than not, when someone did, they would win the ball back a second time, something you rarely see today. On the second occasion, Ron

Leslie May and I, left of middle row, show off our first ever trophy for Park Walk. With Mr Robertson, our coach, and Mr Cope, our headmaster, in 1962.

Assistant manager Ron Stuart gives Tony Frewin and myself a few tips on how to keep away from the King's Road while at Mitcham training ground in 1968.

Day of the 1970 Final, and I can only make the head tennis team. The famous 'Cage' is in the background – the other Wembley.
(Evening News)

(Opposite) Getting young Allen ready for the big time as quickly as possible at the Bridge.
(Daily Mirror)

One of my modelling jobs while at the Bridge, this one for Limited Edition Shirts in 1972.
(Daily Mirror)

Leaving the Bridge after just putting pen to paper for Tony Waddington in January 1974.
(Press Association)

Capping Stoke's first win at White Hart Lane for 100 years by getting our second goal, 1974.
(Press Association)

In the match at Stoke where Bill Shankly came into the dressing room afterwards with that wonderful compliment, 1974. *(Coloursport)*

Just returned to training after the summer break of 1974, with Dennis Smith and Geoff Hurst at the Victoria Ground.

Something that was a ritual for me, doing my sit-ups before the Germany match in 1975. *(Daily Mirror)*

One of my all-time favourites, Alan Ball and I discussing our night out after just beating Germany 2-0 at Wembley on my debut in 1975.
(Football Archive)

Sparked out at the prefab after celebrating my England debut.
(Daily Mirror)

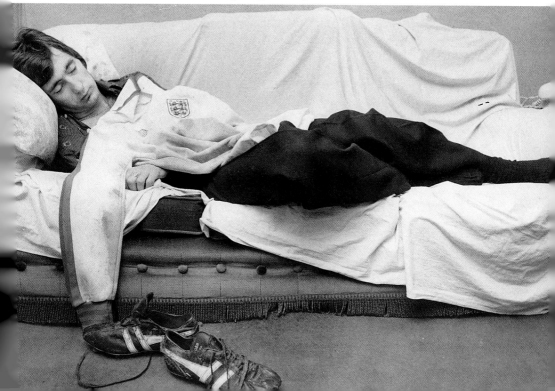

Peter Osgood's testimonial in 1975, George Best's only time in a Chelsea shirt, what a shame that was!

Tony 'Working Man's Ballet' Waddington proudly leads his team onto the Wembley pitch before beating us in L.C. Final. *(Sentinel)*

came flying in on Best, but it was a millisecond too late. On such fractions games are won and lost, especially against George.

I did not play in that match. My usual plan to keep Best out was to deny him the ball; just keep it away from him for the whole game. I could do that by slowing it down and then quickening it up, getting it off the goalkeeper and keeping it out of certain areas, in this case George's. If he was on the left, I would play it down the right and hardly ever direct it into open play in case he got possession of it. I could keep the ball for ages and direct it away from him. It used to annoy him. In one game I said to him, 'You won't be getting it tonight; I'm keeping it all game, George.' He would just shrug and smile that little smile of his. It was like chess. I was a footballer; he was a player. That was the difference between us. George Eastham was a footballer, as was Tommy Harmer. I used to try to outwit them all the time. Gunfighters again! Who was the quickest on the draw? Nevin, in my later spell at Chelsea, was another guy I would like to outwit in training. We saw it as a challenge. Chess, making all the moves!

My shins were troubling me as well as my ankle. I did not play again till nearly Christmas. Then, I was sub against West Ham. Os scored both our goals as we won 2–1. He was finding goals hard to come by at that time, the exertions of the year, Mexico and the rows, all draining his power. Weller was an inspiration. He had a great game at Blackpool, another game I recall as a thriller. At half-time the Blues were 3–0 down and the position remained the same with 20 minutes left. John Phillips was making his Chelsea debut in goal and he must have thought that the tower had fallen on him in the first half. Dave Sexton gambled for once and replaced Baldwin with Charlie Cooke. Peter Houseman went to left-back (the position he was to finish his Chelsea career in), Ron Harris went to the right-back slot – he could play anywhere in the back four, as long as he had a target – and Paddy went to centre-half, with Webb pushing up alongside Weller. Between them, they scored three goals and then in the very last minute Weller's centre was knocked into the Blackpool net by one of their own defenders; a truly astonishing result.

The following season at Blackpool I was escorted off the bus by two policemen because they had received a threat on my life.

Things were really hotting up for me. I'd always felt the need to be wanted, but not this way! An amazing turnaround! I cannot recall Chelsea playing in a game like it since; proof of the sky-high spirit we had at the club at the time.

Webb scored in the return match against the CSKA side. Once again the defence smothered their dangerous forwards and we went through with ease. As 1971 dawned, we were all confident of more glory.

6

The Year of
Living Dangerously

'I did not make it baby/By playing by the Rules.' 'Troubleman',
Marvin Gaye

1971 opened with Chelsea defending the FA Cup. We were drawn
away to Palace, of all teams. I missed both the games we played
against them. Webb set Osgood up for the first goal early on. How
Palace must have grown sick of Osgood scoring against them! They
hit back, though, and led 2–1 at the break, Alan Birchenall scoring
against his old club with a fine shot to put them in front. The pitch
was frozen and would have suited a John Curry more than a Tony
Currie. The snow had been down since Christmas. Layer upon
layer had crystallized and hardened into abstract shapes. Cooke,
not having a happy season up until then, was the title of this book
performing. He was floating over the most difficult surface with
such grace, and with the ball under complete control. He set up
chance after chance which the Chelsea forwards contrived to miss.
Eventually, Tommy Baldwin converted one. Near the end, Charlie
almost brought down the bar with a mighty shot. Weller was the
star of the replay. He put Tommy in for the first goal and

Houseman scored the second after the Palace keeper Jackson pushed out his cross.

Only a player with Charlie's balance could have given such a display of sheer magic. When Charlie really had it in his mind to do it, there was no finer sight in our game. Second to none of his peers. I remember the first time I ever saw Cooke do his famous drag-back, or roll-over, in a match against Liverpool at the Bridge. I was still in the reserves and was studying him. That night I was fortunate to be sitting right behind him as he picked the ball up about twenty yards from their right corner-flag. Emlyn Hughes, Tommy Smith's pal, was his prisoner. Charlie showed him the ball, and with his magic wand rolled the ball towards Hughes as if he was giving it to him. Just as poor old Emlyn bit, Charlie was rolling the ball back, leaving the Liverpool captain on one knee. It was the first time I'd seen this done and immediately worked on it. While Charlie was waltzing into the box the crowd was silent, still watching Hughes trying to get back to his feet. This was worse than being tackled by Ronnie. To be sprawled out on the floor without being touched – poor Emlyn! Couldn't happen to a nicer fella! Only Charlie, though, could have done that one. Oh, to be on the same pitch as Best and Cooke, a dream in my first season. They say you must keep your eye on the ball when defending. Emlyn might differ, and there are plenty who have tried to keep their eyes on the ball against Besty.

This was the time of Dave Sexton's 'fiver' ball. He promised a fiver to anyone who scored using a complex passing movement he had devised. It involved knocking it over the head of defenders and various players spinning off in different directions. It would certainly fool defenders, as even our lads could never quite grasp the implications of what exactly was required of them and what was involved. Peter's goal, his first since Wembley, seemed to contain some of the elements that the Chelsea manager was seeking, so he happily donated a Jacks to Peter. Fitting that his favourite pupil should win the prize! Os would look puzzled at the whole thing, as did Baldwin. Had either of them been lucky enough to win this generous prize, I would like to have seen Sexton's face. Doubtless it would have gone direct to the Markham Arms, or in Tommy's case the Trafalgar.

It was no surprise that Sexton's other favourite, John Hollins, would try the 'fiver ball' given any opportunity. I would go square for the ball and watch Holly hit it fifty yards over the top of defenders through to their keeper. The 'fiver ball' was an option which should have been used as a 'get out' only. It was rare for a tactic like this to catch defenders on the hop, and it was becoming a hindrance to our team. We were a passing team, like all great teams, and this new ploy was to lose us the ball much too much for my liking. It was fine for Holly because he loved chasing to get it back – I can't say the same for Ossie. (Later, Dave Bassett and Graham Taylor were to make careers out of employing these tactics.) It was far better to keep possession and, as I say in my coaching of the game, 'Suck 'em in and spit 'em out!' Like Charlie did with Hughes.

I was back in the side a few days later when we played Manchester United at the Bridge. Once again the gates were locked. Best had gone walkabout. He had missed the train to London and was dropped. I think he was cased up with an actress then. She must have been good for him to miss a Chelsea–United clash, which was always a humdinger. I suppose she was; George never confided in me. Os and Weller missed the game for the Blues. I do not know if any actresses were to blame; I do not think so. Unless Raquel Welch was back in town.

With an hour gone, I scored to put Chelsea ahead. This shot did hit the back of the net. Paddy Crerand set it up nicely for me, square-passing in his own penalty area. I have met Pat on several occasions and never seen him without that massive grin on his face. This day, he bent down with his head in his hands, I don't know what he must have been thinking. Crerand was like all my other peers that I admired – a wonderful player and a terrific guy. The ground had absorbed so much cold that the rain made it very slippery. United had not won for ages and we should have murdered them. We let them back into it though, and Willie Morgan, who always reminded me of the guy in The Hollies, Terry Sylvester, scored from the spot after Denis Law had cleverly won a penalty off John Boyle. Just on time I headed (that's right, headed!) against the bar. The crossbar, that is! I do not think it bothered me in later life.

In the closing seconds United broke away to score. Alex Stepney
cleared with a punch that would have floored Ali. Gowling picked it
up and swallowed half the pitch without a serious challenge going in
on him. He put in a shot that Bonetti blocked. Trouble was, it spun
over Peter like a ping-pong ball, he dived backwards (as always, as
agile as the cat he was nicknamed after) and scooped the ball back
via the post. The ref gave a goal. I do not know if he came from
Crewe, or possibly Ipswich. First time I ever saw a goal given for
hitting the post. (I am leaving the 1966 World Cup out of this
particular debate, as I once lodged with the man who scored a
hat-trick in that game). Anyway, a goal was given, as absurd an
event in its own way as my shot against Robson's team. Who says
what goes around comes around? I do not know what George Best
would have made of it all.

George Best had left the building, as they used to say in the Elvis
concerts. Manchester teams gave us a lot of problems that month as
City thrashed us 3–0 in the fourth round of the Cup. At the Bridge,
too! I had got the taste of Cup football – always had, mind you –
and was bitterly disappointed leaving the ground knowing that all
we went through the year before, ankle and all, had been thrown
out of the window by Dave's team selections.

I missed that game as well. Fayeknights. Dave Sexton was toying
with the idea of playing Marvin Hinton in a midfield role. He
played that role against City to the exclusion of Alan Hudson. I
guess that was the time Dave was looking at Steve Kember down at
Palace. He was contemplating using me wider, which was rather like
using a Rolls-Royce as a mini-cab. City overran us in midfield,
Colin Bell had the run of the park. Players like Hollins were
exposed by the likes of Bell. I excelled against him, for I would
keep possession for long periods, not allowing him to use that
unbelievable engine of his (they called him Nijinsky). He scored a
great goal from near the corner flag. Ian Bowyer, always a nemesis
in Cup games, also scored that day.

It is the first tap that cracks the Ming vase, the first lie that
destroys the truth, the first adultery that ruins a marriage. After
that, it is only repetition. I was concerned about the defeats. I was
worried that the pressures outside might destroy what we had built
up: the finest footballing side of its generation. The team needed

fine tuning, a little tinkering with here and there. We called for a forum where we could all have our say and clear the air. It was vital that Sexton was present to thrash out any problems. I had missed both Cup defeats and didn't like it!

Following the Cup exit I was back in the team the following week against WBA, and felt that old form coming back. I recall standing in the Ifield Tavern and telling my uncle George that I was on my way back, but only if the grounds could stay soft. Now I know how these horses hate the firm going, I really can relate to that. I am sure my good pals Steve Smith-Eccles, Graham Bradley and Peter Scudamore would agree. McCreadie made his first appearance of the season and we ran out easy winners, 4–1. I made one of them for Hutch. Also on the scoresheet was a young lad called Derek Smethurst. Os had been banned for a staggering eight weeks. His only crime was collecting three bookings. In one of their periodic fits of morality, the FA made an example of him. Echoes of Cantona or George Graham?

None of us really knew where Sexton obtained Smethurst from, only that his old pal Eddie Firmani used to show up at our training ground once in a while. He fitted the image required by the management, so was given a place in the team. His type of player never really went to the edge. Consequently there was no danger, no menace, no real excitement. In my view they lacked the real talent at that highest level. I had seen a lot of youngsters come and go in my time at the Bridge. A lad called Ian 'Chico' Hamilton always stuck in my mind. Tommy Docherty gave him his debut at White Hart Lane, of all places. He was just turned sixteen and, just like Greaves, scored on his debut for Chelsea, heading in a corner to go into the record books. My father had a bet with Frank Blunstone as to who would make the biggest impact, 'Chico' or his son. Hamilton only played a handful of first-team games for Chelsea but he did have a good career in the game, playing for Villa and Sheffield United, and later I caught up with him while he was playing in Minnesota and our Seattle team were visiting. I always found it odd that we only ever played together in the youth team and a couple of reserve games. I thought that Chico would go to the very top, but he was gone by the time I reached the first team. A real nice guy, another who went on the missing list.

A few days after the WBA game we left a freezing February in
London to fly to the 85-degree heat of Kingston, Jamaica to play
against Santos of Brazil. I visited Jamaica again recently and realize
that the magic was not just Pele. I can understand why Ali
Campbell wrote such a wonderful song about the place. Edu was
playing alongside the 'Black Pearl'. A chap called Douglas (not the
one who played for Blackburn) scored the only goal of the game,
late on. It was amazing to be on the same pitch as Pele; he was
everywhere, and was everything I had ever imagined as a player.
Powerful, wonderfully balanced, beautifully built, and with a touch
like an angel. In the space of a few months I had played against the
two biggest names in world soccer, Cruyff and Pele. Thirty-three
thousand people watched the game, the biggest crowd ever
assembled on the island for a soccer match. Most of them spilled on
to the pitch when the goal went in. The match was held up for ten
minutes, such was the excitement, but it was all in the best of fun
and nobody got hurt. When we flew back to Heathrow, though, the
carnival had been turned into a riot by our media – we were greeted
by headlines of 'Chelsea in riot match'. But it was hardly the
Millwall Cup replay. Kingston was the home of Robert Nesta
Marley, better known as Bob. He was soccer-crazy, and it was said
that the cancer that killed him started with an untreated soccer
injury. His toe was slashed by another player's pair of rusty spikes
whilst playing football on the Boys Town recreation ground in
Trench Town. Marley's best mate was Skill Cole (no relation to
Andy), who played for the national side of Jamaica and in Brazil.
Marley's team was Santos, and he was a mate of Paulo Cesar. When
he lived in London, he played every day in Bishop's Park near
Fulham's ground. It was said that he wanted to be a footballer more
than anything.

A few days after the sun and fun of Jamaica we visited another
beauty spot, Newcastle. I was certainly racking up the air miles, not
that they had any then. Pele one game, Barrowclough the next. I
scored the only goal of the match from an acute angle. I picked up a
ball just inside their box, and after dummying past ex-Scotland
skipper Bobby Moncur I found myself on the by-line. I looked up
and saw Hutch standing there, screaming for it. As I went to play
the ball to him, I saw McFaul just leave me a little gap on his near

post. Very inviting. I just screwed my foot around the ball at the last split-second and the ground went silent. Not just because I scored, but because they could not believe what had happened. Pictures of the goal do not even show me. All right, I will say it again: there is always something special about an Alan Hudson goal. I got the idea after watching Pele. Try something out of the ordinary and see what happens. It was the first time I was to meet the great man. He walked into our hotel bar with a drink in one hand and a stunner on his arm. Johnny Boyle and Tommy Baldwin were my drinking partners that night, and it was the first time I had ever seen three chaps take absolutely no notice of such a beautiful woman. Pele was a gentleman, having a quick drink with us. He had no choice but to have a drink really, as he had both arms firmly held by us and was going nowhere. We were in the presence of sheer magic. He oozed class, he had an amazing aura. We asked him if it would be OK if we called him God. He had no choice once again, we didn't think Pele sounded right. I don't think Sexton would have had him in the Chelsea team. Pele had that awful smell on his breath, the one that Dave just didn't like.

My goal at Newcastle was inspired by meeting the great man, I know it was. I felt my confidence returning, and Pele was the lift I needed, although he did nutmeg me in the match. My privilege!

The honours were coming in thick and fast. I played at Hampden Park for the Under-23s in a 2–2 draw. Hutch was also in the side. We spent the night without a bathroom, as it was occupied by a famous Arsenal player and a lady friend! I was still indulging my passion for clothes, always in the Squire shop, Village Gate or Stanley Adams. Best was the role model. He wore a lot of velvet suits, which have not aged very well. People who got married in such garb at that time cannot show their wedding pictures to anyone!

In the late winter, Micky Droy made his Chelsea debut at Wolves. We lost to a Kenny Hibbitt goal. Kenny came over to Seattle and performed brilliantly while on loan there. I used to think of him as just another good player, but he showed me that he was much more than that. He played some great football and scored some superb goals, one of which took us to the Soccer Bowl Final. I had a lot of time for Kenny, he was another one from our kind of upbringing. His brother Terry died just before he arrived in the States, Terry having played for our old enemies Leeds United. Droy was huge. I think at the time he was the biggest player in the League, 19 years old and 6ft 4in. He came from Slough Town. Bruce Dern, the American actor and Chelsea fan, once described him as 'the big guy who looked like he ought to be in jail'. In fact, he was a hell of a nice guy. We became great pals from day one and I'm delighted to say we still are. At that time he found it hard to break into the first team. Chelsea had so many good centre-backs such as Webb, Dempsey and Hinton (when Sexton wanted to use him), and Ron Harris could play there too. Droy lacked a little confidence at first, being star-struck by the set-up he was in. I suppose it was the blend of players and styles that was so lethal. Like so many young players, he was launched into the stratosphere without the breathing equipment. I was lucky, I had my father and a deep-rooted belief in my talent. I always knew that I could hold my own, in even the most exalted company.

The team knew that players like Smethurst would not be with us for long. He was later sold to Millwall after the promise Dave Sexton had seen in him fizzled out. In Greek mythology it is said that when mortals encounter the Gods, they come away dazed and confused. Droy established himself after the break-up of the great side. Just before I came back to Chelsea in the early 1980s, the club came within a couple of points of being dumped into the then Third Division. Only Droy and Clive Walker kept them up. In the penultimate match at Bolton they never played better, as Chelsea scraped a vital win. Walker scored the winner and Droy played like three men.

Clive, an explosive talent on his day, was rewarded by being sold soon afterwards. He is still knocking them in for Woking. Revenge is a dish best served cold though, and he almost single-handedly knocked Chelsea out of the Milk Cup whilst playing for Sunderland. Joey Jones was playing at full-back for the Blues that night, and Walker took him apart as comprehensively as Gray had done Webb. Walker had given Jones the same melting when he played for Liverpool and Clive was at Chelsea. After the Sunderland defeat, as damaging to the Chelsea 80s aspirations as our defeat at Orient, Walker was involved in a fight in the players' bar. Droy broke it up, I think. He was once promised a job for life at Chelsea, he was regarded so highly. He once had a garage in Battersea, not far from where Peter Houseman was born. Micky was the most gentle of giants, to me anyway.

The Sunderland match saw Chelsea play another fine young player out of position: Dale Jasper was a talent in the Hoddle mould. How Chelsea could do with a Jasper or Fillery now, even with all their expensive overseas players. You must never overlook your gifted youngsters, and Dale and Fillery were two of the special ones. Dale was a truly sensational prospect. I mean, he could have won many caps with the right guidance. But at the time, Chelsea, coached by Hollins, just wanted the ball as far forward as possible. Does that remind you of the 'fiver ball'? I was getting very despondent watching young players like Dale Jasper neglected. I later tried to get Stoke to sign him and told our manager, 'Get Jasper up here to play alongside me and he will put his name alongside the already great ones like Greenhoff, Eastham, Dobing, Vernon, Viollett and myself.' I cannot leave myself out, for I love just being mentioned in such exalted company. That's how much I thought of Dale. I spoke to his father and he said he didn't want him leaving London – the worst day's work his father ever did. It reminded me of when I first went to my Dad about Mr Waddington. My father had started to pack my bags before he finished talking. That's the difference: my old man had such tremendous football insight. I hope I have inherited some of that quality. I'm so glad he was right behind the move to Stoke. City never got to see the Jasper brilliance. Neither did Chelsea!

Spring came suddenly. We were paired with Bruges in the quarter-finals of the Cup Winners' Cup. They were a good side, very good, as we were to lern. They had not been beaten at home in domestic competitions for three years, and they included two talented forwards in Lambert and Rensenbrink. In the first leg Bruges had an overwhelming advantage, with their tiny, cramped ground and screaming fans. I cannot ever remember such a small crowd – 23,000 – making such a racket. The din was deafening. They came out of the traps at us like tigers. They got the dream start all clubs want in those situations, an early goal. Lambert put in a near-post header from Thio's corner. John Phillips was making his European debut and was powerless to stop it. Lambert was surrounded by Chelsea shirts, but still scored. This gave them a tremendous fillip and they started to play with great assurance, pushing the ball around and taking men on all over the field. We were stunned by their early onslaught and found it hard to get going. Passes were dropped short of their intended target and we became hurried and anxious. I started to forage for possession further down the pitch. The Bruges side had exceptional all-round skill and must have been very well coached in how to play against us. We missed Os and Hutch a great deal in a game like that. Ossie could switch the play when required and was always likely to chip in with a goal out of the blue.

Luck was against us when we put in one of our few attempts on goal. Tommy headed on a Weller cross with the Bruges goalkeeper going the wrong way. It looked a certain goal, but Sanders, their keeper, stuck out an arm and somehow punched the ball against his own bar. It was scrambled away. Just before half-time, they went two up. Another Thio corner and the impressive Rensenbrink powered it towards goal. Their centre-forward, Marmenout, tried to get out of the way but it struck him full in the face and ricocheted past Phillips into the net. We were devastated, and only a string of fine saves by our goalkeeper pegged the score. Tommy nearly slid one in near the end, but we were completely outplayed. It was a huge shock to us. Since I had been in the side, it was the only time we had been so completely outplayed apart from the aforementioned Everton match.

Trouble marred the end of the game. The Chelsea fans attacked the Bruges fans and there were some ugly scenes. It is tempting to add that little has changed. The fans that followed us into Europe up until then had behaved splendidly. They had even turned up in Bulgaria.

The leader of the Chelsea fans in those days was a chap called Michael Greenaway. He was a huge influence on his followers and had an amazing chant of 'Zigger, Zagger, Zigger, Zagger!' Often, in quiet periods during games, or when we were losing, he would unleash a chant and it would lift the whole team. It seemed a lot more humorous then, too. This was before the real violence of the mid 1980s.

The northern clubs were the pioneers of the aggression, I always thought. The first time I ever saw trouble at Chelsea was in 1966 when they played (wait for it!) Leeds in the Cup. I stood in the Shed, not ever thinking that I would be playing against them in a few years. It was a tremendous match. Bobby Tambling shot Chelsea in front early on. That was when Docherty, with the cameras on him, roared on his 'Diamonds' and the legend was born. From then on, they were known as 'Docherty's Diamonds'. The following season Chelsea got to Wembley and I recall seeing a huge 'Docherty's Diamonds' banner in the ground. After we had lost the game, I saw the banner in the gutter, crumpled and torn, like a discarded pennant at a medieval battle.

Chelsea, just as they would in the Cup Final, hung on to beat Leeds, Bonetti making a point-blank save from Jack Charlton in the last minute. As the whistle blew, Leeds fans pelted the Shed (Alan Hudson included) with coins, stones, ball-bearings – anything they could lay their hands on. I never stood there again, and as my son grew older and wanted to watch games, I was very careful where he went. Of course, Chelsea fans were no angels even then, but like the gunfighters again, they attracted trouble. The media seemed puzzled when the hooliganism thing came back into vogue when Chelsea were next in Europe. Of course, it is a different generation and a different type of hooligan.

Just as when Bruges lost to Chelsea in the 1995 Cup Winners' Cup their side was not a patch on the 1971 team (I know I am biased), the 1971 hooligan was not in the same league as his modern counterpart. In 1971 it was boots and fists and lots of charging aimlessly around backstreets. Today it is glasses, Stanley knives, CS gas, mobile phones and arranged meets. Bugsy Segal (he owned a nightclub too) claimed in the 1940s that his gangsters 'only shot each other'! The bad boys who followed Chelsea only fought with other gangs: West Ham's ICF, the Cockney Reds of Man United and Spurs' 'Park Lane Crew', to name but a few. This is not to glamorize it, merely to explain the heritage behind it.

The Chelsea crowd never gave us more fantastic support than they did in the return against Bruges. That was about the best we ever played, in my view, as a collective unit. Chelsea fans who were present that night still talk to me about it. The tragedy was that it was never captured on film for posterity. A video of it would make a best-seller. Real edge-of-the-seat stuff, not as violent as Quentin Tarantino but a real classic. Pulp Football. Peter Houseman scored early on in the game, which lifted the crowd and gave us hope. Os was back in the team, playing his first game for months. In that time he had moved house, and the upheaval had been very demanding. Nothing seemed to be to the detriment of his skill, though. The bigger the match, the bigger the challenge.

With only nine minutes left we were still 2–1 down on aggregate. The crowd had been staggering. In lesser matches sometimes they could be on our backs, the expectations were so high. They knew what we were capable of and expected it. In the big games, though, especially when the odds were stacked against us, they seemed to have a different attitude. Even when mistakes were made on the pitch, they still roared us on. Willing, pushing! Like at Old Trafford in extra-time when they propelled Chelsea on to score with the old mantra, 'Chelsea, Chelsea, Chelsea'. We could feel it coming down in waves from the back of the Shed, across the stands. It filled the terraces, the pitch, our very brains. Bruges had played so well, but they sensed it too, and started hacking the ball away where before they had passed it.

Nine minutes from oblivion, Osgood scored. It was not one of his super goals. In a catalogue of his wonder goals (Arsenal, Milan, Derby) it would not have rated very high. Like Houseman's equalizer at Burnley, though, it was a lifesaver and paved the way for glory. Thus in that context it was priceless. The big centre-forward turned a shot in by the far post. He was surrounded by defenders but the old gunfighter's reflexes made sure he got to the ball first and turned it home. Maybe his goal at Old Trafford was more emotional and better crafted, but this was probably the most cathartic moment in that particular team's history. We all thought that Os had been treated so harshly, and for him to come back and score such a vital goal unleashed a dam of hysteria, passion and frenzy.

All the good things in the game! Not sleaze or drugs or corruption! Fields of Gold, as the man sang. Os went off somewhere, celebrating. Just as he had kept his record of scoring in every round in the FA Cup when we won it, he kept his word to the fans. How could they fail to love him? That's why they have an 'Osgood's' bar in the ground now. He had scored at the end that the new North Stand now overlooks. He vaulted the little fence where the dog track was and ended up in front of the benches. The crowd were already steaming down to mob him. In those days, a hot-dog truck trundled around the perimeter, and in quiet games we could smell the burgers and onions. This was all pre-Big Macs and Burger Kings. Os dived on to the trolley, the buns went flying and the crowd engulfed him.

Sometimes in your life you try to recreate certain moments and feelings. That was always a special moment for me. I think we all knew then that we could go on and take the Cup. The game went into extra-time. It was ours for the taking. Bruges seemed to sense that it was all up with them. Funny, I still think to this day that if they had attacked us at the Bridge, they might have gone through. They were a talented side, better in a way than the teams we were to meet later on in the competition.

I set up Os for the third goal, which put us in front for the first time in the tie. It was the oldest trick in the Osgood–Hudson songbook. The old cut-back from the by-line and Os was in again, like Dettori riding for Sheikh Mohammed. A terrific interplay between Cooke, Os and myself put Tommy Baldwin in for our fourth goal. I remember weighing out 10lbs lighter after the match, feeling weak and shattered, such was the hard work and emotion. I couldn't help thinking about our first-leg lifeline and was going to do anything in my power to take that lifeline. I recovered, after sitting in our beloved Alexandres to get my strength back, and then went on to the Aratusa with Sponge and Charlie! Cooke was brilliant that night. What made him such an awesome opponent was his accuracy. He was ruthlessly determined to win honours then. In the closing stages of the game he seemed to get stronger, just as in the Leeds replay.

My father was steeped in the history of Chelsea Football Club. He used to tell me about Hughie Gallacher, who was a legend in the 1930s. He could dribble like Cooke and score like Os. Like those two, he was a 'big match' specialist, saving his best performances for the special occasions. He was always in trouble off the pitch, getting in rows and drinking (sounds familiar!). He left the Bridge after a huge bust-up with the management (sounds familiar!). Tragedy followed him around, though, and he ended up taking a flying header under an express train. He still has the record for the most hat-tricks for Scotland.

On the following Saturday, Leeds came to the Bridge. We were up for it. We crushed them 3–1. Os scored another great goal. This win effectively set Arsenal up for the Double. Our legends were growing. In football I was known as 'Huddy'. Ken Bates tells me the next bar he is going to name at the Bridge will be the 'Huddy' bar – named, he jokingly says, after the comedian Roy Hudd. However, I suspect that the next bar at the Bridge will be named after a certain gentleman pictured on the back cover of this book with myself and the England manager.

The Chelsea fans nicknamed me 'Hud'. For a while, we contemplated calling the book 'Hud'. I got the abbreviation from the 1963 Paul Newman film. They used to show it on TV a lot around that time. Adapted from a novel by Larry McMurty called *Horseman* (no, not Houseman!) *Pass By*, it won three Oscars and was a huge box-office hit. How come, then, no-one else I know has ever heard of it?

7

Greece is the Word

'When there is no vision, the people perish' Proverbs 29

The years can take away the looks, the money, the suits, the friends, even the medals, but never the glory – never that. Memories: the living with them and the killing of them. A lot of that late spring, early summer of 1971 is blurred.

A little while after beating Leeds we went to Arsenal. The biggest crowd of the season, more than 62,000, watched us lose 2–0. The previous biggest crowd had been when Tottenham won by the same score at Stamford Bridge the previous November. I had been injured and missed the match. How I got depressed missing such matches as these. I recall it was played in torrential rain, like something out of *Bladerunner*, and Tottenham's Pat Jennings made a point-blank save from a Baldwin header that was the equal of Banks's classic save from Pele in the World Cup earlier that year. I was later to see Pat do that so many times during my stay at Highbury. Spurs scored both their goals in the dying seconds. I was on my way home. Mullery scored one of them. What a shame I missed it!

At Highbury, Kennedy, that man again, scored both of Arsenal's goals and Peter Storey hit a post from George Graham's cross. Graham was superb that day, slowing down the pace as the tension grew. He must have done more for Arsenal on and off the field than any living person. It's a story to make one weep, even now. Our minds were on the clash with Man City in the semi-final of the Cup Winners' Cup. City were the holders and we would have preferred to meet them in an all-English Final. It would probably have been played in this country. Chelsea were on course to play Arsenal in the Cup Winners' Cup Final 24 years later, but that was not to be either.

The first leg was at home. We wore yellow, City wore shirts the colour of the tablecloths in Alexandres. It was not a great game and lacked the passion of the Bruges match. We did not play well, and injuries to key players on both sides disrupted the balance. Mickey Droy made his European debut and John Phillips kept his place in goal. I played in the number seven shirt. Smethurst scrambled the only goal of the night. Our fans wondered if it would be enough to take us through to the club's first European Final.

Ever the optimist – every Gemini knows that there are a number of ways to perceive any situation – I figured we would have more room at Maine Road. The blindspot between their centre-back and the ageing full-back Tony Book could be attacked. If we could drop off into the space and push Weller or Houseman against Book, we could get something. It worked a treat. Keith Weller scored the only goal with a free-kick in the first half. The City goalkeeper, Healy, could only punch his dipping cross-shot into the roof of the net. In one of those strange fixture quirks, we had played there in the League a few days beforehand. Keith scored in that game too, losing his boot in the process. Near the end of the European tie, Houseman hit the post with a flying header as we found space. Chelsea took 10,000 fans up there in the middle of the week. There was a lot of trouble in the streets after the game as the Chelsea boys fought their way back to the station. The trains were bricked as they left Manchester Piccadilly. It was almost a year to the night since we had won the Cup. Winning was getting to be a habit, especially in Manchester.

Now we had to finish the job and win the Cup Winners' Cup.

The Final was held in Athens, against Real Madrid. I suppose they were what Liverpool are today, a good side but a shadow of their glorious predecessors. I saw the early sixties version who had made the European Cup their own personal property. Di Stefano, Puskas, Gento, Kopa and Santamaria: a footballing hall of fame. The team we met, shorn of those players, were (dare I say it?) a somewhat stodgy side, but certainly no pushovers. They played with a pessimistic outlook and were too traditional to please the more sophisticated fans. Easily their best player was the midfielder Pirri. He was one of the best balanced players that I had ever seen. He ran the midfield like a game of chess; the type of player that I relished playing against, as we had to outwit one another. He used his team-mates like pawns, working gambits. At the highest level of a European competition, it really was like playing chess in a championship tournament. A battle without armour, a war without blood.

I had a great chance to put Chelsea ahead in the first half. I would love to have scored in a European Final but, put through with only the goalkeeper to beat, I was brought down from behind. It was a blatant penalty but nothing was given. It was one of the biggest disappointments of my career. The guy 'dead-legged' me, and as the game wore on I was feeling the effects. I drove myself harder, telling myself at least I was playing in a Final, which had to be better than the heart-break of missing the Leeds games.

Os, once again, put us in front with one of his specials. That looked as if it might do it for us, but Pirri had other ideas and pinned us down with his masterly football. Chelsea, then as now, were never as comfortable holding a lead as chasing it. Twenty seconds from the end, Zoco capitalised on a mistake and equalized for Madrid. We had breathed the fire of a dragon. Chelsea had come so close to lifting the Cup, but had not managed it on this occasion.

This game had been played on a Wednesday. Most of our fans had come over for the day on special flights, I think it was £24 for the package. I doubt if you could fund a trip to the Bridge on that now, let alone Athens. The Chelsea fans, virtually to a man, stayed on for the replay on the Friday night. They had done most of their dosh just getting there but pooled funds and slept on the beach.

Incredible people, like an army they could endure any hardship as long as they could be with their team. The atmosphere in Athens for those days was magical. The whole town was buzzing; not only with flies, but with chat and merriment from the Chelsea boys. The pickpockets and ladies of the night were on overtime and the streets were full of jugglers, dancers and music.

Thursday was ordered as a complete day of rest. Dave Sexton gave strict instructions that there was to be no drinking whatsoever. My leg hurt like hell. It was so stiff that I had a feeling of déjà-vu. Surely not another Final I would have to sit out! I had the feeling that Sexton was trying to talk me out of playing in the replay, so that he could bring in one of his favourites. By now I sensed that soon all-out war would erupt between the club and myself. I had this feeling of excitement tinged with fear of the future. That long Thursday was solitary and almost surreal. As lunchtime approached, Os, Tommy and Charlie Cooke strolled up to the Athens Hilton. I went to the flea market and found neither fleas nor a Squire shop. On the way back, I thought I would check on the chaps at the Hilton. I found them by the pool, throwing down tropical punches. They were drinking as if the planet was going to explode the moment they left, and Os was throwing back the most. He loved a good watering-hole in the sun. A few years ago he told me of a drink he found in the States called a White Russian. This consisted of vodka, coffee liqueur and cream. Way to go, Os! Cooke had had a few too. He had a darker side to his personality which drinking sometimes brought out, particularly when he drank brandy. When he 'went into one', he could give you a hard time. When I first broke into the side, the year we won the FA Cup, he always regarded me as an outsider at first at the drinking sessions. I recall going to the Palmerston once with my pal Tony Frewin, and Cooke questioned my right to be there. At that time he regarded me as a kid. I was 19, and yet to prove my ability to hold my own in both the team and the drinking bouts. I soon showed him, on both fronts.

Charlie's best pal was Tommy Baldwin, who took on the Terry McCann role of 'minding' him. Tom was everybody's pal. He had that way with him, he still does. Os had that affable nature on the surface. I challenged him about the marathon drinking when the next day we had our biggest game ever.

'Go home, son,' he said. He was wearing a striped shirt, Chelsea shorts and sandals. Cooke had a white jacket and was carrying expensive brown sunglasses. 'Rest your leg,' Ossie said. 'Don't worry. I will win us the game.' He raised his glass again. He had such belief in his talent, such certainty! They stayed by the pool until 8.30 pm, by which time it was pitch dark, still drinking the wallop you could fly Concorde on. On a side-plate were soft marzipan cakes which the waiters kept serving with wine, coffee and beer as quick as they could, arguing with the drunks while adroitly attending to the not-so-drunk Chelsea players. Alongside these three was Johnny Fennell, one of the Cromwellian squad.

The next evening Os repaid everyone's faith in him by scoring our second and what was to prove the winning goal. Tommy, playing in place of the injured Hollins, gave Os the shooting chance from about twenty-five yards and the ball powered in. Sexton gambled on playing an attacking formation and it worked to perfection. John Dempsey, of all people, scored the first goal. Baldwin started it off by firing in an angled drive that the Real Madrid goalkeeper Borja just tipped over. Cooke, on peak form, arched over the corner and Dempsey volleyed in a piece of history. I was so pleased for him! He had let Madrid in for the last-ditch equaliser, and it was good to see him make things up. Dempsey had even survived a penalty claim against him by Madrid just before he scored. Pirri, such a force in the previous game, was quieter that night. He played with his wrist in a plaster cast. Maybe the injury had something to do with it, maybe not!

The 'Athens Hilton Beach Party' played superbly – Cooke had probably his finest game for Chelsea. In the second half, Bonetti kept the Spaniards out as they put up a stupendous fightback. Os was suffering from the dreaded ankle-pains (sounds familiar) and limped off to be replaced by Smethurst. Gento came on as sub for Madrid in a last-ditch effort to save the game. He was another hero of mine, at his peak the fastest winger I had ever seen. He had passed that, but was still an inspirational player to them. A great dribbler, he could bring his leading foot over the ball (like Rivelino) passing from outside to inside. This gave the impression that he was attempting a diagonal shot. He would then touch his foot down just inside the ball, the outside of the foot setting him up for either a shot or a pass, or enabling him to continue his run. The deception, executed at speed, was devastating. The thing that I remember most about him was that he was wearing a wrist-watch, the first time I had seen one worn on the pitch. I do not know if he had merely overlooked it or was anxious to know how long was left, but the bench made him take it off, at top speed. He threw off his time-piece whilst gliding past a bemused Johnny Boyle. Velazquez had gone off, but the other winger, Fleitas, was a handful. With fifteen minutes left, he robbed Webb, ran twenty yards and beat Bonetti to put Madrid back in it. Zoco tried to tie it all up, but Peter made a great save. I was so tired, but suddenly broke upfield. I set Smethurst up with an easy chance but he missed it. I do not recall the final whistle.

Must mention Dennis Darcy being buried in my Cup Winners' Cup shirt. A Fulham lad, a good friend of our family and a lovely boy, he was dying of cancer. I visited his home and he was so pleased to see me with the look of a European Cup winner. I had no hesitation in taking my shirt for him to be buried in. There are certain things in life we cannot account for. Where did this go? Where did that go? Or I wish I'd never done that. This shirt went to the right place!

The BBC's seventies football show, hosted by Dennis Waterman, barely touched on our achievement in winning the second most prestigious trophy in Europe. Chelsea had lifted two cups in just over a year. The team was young and strong. It should have been the launching-pad to the stars. We should have taken a string of championships and strangled English football, won so much that the public would have been bored.

That night it looked too easy, much too easy.

8

Such Dust As Dreams
Are Made Of

'Which of us has his desire? Or, having it is satisfied' Vanity Fair,
Thackeray

We flew back to London the next day. It was blindingly sunny, as if
we had taken the Athens heat with us. I had been up all night: a
combination of heat, my aching legs and excitement. I had a few
drinks, but the more I drank the more sombre I felt. A dream
within a dream. I watched the sunrise from my balcony, too tired to
sleep. The stone floor soon became hot under foot. The sun hit the
white houses down by the beach, near where Ossie and the chaps
had been drinking. The white houses soon became as pink as the
geraniums that stood in the pots on the balcony.

The scene at the airport was like something out of the old footage
of the Beatles when they returned from conquering America. I
suppose it would be Oasis or somebody else now. Twenty-five
summers have passed since that day, but I can still remember it all.
I travelled on the open-top bus this time. I was part of it. I had been

there, seen it and done it. Pictures show me wearing a striped shirt, probably a Ben Sherman or a Take Six. Ben Shermans are still fashionable today. I thought of Tony Frewin, who by this time had gone to South Africa. That was the difference in football at that level. You could be on the bus with the Cup, or going out of the game. I should know about that, even at the tender age of twenty.

The summer was uneventful until Dave Sexton told me about a player he was buying, Steve Kember of Palace. Oh yeah? The Chelsea manager told me that Kember could only play in one position, in the middle of the park; yours truly's place of work, my manor, my little world. I should have smelt a rat then, but I went along with it at first. Keith Weller went abruptly, and Sexton had pencilled me in as his replacement in the right-wing berth. Dave liked me there because I could run all day and go past people. I was dead against it. Playing wide was too peripheral for me; it all went back to the League Cup game against Leeds, the season we beat them in the FA Cup Final.

That was the game I nutmegged Terry Cooper, my all-time favourite English left-back, but that came in the second half of the game. In the first half I was up against Leeds's utility giant Paul Madeley, and the big 'Revie Robot' kept making runs and taking me deep into my own half. This was a test I could not pass. I was totally run off my feet. It taught me my biggest lesson so far – you had to be 110 per cent fit! From that day on, I worked even harder on my cross-country runs. I vowed that it would not happen again, and it never did! At half-time, Sexton spotted the obvious and moved Johnny Boyle to run with Madeley, freeing me to attack Terry Cooper. This gave me a chance to get my breath back and I had a very good second half – which didn't do me any favours for the future, as it gave Sexton the ludicrous notion that whenever Chelsea were struggling he could move me to the wing. Ultimately, this move led to me leaving Chelsea.

I always think of wingers as bird-watchers, and only if Raquel Welch had been a season-ticket holder at the Bridge would I have wanted to be a winger. My game was to be involved all the time, setting up the plays and making things happen. To be isolated on the wing and out of the game for long periods was totally alien to me. I did not want to be chatting to a full-back and not involved. I would be limited in my choice and timing of passes. This was not going to be an easy adjustment for me, and why should I alter my role anyway? Had we been starved of success of late, or what? Thinking about it, that is when I should have left. At that time my stock was so high I could have walked into any midfield in the land. I could have done a good job for the next ten years, such was my ability. I felt that way, anyhow. But by then the poison had been poured into every ear that would listen.

Dave Sexton's plan was for me to feed Kember. Chris Garland had joined the club from Bristol City by then, the first player with the name Chris to play for Chelsea. Not a lot of people know that! Chris is ill now, suffering from the same affliction as Ray Kennedy, but is fighting with the same determination he showed battling up front for the Blues. At that time he was the new kid on the block. He always reminded me of the actor Ben Murphy from the hit TV show *Alias Smith & Jones*. Chris was another of those 'pretty boy' strikers that Chelsea purchased in that era. They were always popular with the crowd. The media used to typecast these players and burn them out fast. Garland was bought to give us more firepower up front in the continued absence of Hutch, who was never to regain his full fitness after the catalogue of injuries he sustained. The night we won the Cup at Old Trafford, Hutch looked indestructible. He was not. Altogether he suffered two broken legs, two cartilage operations, a broken arm, nose and marriages. Funny story about the broken nose and arm; he got them in the same match, playing against Forest's Sammy Chapman. Now he was a real hard man. He elbowed Hutch and broke his nose. When Hutch retaliated, he injured himself again, breaking his arm. Both left the field for different reasons.

Around that time AC Milan had enquired about me. They had been trailing me since the FA Cup run and were looking to import some names. Funny! If things had worked out differently, I might have ended up living in a seventeenth-century *palazzo* with a rack of Armani suits and one of those nice yellow sports cars in the drive. In Italy no-one ever dreams of being a train driver. I am sure going to Milan would have been right down my street. I especially liked Inter and all their superb inside-forwards, particularly Suarez who played nearly ten years for them after moving from Barcelona. He was nicknamed 'The Architect' for his ability to construct the pattern of play. Sandro Mazzola was another legend who started his career as a striker before switching to the playmaker's role. Liam Brady, whom I played with later at Arsenal, also played for the *Nerazzurri* (the Black and Blues).

I remember my first Chelsea youth trip to Switzerland alongside the Inter Milan Under-17s and I came away very impressed with how classy they were on and off the field. Tommy Docherty wanted Chelsea to wear the black and blue strip as their colours. In their disappointing semi-final defeat against Sheffield Wednesday, Chelsea actually sported the Milan strip. It was never worn again and ended up being worn by a Sunday morning team Johnny Hollins coached.

In the first League match of the 1971–72 season we went over to Highbury to meet the Double winners. They blasted us 3–0. Before the game, played in blazing sunshine, Arsenal displayed their two trophies. We brought our family silverware to the party. What a time for London! The old town had never seen so much booty. We could never get going in conditions better suited to a barbecue than a football match. When McLintock headed Arsenal in front, the defence must have been dreaming of sausages and cold beer! Our friend Kennedy scored his obligatory goal.

Osgood was transfer-listed by Sexton after Manchester United had beaten us on our own ground on a scalding late summer night. It reminded me again of Athens, it was so hot. Best was sent off in what was to be a troubled season for him. He had dyed his hair blue-black like Elvis (he was entering his Elvis/Albert Goldman phase). Charlton (coming out of his Bobby Charlton phase) hit the winner with a shot that threatened to decapitate Phillips. I think he ducked down at the last second and the ball went over him.

Charlton is another myth that I would like to debunk. Whenever I played against him, all he did was moan to the referee. Being an icon, his voice carried some weight with some of the officials that were unfortunate to come up against him. Once, Webb accidentally (and I must emphasise this) nutted Charlton, brother of the more famous Jack (only because of the Shredded Wheat!). He played in Mexico but was effectively spent as a force. But for my injury at WBA, I might have edged him out. I knew from the start that if I could hold my own with the likes of Sir Bobby then I could go anywhere. Charlton was every schoolboy's hero. At that time, nobody in England wanted to be a train driver either. I was vaguely disappointed in him. Tony Bennett once sang a song 'Is that all there is?', all about disillusion and hollowness! When I saw people like Charlton for what they were, I would think of that song.

Denis Law was my favourite in a red shirt before the arrival of Georgie. Ron Harris said that he was the best player that he ever marked. Law knew that stick was being dished out and expected it. It made him try even harder. He was the first of the superstar players. Best was the first pop-star footballer, which was different. Law was the first player to wear his socks down, his shirt outside his shorts, and the first to punch the air. His influence over a whole generation of players cannot be overestimated. It was said that Rodney Marsh used to practise that salute in gladiator fashion in front of the mirror. Sounds like the beginning of Rodney's love affair with a mirror!

Another ex-Fulham striker, Allan Clarke, tried all the moves from the Law bag of tricks. Another Rodney, Stewart, always saw Law as his alter ego. At the time Kember joined Chelsea, Stewart's first global smash, 'Maggie May', was breaking. Everywhere I went I would hear it playing. If Chelsea had been a pop group they would have been Rod's good-time band, the Faces (ex-Small Faces). Ronnie Wood was later to join the Rolling Stones, who had started their career a hundred yards from the 'Cage'; and the original Small Faces, led by the late Stevie Marriott, lived together close by in Pimlico for a while. Ron Wood's drinking chum these days is one James White of Tooting, superstar snooker ace and Chelsea fan.

Law was the first player to bring the 'bicycle kick' home from Italy, a spectacular method of kicking which enabled shots to be taken when an attacker was facing the wrong way and did not have the time or space to turn. Jimmy Greaves had devised a 'scissors kick' on the basis of getting his feet into the position occupied by his head. He used to practise this in training and used to shatter car windscreens such were the dynamics of the forward thrust of the kick. Gianluca Vialli demonstrated his scissors kick on his Premiership debut for Chelsea. Law was such a daredevil that he risked injury each time he fell, after kicking backwards over his

shoulder. Law always had the 'suss' to try and play the ball over
and behind markers like Ron Harris. No defender relishes that, and
in the modern game that is why players like Ian Wright are so hard
to counter. Harris loved players having the ball played up to them
with the goal behind them. He would never let them turn and face
him. The odds were always stacked in his favour, and when he put
in one of his shattering tackles the forward would go down writhing
in pain.

In the 1994 World Cup held in America, it was noticeable how
players like Romario and Baggio would receive the ball on the
half-turn, thus giving them sight of the defender as they came in on
them. I am not blaming him, but when Bruce Rioch tackled me in a
match involving Derby and Stoke I ended up with a broken leg.
More of that later, but the point was that I broke my father's golden
rule of never turning my back on the defender. Watch today's
Premier League games and see how many strikers receive the ball
with their back to goal with at least one defender on top of them.
Players without the swivel of an Osgood would have had to
pas-de-deux quickly to find any space. Even mediocre defences
could snuff out such attacks provided they held their shape.

Our first match in defence of the Cup Winners' Cup was against
Jeunesse Hautcharage of Luxembourg. It rained goals, and we set a
new European record which I think still stands. In the away leg we
hit eight. Os powered in a hat-trick, Houseman scored two solo
goals, Webb, Tommy and John Hollins's penalty were the others.
In this match it wouldn't have mattered a jot had Hollins missed the
penalty. Jeunesse were amateurs. One of the team only had one
arm. No, he did not play in goal! Perhaps he was the mysterious
one-armed man that Richard Kimble was looking for in *The
Fugitive* TV programme that showed then. In the game, Os hit the
post twice. He could easily have scored five.

That is exactly how many he did score in the second leg at the
Bridge. It was another jamboree night for us. With the vital away
goals counting double, we fancied our chances in the second leg. As
in the first leg we were six up at half-time. I scored the third. The
thing I do recall was a section of the crowd barracking Houseman.
It was the biggest ever Chelsea win, smashing all aggregate records
in European history. But they fought very hard, and it was only

towards the end that the goals tumbled in. The crowd were annoyed as Peter found his full-back a tough nut to crack. Like HG Wells's 'Invisible Man', Peter discovered that his gift had its price.

The tragic manner of Peter's death was not in keeping with his modest lifestyle. If any of us had died in a car smash, what would the public have said? 'What we expected! So long, sucker. You had a good time.' They always say, 'Where were you when you heard of Kennedy's death?' I always remember where I was when I heard of Peter's. It was 3.30 one Sunday afternoon, in the Imperial. We had both left Chelsea by then and the sea of life had started to take all of the lads in different directions; eddies and currents had started to batter us. I was in the pub with my mate Les May, who was also to die tragically young. Sunday afternoon was always a late session. We would get home late, have dinner, doss out and maybe go down the King's Road on Sunday night for a couple. My mum rang: 'Peter and Sally are dead, killed in a car smash.' I felt sick. Like vodka-sick after a bad night, like ankle-sick when I got hurt at West Brom. Like 'somebody was killed' sick.

I started to cry, really out of character for me. Gemini thing again; hide your feelings. When you miss the Cup Final, smile and shrug. Bust up at Chelsea, their loss. Control, see? Get a right-hander off the ball, smile at them and run them dizzy. Control ... it's just that I cannot see at the moment. For Peter to die in a car smash was unbelievable. He used to get the tube home after some games. I never remember him driving. When he was killed, he was just a passenger.

My memory of Peter, apart from all the games and the goals, was a boat trip. The time we were in the West Indies, we all went fishing. It was like the scene from *Jaws* when the shark hits the side of Robert Shaw's boat. Actually it was more like *The Poseidon Adventure*, where the boat turned over. I think our pal Caine was in it. Anyway, we were all so battered that nobody would have noticed had one of us fallen overboard. Peter Houseman and myself were up at the front of the boat. He had drunk more than he usully did and had chilled out. Drink always loosens people up, I find. Like most people, I drink for the effect not for the taste, unless it is the finest bourbon or coconut rum. With inhibitions gone, the conversation, like the drink, flowed. We got to know each other very well. I sensed that he would have liked to be that relaxed all the time. Maybe the restrictions placed on him made him so quiet. I wish we had had more drinks together, been even closer. Perhaps he saw me as a younger brother. It was a moment that had both an infinity and an evanescence, an intense closeness, yet no more durable than the tiny shimmering organisms in the water around us. Loss! We should never be together like that again. Perhaps I knew that then also.

Perhaps because Peter was so quiet, Os and I did not pass to him as much as we should have. Out on the left, he was often neglected. 'Get it more to Nobby,' Sexton would always insist. Peter would just nod his head, his lazy, ironic eyes shining. Thinking about that trip if we had hit anything or if a sudden storm had blown up, we would have all gone down. Chelsea went down quick enough after I left anyway. 'Peter's dead' – perhaps all that flashed across my mind as I heard the words. It is the age of flashbacks, after all: the seventies, wind a tape; the sixties, watch the dish. Years afterwards, I would dream about the boat and always take a trip on one when abroad in an attempt to recapture those memories.

In some parallax way, the Silver Jubilee reunion at Chelsea brought it back. None of us spoke about Peter. We hardly did when he was alive. He was such a part of things, I suppose. We even called him the 'ghost' when he set up so many goals by sneaking through to arrow over a cross. I felt his presence especially on the pitch that sunny spring afternoon. Ultimately people are remembered for what they are. For example, Marilyn Monroe is remembered for herself more than her acting. Similarly, Elvis is not remembered so much for his singing but for his overall image. I am not ranking the Chelsea personalities of the seventies on such a high plane, but in terms of football history and public consciousness they are legends.

Steve Kember made his debut at Sheffield United. He was dazed by the ball early on. Sheffield had made a tremendous start to the season, almost as good statistically as when Spurs took the Double. Our nemesis, Scullion (you will recall him from the semi-final against Watford), scored the game's only goal. In the last minute, Webb, up on a suicide raid, headed down to Os who was standing literally on the goal-line. In one of the most remarkable misses ever, he volleyed straight up in the air and over the bar. It looked impossible to miss from such a position. The shot was almost perpendicular. The only miss I have seen from closer range was when George Graham, playing in his last game for Chelsea, dribbled round the Blackpool goalkeeper Waiters and was practically in the back of the net when he blasted it over. Missed chances! It was to be the story of that season.

This was never more so than in the second round of the Cup Winners' Cup against the Swedish side Atvidaberg. We should have scored at least six over there, but settled for 0–0. The pitch was awful and my ankle felt it afterwards. We flew back to London confident that we could finish them off at the Bridge.

The day we played the return match, I visited a Chelsea boy who was dying of a very serious illness. Hutch came with me. Robert Drewitt was an old school-friend of mine from Elm Park Gardens. I was told that he would like me to visit him. I think it was leukaemia. I was only too pleased to oblige. In times like this, it was not only to help the person so wickedly struck down; it also gave me the opportunity to really appreciate not only my God-given talent but thankfully my health and strength! Again, the sentimental side of me! But the realistic one too. Robert Drewitt came on to the field with me that evening. I can honestly say that when the ball left my foot from twenty-odd yards, it was him hitting it! A sweeter volley you have never seen! An Ossie special! Robert had played for Chelsea in Europe! I told him I would score a goal for him specially, and I kept my word. I think at certain stages in your life God either sends people to you or they cross your path to remind you of the fragility of life and the uncertainty of it all.

We dominated but finished wretchedly, especially Os. At half-time, Sexton switched Webb and Hollins and substituted Hinton for Paddy Mulligan. Fifteen seconds into the second half I scored from the edge of the box. That seemed to be it against a side who appeared just to be concentrating on keeping down the score. The only player they had was Roland Sandberg. In Sweden, his robust play had set up a couple of chances. After 63 minutes we should have wrapped it up. Hollins stepped up to take a penalty. I had asked the Chelsea manager why John took so many free-kicks and spot-kicks. He took the penalty and missed. The ball skimmed the outside of the post. Three minutes after Hollins's miss, Sandberg ran on to a peach of a ball from Lars Andersson and comprehensively beat Bonetti. The Swedes held out, and we crashed out on the away-goals rule.

The next week we had almost a repeat performance against Bolton in the League Cup. I scored again. We had nearly all of the game but it ended all-square and we faced a tricky replay. The Atvidaberg game haunted us. I had never played in such a one-sided tie, yet we had lost. The vital, lucrative route to Europe had been severed. The damage to the club's finances was immeasurable. Our form in the League was patchy. Arsenal completed the double over us at a rain-drenched Bridge, Kennedy (not the President!) scoring both their goals. George Graham had a great game. We had a couple of meetings in the Markham to try and sort things out. We had taken a bit of stick in the press, who were quick enough to latch on to the King's Road angle and play it up as a glamour thing but were merciless in throwing it back in our faces when results went against us. We were very determined on the night of the Bolton replay and hit our best form of the season, scoring six. Tommy bagged three of them. That was my first meeting with my Seattle pal and team-mate, Roy Greaves.

Another bizarre Hudson goal came at around that time. We beat Palace 3–2 at Selhurst, and I scored direct from a corner. I got the idea from watching Cruyff, pre-season, curling over his crosses. Os scored the winner when he pivoted on his standing foot and blurred home a great shot. Poor old Palace, he always had something to punish them with.

A few days before Christmas 1971 we met Tottenham at the Bridge in the first leg of the League Cup semi-final. It was our Christmas treat for the fans, a truly unbelievable match. Osgood put us ahead near half-time, but early in the second half Spurs hit back with two goals in a minute from Terry Naylor and Martin Chivers. Chivers was having his best season for Spurs, playing with great aplomb and scoring at a prolific rate. Coates (a thorn in our side since his Turf Moor days) was a handful. Chris Garland was Chelsea's best player that day, hitting the bar in the first half, then almost equalising when he robbed Cyril Knowles and flicked the ball into the side-netting when he had a clear shot. Sadly, Knowles died a few years ago. He was a cult figure at Tottenham. They had a lot of cults. I remember Docherty calling them the biggest cults in the game. Cyril even had a record made in his honour, 'Nice One Cyril'. Of course, people recall our own foray into the pop music business, and Tottenham's effort was not in the class of our little gem.

Knowles had a kid brother called Peter who played for Wolves. He was a real livewire, forever getting into scrapes and being booked. He would have fitted in well at Chelsea. The story went that he found religion and chucked it all in to become a Jehovah's Witness. He was still banging on people's doors last I heard.

Charlie Cooke came on for Tommy and the crowd went into a frenzy. Chris equalized for Chelsea with a header from Houseman's cut-back corner. Just how good Peter's crosses and corners were it is hard to say, because when Hutch was fit he would go for anything, throwing himself into a sea of boots and elbows. When Ian first came to the club, I played against him in a practice match. At corners and other dead-ball situations he would scare the life out of me. Like an eagle, he would get on the end of anything. I stopped going into the box and challenging when he was soaring in. I know how defenders felt.

Wingers can make forwards, as Nevin did for Speedie and Dixon, and conversely forwards can make wingers. For example, when Jimmy Carter was at Millwall he had two exceptional headers of the ball to supply: Tony (we don't need another hero) Cascarino and Teddy Sheringham. They had more air-power than the Luftwaffe, and Carter later joined Liverpool and then Arsenal without really having great success. Great to see Teddy Sheringham doing so well, though. I met him in Scribes one night and was impressed by what a nice fellow he is. I told him I thought he was good enough to have played in our side, and I cannot say that about many modern strikers.

Near the end of the Spurs game, I found Paddy Mulligan breaking on the right. The Irishman chipped back into the box, I ran on but Naylor handled. I wanted to take the penalty but Hollins insisted and scored. It was a hard game. Os had a running battle with Mike England all night and Webby collected five stitches in a gash that looked as if he had been 'bottled'.

The return game at White Hart Lane made the first encounter look like a reserve match, such was the drama and excitement. Chelsea aficionados rank it alongside the Cup Final replay and the Bruges matches as one of the all-time classics. The nearest game of modern times would be the Cup replay at Newcastle in the 1995–96 season. With Kember cup-tied, I played in my usual role. I am not claiming that had anything to do with our display but ... 3–2 was not a big lead to take to Tottenham. Spurs threw everything at us early on and squeezed us back into our own half. We hung on grimly. In first-half injury time, though, Coates got to the line, Peters's head brushed his cross and Chivers, close in, thrashed home a great goal.

At half-time we sat in the dressing-room looking at each other in a manner not dissimilar to when Watford were giving us problems in the FA Cup semi. I did not worry though; White Hart Lane was my lucky ground. Garland scored early in the second half, probably his best goal in Chelsea blue. Sexton had moved him up alongside Os. He received the ball on the right-hand side, cut in and bulleted a shot in to the top of the net. Jennings was a hell of a goalkeeper, and to beat him from that range needed real power. It lifted the whole team. The Chelsea fans in the 52,000 crowd went crazy. Once again, you cannot underestimate their value in games like that. Cooke, back in midfield, started to find the form he showed in Athens. Seven minutes from time, Spurs drew level again. I was back in defence trying to set something up when Chivers's long throw hit me. A penalty was awarded. The ball had skidded off the mud-heap pitch on to my right arm. It seemed a harsh decision – half arm, half chest. Peters coolly drilled in the kick and it looked all set for another half-hour.

But in the dying seconds, Os launched one last raid on the Spurs goal. England fouled him, as he had repeatedly. The foul had taken place out on the left near the corner flag. I trotted over to take the kick. No sign of Hollins. I was really tired and did not fancy the prospect of extra-time. More importantly, a special party was being arranged for us at Alexandres if we managed to get through to our third major Final in three years. I fired in a low drive. Everyone was expecting a lob to the far post. I reasoned it might confuse Jennings, who was superb in the air but, being such a big man, found it harder to make the ground shots. Perhaps he would scramble it around for a corner or Os might get on the end of it. Webb was staying back; no-one wanted to lose a goal that late in the game, there would be no time to pull it back. Pictures of the goal that took us back to Wembley show no Chelsea player in the box. One Spurs defender, Knowles, skied his clearance; the ball hit the far post and rolled in. Gilzean was back there, and England. Jennings was at the other end of his goal, unsighted.

The Chelsea fans went wild. I read later that they smashed up Seven Sisters station and the pub near where Sam Fox later had her club. Spurs, to this day, are Chelsea's bitterest rivals. In 1967 when Chelsea lost the 'Cockney Cup Final', the bad feeling between the fans started. This victory over Spurs confirmed us as top dogs in our own town. Arsenal had the Double, but not the flair Chelsea oozed. Only Charlie George, my old mate, and the other George, Graham, would have gained a place in our attack and midfield. We were the real London Lads.

Today a lot is written about the cult of the 'Lad'. Magazines are full of it and TV ransacks the 1970s for its shows. At the time, Adam Faith was starring in the quintessential London Lad show, *Budgie*. Faith was a pal of Venables (I always saw a lot of Terry in his character) and Hollins. Richard O'Sullivan (a great Hutch fan) was in *Man About the House*. We all liked the blonde in that. Once when interviewed O'Sullivan was asked, if he had the choice who else would he have been? Alan Hudson, was his reply. Thanks, Richard, I don't think I would have swapped places. Rodney Bewes (a great Weller fan) was in *The Likely Lads*. Dennis Waterman was in *The Sweeney* which later metamorphosed into *Minder*. Caine had already been in *Alfie* and Patrick Mower was in *Special Branch*. The common thread of all these shows was the references to Chelsea contained in them. I cannot emphasise the showbiz connections too much. This is probably why Chelsea had such media attention over the years, even though honours eluded them. They were such a part of the nation's consciousness.

Programmes like *Budgie* were never understood up north. He was seen as a fantastic figure, but in the capital you could actually meet people like him. I grew up amongst people like him. Today the 'Budgies' of this world would be found in Scribes. I grew up near the King's Road. The flash clothes, the fancy eating-houses, the bims and bos that were always tantalisingly in sight. My ambition and comfort with it grew out of growing up amid the contrasts of cosmopolitan life, where the different classes lead their vastly different lifestyles side by side in a way that does not happen up north. That is why someone like Coates, stepping out of a community like Burnley, found Tottenham such a vortex. They tell me the other Le Tissier brothers were better prospects than Matt but did not want to leave their rural background, and Matt told me recently of his apprehension about joining a 'bright lights' club. The Chelsea showbiz connection is still carried on today. Phil Daniels goes to the Bridge with one of the biggest pop stars of the day from Blur. The singer from Madness, Suggs, is another fan. They all wore the Chelsea shirts and dreamed of scoring the winner at Tottenham. Weller (Paul, not Keith) had the cover of his *Stanley Road* CD painted by Peter Blake, the artist who constructed the cover of *Sgt Pepper* by the Beatles. Weller's record had a drawing of Paul's hero, Osgood, on it. When the artwork was completed, though, the picture was scrapped because it depicted Os in the red and white of Southampton. Matthew Harding was a fan of both the Wellers.

Os features in the story of our celebrations at Alexandres. Earlier there was an argument between Alan Mullery and my father at White Hart Lane. Why did the concept of 'Mullers', as he calls himself, on a phone-in show make me uneasy? The stench of victory was heavy in the air. We were all so buzzed. Games like that gave you an adrenalin it took days to burn up. The waiters in the place were all gay. They made a huge fuss of us all, especially on nights like this when we were the conquering heroes. The party broke up at about 2.30 am. We hit the night air. It was unusually warm for January. We were singing 'We're on our way to Wembley', or something stunningly original like that. I remember that night as if it was last week. I had some kind of baked fish with a head and tail and a plate of linguini with clam sauce. There was just me, Os, Chris Garland and my pal Danny Gillen. He spent the summer with us, family and friends in Cornwall. Now he works for Phil Collins as his minder. The next few minutes were like something out of the Collins movie *Buster*, as we were surrounded by an army of police, squad cars, vans etc. About the only thing they did not have with them was a helicopter. We were told to quieten the din. Os started to argue and a scuffle broke out. The evening ended with Os and Danny spending the night in the cells of Chelsea nick. The papers wrote it up as if Os had been doing some anti-Semitic chanting. Today they would have made it into *Schindler's List*. Later, Os was found not guilty of being Schindlers and disorderly. We were in another Final against Stoke City. Some hicks from the sticks. Managed by a fellow called Waddington.

9

When You Come Undone

'But I am Senna.'
The late Ayrton Senna when it was pointed out that he hindered
other drivers.

The chalkmarks that were drawn around us were already getting blurred by rain. 1972, Bowie was singing about *The Man Who Sold the World* (Ken Bates). Hurricane Higgins won the world snooker title and £480. The future looked so bright we should have worn ray-bans. Inevitably, Real Politik intervened. Already through to Wembley, we also had our eyes on getting the FA Cup back and into Europe again. Blackpool and Bolton (our whipping boys that season, as Palace had been) had already been dismissed. We were drawn away to Orient in the fifth round. It looked easy, too easy. My mate Ray Goddard kept goal for Orient. We had grown up together and played for hours in the 'Cage' near where I lived. Ray was in goal even in those days. I would not have guessed that our paths were to cross again. Ray was a real nice lad, like most of the youngsters in the Chelsea Boys Club team managed by my father. Our first taste of glory came at Craven Cottage when we won the

122

National Federation of Boys Clubs trophy for under-14s. Johnny Haynes presented the trophy, and I had no idea at the time that one day I would wear my hero's number ten England shirt. Ray was two years older than me. He still is.

In the League, our form improved. Like the M People sang, we were moving on up. We beat Man United at Old Trafford, as lucky a ground for me as White Hart Lane. Os scored the only goal of the game after we had tricked the Manchester defence with a 'one-two' from Webb's quickly-taken free-kick. United attacked us flat-out near the end, but we held out. Kember nearly scored a second. United were knocked off the top spot. George Best was taking tremendous flak in the media, it was about as much as Lady Di gets today. Best was with Miss World, Marji Wallace, then. I recall some scandal and a lot of headlines about a fur coat – Ron Harris was an easier opponent than some of his female friends. I always enjoyed playing against Best. Like the other legends referred to in this book, he raised your game and brought the best out of you.

We blitzed Everton 4–0 at the Bridge. Os hit two of them, one a screamer on the run from a Hollins through-ball. Without the real Ball, Alan, by now at Arsenal, Everton lacked the power of previous seasons. We were still only cruising in mid-table, but looked to be running into peak form for the Cups.

Around this time we cut our record *'Blue is the Colour'*. Period trappings, but one of the most successful football records ever made. One of the few that you could listen to without cringing! It was a top ten hit, and if we had not suffered such traumas in the ensuing weeks, who knows how high it would have climbed? The video age was not with us yet and only a few photos remain of the recording session. I wore a white cashmere polo-neck sweater with a cardigan, both from Cecil Gee. My hair was still long, so going in the studio I looked the part.

I was starting to make friends in the pop world. Frank Allen of The Searchers was a constant visitor to the prefab. He was a neighbour of Barry Lloyd, who should have been a much bigger name in football. He was unlucky that there was so much talent at Chelsea at the time. He would come round with Frank in his open-top E-type and park it outside for all to see. We would cruise the King's Road and end up in Soho's La Chasse club. Frequent visitors here were Long John Baldry and Keith Moon of The Who. Moon was an amazing character. In a hardened school of drinkers, he was top man. Stories of his drinking were legendary, he could out-drink Ollie Reed and Lee Marvin on film sets. He drove a Roller into a swimming pool and left a trail of devastation behind him. I found him thoroughly charming and likeable. He had a habit of taking the slice of lemon from his glass and chewing the rind whilst talking to you. I admired The Who, West London lads who had taken the world by storm. Around this time, Jim Morrison had taken the same trip as Moonie's Roller. The Doors' music was playing in the hip shops on the King's Road where I shopped. He was dark and damaged enough to have been a 'maverick' had he played English soccer.

I only saw one 'door' that day, though; the one that I was shown by Peter Osgood. It was a funny tale. I had been chosen to do the start (actually just a voice-over introduction) to the Chelsea cover version of *'Chirpy Chirpy Cheep Cheep'* (part of the psychedelic hierarchy, you must have heard it!). Problem was, the night before the session I had been having my own session. This would not have been archived by John Peel, as I was celebrating the birth of my son Allen; wetting the baby's head. If you cannot celebrate the birth of your first child, what can you do? Os, the Phil Spector of Stamford Bridge, did not think I was up to the task and I was sent off. On our way to the studio we saw the Bee Gees leaving. They are like the 'Chaps' in that they have been around a long time, been to the bottom of the sea and back, and are still functioning. Probably came out of it with a little bit more cash, though. They were polite and friendly. I hate people who pull attitudes. They originally hailed from Manchester but I do not know if they were football fans or not. Barry Gibb had an expensive Italian suit on and his hair was combed back slickly. They still play *Blue is the Colour* at the Bridge today. Everything that team did had class, and cast a shadow that even now is the standard that all others must be judged by.

The week before the Orient game, we beat Leicester 2–1 at home. Osgood celebrated his 25th birthday with both our goals. Weller, now playing for Leicester, gave us a torrid afternoon as he attacked the Chelsea defence throughout the game. It did not seem to register at the time but teams were going at us much more. At the end of February we travelled across London to Brisbane Road. It was a cold day, but bright. I can still remember it well, it made such an impression on me. We wore yellow shirts in front of a crowd of 30,000, and were later watched by millions on TV. Webb, playing against his old club, headed us in front. Houseman had his first corner cleared and whacked his cross back in. Webb, as he had done so often before, put it in. Shortly afterwards, another corner from Cooke was headed home deftly by Osgood. Minutes before half-time, the Orient full-back Phil Hoadley scored their 'goal of the century'. Twenty-five yards out, he smashed in a vicious shot that Bonetti could only help into the net. Just as the Spurs goal before the break in the semi-final had rejuvenated them, this truly amazing strike set up Orient.

The theory about Chelsea losing games they should have won at a canter, and snatching games when all looked lost, was displayed once again. Experts used to say that the more Chelsea had of the ball, the less they made of it. Possibly an element of predictability had crept into the side. The loss of Hutch was incalculable, particularly in a game like this, away to a lower league side in the Cup. Raggle-taggle, scuffling sides who chased everything were always hard to overcome. Up front we were unsettled. Smethurst had gone from the club, Tommy Baldwin was in and out of the side, and Chris Garland was still adjusting his game.

Five minutes into the second half, our defence got in a terrible tangle. Micky Bullock ran the ball into the net after a bad mix-up between Webb and Bonetti. It was a joke goal; one of those that look as if they are taking place in slow motion. I still thought we would win it because we were so much in command. If we had scored another then, I think Orient would have folded and we would have gone on to win easily. Ian Bowyer took a hand in proceedings though. He had been instrumental in taking the Cup from Stamford Bridge when Man City won there. He had left City abruptly, under a bit of a cloud. He was in a different class to the other Orient players. Later, Brian Clough rescued his career and he won a stack of honours with Forest. He could swivel explosively on his heels and flick the ball with the outside of his foot, which is easier said than done.

In the closing minutes he set Barrie Fairbrother up for the third

goal, after another catastrophe at the back. We stormed back down
the field, straight from the restart, and had enough chances even
then. I put in a shot, but Ray Goddard fell on it just as he had in the
'Cage' all those years before. *Two Little Boys* – that song came into
my mind for some extraordinary reason.

'You don't know what you did, Ray,' I mumbled. He looked at
me. It was something I will never forget. It all flashed across my
mind, like some *Star Trek* vision. I could see the team breaking up
now. With this defeat, Sexton would be able to bring in the reforms
that I knew he had in mind.

Right on the whistle, Webb, on some last-ditch raid, found
himself smack in front of goal with only Goddard to beat. To his
dismay, he blazed it into the crowd behind the goal. It was another
appalling miss, on a par with Osgood's at Sheffield or Hollins's
missed penalty in Europe. The game ended in pandemonium as the
Chelsea fans tried to get on to the pitch to stop the game. They
kicked a wall down in the corner of the ground, but luckily nobody
was hurt. It was no *'Wonderwall'* for Chelsea. The Orient
goalmouth was packed like a tube train as we threw everything
forward. I looked across at Sexton chewing his lip.

A piece of us all died that day when the whistle blew. The team
and the club were never a force again. It was one of the biggest
shocks for years. Not that we played that badly; we made so many
chances. Had we played another ten minutes we would simply have
overwhelmed them. It was as if some power, some spirit was against
us. In the years that followed, Chelsea went from being a
superpower to a dreadful Second Division side more famous for its
hooligan element than its team. The whole place became a rancid
meat pie, crawling with maggots. The collapse of the club, its
downfall, was, I guess, triggered by the events of that awful week.
Perhaps we had been living dangerously, but to us it was the only
way. The talismanic quality of people like Hutch had gone.
Nietzsche (I do not know who he played for) said that if you only
live one life, it might as well be extraordinary. It was the most
extraordinary period of my life.

No less extraordinary were the rumours that circulated in Fleet
Street that week. Ron Harris was to lose the captaincy. He had been
at fault for the Orient Express's third goal, but to some extent we

were all to blame for the defensive errors and missed chances. The old drinking stories and rumours reared their heads; we were a cocky team, but never vain. Vanity was going too far when players started talking to themselves in front of the mirror. Not Guilty. Guilty of having a good time, yes. Guilty of being in the company of showbiz stars and attractive women, yes. I suppose anyone at our age, given those circumstances, would have done the same thing. I would have been silly not to. Guilty of having a few drinks, yes, but I was never a great one for parties. (And if you believe that...!)

We were accused of being poseurs, but to me that adhered to being something stagnant and empty. We were never fakes, never. People could never figure out whether I was very complex or totally uncomplicated. I have no idea. Perhaps the whole thing can be best summed up by the Latin proverb: *Ars est celare artem* (Art lies in concealing the art). The image of us all as hell-bent hedonists, forever living on the edge, constantly chased by demons intent on destroying us, suited the media. Perhaps our talent was narcissistic.

Chelsea had won two Cups because we were so buoyant, so cocksure, so secure behind our brash displays. After that week I needed someone to tell me that I was a star, not a dilettante. One morning I found myself on Battersea Bridge, early. As I sipped my tea at a little stall there, I cast my mind back to my early days at the club. I wondered where it would all end.

On the first Saturday in March we went back to Wembley to play Stoke. Let us not forget, it was not Orient we were facing but a fine football team which had been geed up and prepared to give us one hell of a game. They played for the people of Stoke-on-Trent, whom I later got so close to. This was Stoke's first taste of the big stage as a team, but Banks, Eastham and the brilliant Greenhoff had the experience, and they were no pushovers. Greenhoff and I later struck up as poetic a playing relationship at Stoke as I enjoyed at Chelsea with Osgood.

The worst possible thing happened to Chelsea when Stoke scored an early goal. Conroy, the fiery Irish striker, headed home after a long throw from Peter Dobing. It was another mix-up in our defence, and gave Stoke the confidence they needed.

Chris Garland was probably our best player that day. He made some powerful runs and was unlucky not to score. Pejic brought him down as he broke through. He was booked, as was Bloor for the same crime. We ran the midfield and started to take a firm grip on the game. Near half-time we equalised. Cooke passed to Os inside the box. The big fellow stumbled. Earlier in the book, we discussed how the truly great strikers could score from any angle instantly. They did not need to waste valuable time teeing up a chance. This was text-book stuff from Os: although down on one knee and ringed by defenders, he still smashed in a shot to put us level. That should have been enough to propel us onwards to win the game. It would have given us a hat-trick of major honours, but ...

Paddy Mulligan went off at half-time. His studs caught in the turf and he jarred his ankle. (Ooooohhh, I had my flashback to West Brom!) Tommy Baldwin came on and Peter Houseman went to the left-back slot. We continued to press very hard, but the injury to Paddy had upset the shape of our team. We continued to make and miss chances. I set Tommy up but he missed. Later, as he burst into the box, a strong tackle decked him. The pattern was the same really as in the Leeds game, and just as we had dominated at Orient, we again got nothing out of it.

We had outplayed Stoke, or so I thought, but they got the decisive goal. Conroy was involved in a snarling match with Os all afternoon. It was the Irishman who crossed for the lanky Ritchie to nod down. Greenhoff smashed in a shot that Peter Bonetti parried and would usually have caught blindfolded. The ball ran loose, as it had at Brisbane Road. George Eastham, a veteran amongst veterans, scored from about a yard; a fitting end to an immaculate career. The trouble was, it was at Chelsea's expense. I do not think City got out of their box in the last quarter. Banks in goal, reliving his World Cup triumphs, made a great catch from Baldwin as Cooke set up yet another chance. Pejic crash-tackled Garland again as he surged through. Near the end, Banks threw himself full-length to deny Chris. It was as good a save as he made in his career. It was a career cruelly ended shortly afterwards by a car smash. I wish Shilton had been in goal for Stoke instead that day.

The whistle went with another huge assault on the Stoke goal being mounted. We had done enough in that game to win three Cup finals, but we lost to the Eastham goal. In four major finals at

Wembley, Chelsea had failed to win and also never scored first in any of those games. It was Stoke's first honour in 109 years. Unless Banks, Matthews, Eastham, Greenhoff and myself can find some time machine, it may be another 109 years before they win another.

The next day, it poured with rain. 'Just as well we lost,' I thought. 'Think how wet it would be on the open-top bus.' We played out the season in moderate fashion. A sequence of five successive wins was our best spell for three seasons. It all finished a bit tamely though, without any Cup action. I was booked at Wolves and scored in the League against Stoke. Little did I know how much Stoke City were going to feature in my life in the coming years.

10

A Deep Shade of Blue

'Caesar, beware of Brutus, take heed of Cassius, come not near Casca, have an eye on Cinna, trust not Trebonius, mark well Metellus Cimber, thou has wronged Caius Ligarius. There is but one mind in all these men and it is bent against Caesar.' Julius Caesar, Scene III

Early summer 1972. I was at home trying to relax. Coming up was my last full season at Stamford Bridge. The radio was playing; The Kinks with Ray Davies, who shares my birthday. He was thanking someone for the days. Those endless days.

The phone rang, and it was a very displeased Alf Ramsey. At the last minute, I had dropped out of three games on an England Under-23 tour. He demanded to know why. I was in my usual position, skating on thin ice, and it was summer! I was burnt out by the previous season's traumas and my ankle was still paining me. I was having longer lunches where I drank. Something about Ramsey's tone needled me. There was something about his whole personality that needled me. The sound of the whip cracking always annoyed me. When he heard my version, he stated: 'You

130

turn up, or it will be your last time.' Thanks a lot, Alf! I told him to please himself, thinking I would call his bluff. I guess calling his bluff worked – along with Colin Todd of Derby, I was banned from representing England at any level for three years. 'Look about you.'

The reason for my refusal was rooted in the disappointment I suffered in the Home International Championship in May. I had given up a Chelsea trip to Barbados where a few games had been scheduled against the national side followed by the usual boat trip. Instead I kept myself fit in solitary training, after being asked to join the full England squad for the last two games of the Championship. I wanted to go to Barbados. My reasoning was that I would not be chosen for the actual games and would only be watching. I thought that I would be stuck with people that I would not share an everyday drink with, let alone the tremendous camaraderie of the Chelsea lads. I did not expect to dislodge a player like Alan Ball from the international scene. Dave Sexton urged me to join the squad. He told me on good authority that I would win my first England cap. It was common knowledge that club managers would be advised on their players' international standing. It was on this understanding that I went off to join the England squad at Hendon Hall.

I was elated to think that I would be playing for England. Chelsea have had very few England regulars over the years, despite the vast amount of talent that has passed through the club. Wilkins remains their most capped England player, and he left the Bridge after a relatively small portion of his star-studded and varied career. His CV reads like a 'Who's Who' of the cream of Europe's finest sides.

I cannot recall the last time Chelsea bought a current England international. Great midfield players like Mike Fillery and Micky Hazard should have won a sideboard full of caps. Graeme Le Saux was another player who was only considered as an England prospect after he left the Bridge. Another left-back, Tony Dorigo, had to quit Chelsea to enhance his England prospects.

I was still haunted by the Cup chances we had squandered. Exits to sides we should have butchered still rankled, but the prospect of winning my first cap cheered me no end. At my first training session, Bobby Moore came over to congratulate me and said, 'You are in. Well done, son.' This was a sweet sound to my ears. The fact that the words came out of the mouth of Robert Chelsea Moore made it even sweeter, he was the super-hero of all time; a real piece of work. A Chelsea fan sent me some old Esso soccer booklets from that era. All you had to do was buy a gallon of petrol and you were given a little booklet with colour photos and a little bit of text. Amongst them was a great photo of Moore taken in the 1970 World Cup. It must have been over 100 degrees but Bobby was as cool as ice water, as if he had just stepped out of the shower. That is how I always recall him. Cool as a glass of lager on a summer's evening. He seemed to have this aura around him, a forcefield, like a super-hero in a comic book.

Moore took me under his wing straight away. In the sixties, referring to Eric 'Slowhand' Clapton, people use to daub on King's Road walls that Clapton was God. When I got to know Bobby, I began to understand how people could compare some individuals to God. The first time I ever shared a drink with him was in the Long Bar at Wembley. Here I was, just out of my teens, sharing a drink with the only man to lift the World Cup for England. I was never one to be star-struck; I had met them all from Elton to Pele. Moore was a little bit special, though. He was as happy drinking with the pensioners as he was with royalty. He would go out of his way to help the youngsters.

He exuded such charm he could make anybody do anything just by his personality. Always beautifully dressed, he wore a lot of grey with powder-blue tab collar shirts. For a parallel we must go to Hollywood: he always reminded me of Steve McQueen, the movie superstar, who was also to die of cancer at a young age. Moore must have seen the team sheet with me on it. On the lunchtime of Thursday, 24 May 1972, Ramsey called the squad together at Hendon Hall and read out the team. I had been passed over in favour of Tony Currie in Ramsey's experimental side beaten by the Irish at Wembley. When Ramsey read out the team for the match in Glasgow, again I was not in it. Alf must have changed his mind. I could not believe it. The same old tactic of build them up and knock them down. Well now I was certainly down. Bobby Moore came over and said, 'Al, I can't work it out. He told me you were in the team.'

There was something about me and Osgood that confounded

Ramsey. He was never comfortable with us. So what you do not understand, you try to destroy. To play Astle instead of Osgood in Mexico was an amazing decision by the England manager. As I left the room, Ramsey saw my barely concealed disappointment. I had built up my hopes so much I was crushed. 'Don't be upset. You have the Under-23 tour shortly.' At 1.30 pm I left Hendon Hall in a mini-cab alone for the prefab. My personal life was awkward, my wife was eight months pregnant and I really didn't need this.

Colin Todd, who was also banned for refusing the Under-23 tour, was a marvellous defender who had just helped Derby win the League. Later he worked with Bruce Rioch and I wondered why he did not go to Arsenal with him. But then knowing Colin and knowing Rioch ... My favourite story about Todd was when he was playing for Derby against Leeds. He was Man of the Match in a 2–0 win. Norman Hunter shook hands with him as they left the field and asked him what he would do if he did not play football.

'I suppose I would do what you do, Norman,' Todd replied.

I tried to put the Ramsey problem out of my mind. It was very sad; I felt that I had been hard done by, a caution would have been enough. I had set my heart on playing in Munich in the 1974 World Cup. I saw that as the climax to my career and ambitions, but the real damage was yet to come.

The only thing I did learn from the England experience was that some of the Chelsea boys had rivals in the social scene. The evening after England had lost to Ireland, we went back to the hotel under curfew. I retired to my room but was shortly disturbed by a call from Bobby Moore telling me to meet him downstairs. Soon we were speeding down the North Circular in Moore's red jag. On this particular outing were Ball, Summerbee and Rodney Marsh. We ended up at Moore's chum Jimmy Quill's place, with the England captain casually leading us in with his strides over his shoulder and a lager in each hand.

I started the 1972–73 season in cracking form. We whipped Leeds 4–0 at the Bridge, or rather what was left of it. The construction site was where the old East Stand used to be. The famous box in the roof where Docherty would roar on his 'Diamonds', and the bar at the back of the stand where he also punched a Liverpool fan down the stairs, had gone. Memories light the corner of my mind. I felt that the destruction of the stand was symbolic of the destruction of the Cup-winning side. The split was coming and the dismantling of the team was to start.

I felt the win over Leeds was too easy. I would rather have beaten a full-strength side. In the first twenty minutes Leeds lost their goalkeeper Harvey with concussion and Jones with a twisted ankle. Mind you, Leeds had crocked Bonetti at Old Trafford yet could not beat us. I made three goals on that scalding hot afternoon. I set the first up with a long ball to Chris Garland. He controlled it superbly and drove in a shot that Lorimer (deputising in goal) could only push into Osgood's path. Thank you very much! On the hour, I put Charlie Cooke in to score the second. Garland wrapped it up with two late goals, one of them from my pass. Don Howe said around then that I put 'a lot of disguise' on my passing. I was in great form. The incentive of playing for England had gone, but I still had my love affair with Chelsea. We drew away at Leicester and then beat the champions Derby 2–1 on their own ground. Ron Harris scored the first, a real screamer (honest) and a dazzling passing movement set Garland up for the winner. Clough went potty. He hated losing to Chelsea; but who didn't?

Liverpool won at the Bridge in the next game. We conceded two early goals, which gave us an impossible task. Garland headed a brave goal, and Keegan hit the bar. In our next game we beat Man City 2–1 at the Bridge. I had a hand in both goals. The winner was crashed in by substitute Houseman. We were changing in a Portakabin and conditions were not conducive to playing to your peak. In some games we would have our half-time talk on the touchline. Talk about '*Little House on the Prairie*'!

On 30 August we went to Old Trafford where I was injured by Mr Best in a 0–0 draw. I had just knocked the ball away when he came flying in and did a bungee jump on my instep. I do not know what state of mind George was in that night. My policy of depriving him of the ball must have wound him up. Later in the season, with the pressure on him intolerable, he quit Manchester United. Later that same evening, heavily strapped up, I was out clubbing in Manchester with Os and Webb when I bumped into George, also out on the razzle. I challenged him about my injury. He apologised and said he had mistaken me for Ron Harris. Just my luck, one of the greatest players in the world and he crocks me thinking that I was Ronnie Harris! George had not even had a drink at the time.

Ron had more people looking for him than Lord Lucan, but no-one ever nailed him. That was the second time in my career that I was confused with him. On my League debut in the Southampton débâcle, Jimmy Gabriel 'did' me. Years later when he managed me, I found out that he too had confused me with Harris (oh yeah!). Gabriel was no angel, that was for sure. Batty, Vinnie, Bruce etc were ice creams compared to him. He played with a couple of other characters called Jim Steele and Hughie Fisher who were very hard men. Peter Storey snapped Fisher's leg at The Dell and a riot started down there. If the boys want to fight ...

Gabriel did me early in the game. With it being my first League match, I did not know what to expect, probably the worst. In my life that proved to be a pretty accurate yardstick; about par for the course. Os watched the incident from the grandstand and was not impressed. I suppose that is why we were so inseparable – he would watch out for me when I first started out. Harping back to his broken leg, I suppose having such a bad injury so early on in his career made him protective. In the same way, Hutch watched for Os. Hutch would look after anyone in a blue shirt. I can see him now in his early days at the Bridge, coming to the place on his motorbike. In those days he would not go near drink. He was the epitome of clean living.

One of his best early games was when he scored twice at Hillsborough in my first full season. That was the first time that I ever remember getting a right-hander on the field. We were playing very well and cruising to a 3–1 victory. It was pouring with rain and defenders were diving in everywhere. My ankle problems were always less frequent on a soft pitch. I could toe it past defenders and my endless supply of stamina gave me the gas tank on which to fuel my running. Late in the game I went in on Tony Coleman, the ex-Man City winger. Big Mal always claimed that he ultimately failed with Coleman, and in the end he was kicked out of Maine Road and joined Sheffield. The year City won the League, Coleman had played a big part. His running power was awesome, he seemed to be made entirely of blue touchpaper. Once lit, stand well back! Of the modern players, you could compare him to Dennis Wise. He was faster than Dennis, though. Coleman slugged me to the ground. The blow would have stung Tyson, but he was my sort of player. I just smiled at him and shook my head. 'You did not have to do that,' I said.

This was a tough game. In it I saw Ron Harris dish out the hardest tackle I ever saw him make, and believe me he made a few. Wednesday had a full-back called Wilf Smith who fancied himself as a bit of a hard case. He was never in the 'League of Gentlemen' of Storey, Hunter and Tommy Smith. Ron, more than these well-remembered names, had the greatest capacity for personalised aggression. He could always summon up the demons when they were needed. When Chelsea were trailing at Old Trafford to Leeds, his response was to dig deeper. That rainy afternoon at Sheffield, Smith tried to clash with Harris over a fifty-fifty ball. There could be only one winner. The ball came out of something resembling the Eton Wall game and Peter Houseman crossed to the far post, where Hutch headed home. We celebrated and turned back to the halfway line. That was when I noticed that Smith was still spark-out on the turf. Just for a moment I thought he was dead, so still did he lie. Ron just shrugged when I looked at him. That was the end of the match for Smith.

I played with the ex-Sunderland star Shaun Elliott in Seattle. He told me once about how Graeme Souness, playing for Liverpool, put him out for a long spell with an 'over the top' tackle. Bob Paisley was quoted as saying, 'Elliott had done three or four people before he got hurt himself. If you live by the sword you have to die by it.'

The Harris–Hudson confusion still bugs me. Gabriel said that he was on medication for insomnia and was so strung-out during the game that when he challenged me, he thought I was the Chelsea skipper. But Ron had short hair ...

Caviar and jellied eels, the blend of Chelsea. The malignant forces were gathering, though. I was out for thirteen weeks. Dave Sexton changed a lot that season; as he was talking to me I watched his eyes look over my shoulder and also down to the ground. Things drifted. He started to tinker with the team as anxiety consumed him. It was a case of finances starting to hit home. Paddy Mulligan was sold and Gary Locke took over at right-back. He made the position his own and kept it for years. With legs like a kick-boxer, he was the prototype modern full-back. Good enough to play for England, he was very underrated. Had the club kept things together and developed a few more prospects as good as Locke, the future would have been assured. If Osgood and Hudson had stayed with players like Wilkins, Walker, Wicks etc, the ground improvements would have been funded by the rewards of continued success.

Whilst I was injured, I saw Os score one of his greatest ever goals, against Derby in the League Cup. Osgood's striking that season was akin to wine-tasting; each goal a new taste, each one elixir for the connoisseur. Houseman crossed from the left by-line and Os volleyed past Boulton in the Derby goal. Such was the power of the drive that the ball ricocheted from the back of the net almost to the halfway line. It is called timing. Sir Alf was at the match, and Os ran to where he was sitting and made a special point of celebrating one of his greatest goals in front of him. I know that he put a bit on for my sake. What an old ham! What a goalscorer! They compile videos of Le Tissier's goals, but Os would top the lot. I do not think I had seen a ball hit so hard in such a confined space. Once, he thundered shots past Banks and Shilton in consecutive weeks. 'What do I do next?' he asked. That goal against Derby put Chelsea 3–1 up in a tremendous match. Kember shot Chelsea ahead, but Alan Hinton, later to manage me in the States, equalised. Webb put Chelsea ahead before Os's fine goal. McGovern pulled one back to set up a great finale.

I came back against Southampton away, on the right wing. We lost 3–1 in a game we dominated. I kept wandering back into midfield; this would leave the back free and Sexton was angry. It was the start of a very bleak time for me. My drinking increased. Football was my life, but in this intolerable situation I wanted to get away from it. I had no incentive to play for Chelsea or England, and attracted tabloid attention when I was banned from driving for a year.

Bill Garner joined the club in the autumn from Southend. Bill was a real character, popular with the fans and his team-mates. He had played against Chelsea in a League Cup game for the seaside club and impressed Sexton. Hutch had been out of the side for nearly two years with his horrendous injuries. He came back into the side around Christmas and scored two goals against Norwich in a story-book comeback. It was a very emotional moment for us all. Os and I set him up for his second, and he received a standing ovation from the crowd. It was one of the last times that we were all to be together in such a happy situation.

Four days later, Norwich returned to the Bridge in the first leg of the League Cup semi-final. They scored twice in the opening minutes and surprised us with their non-stop running and teamwork. Their best player was the Scotland striker Jim Bone. He had a terrific turn of pace and unsettled Webb, scoring in both the League and Cup games. We still thought we could pull it back at Carrow Road. I scored twice in the match for the only time in my career. Norwich scored three, though, and with only a few minutes left we were 5–2 down on aggregate and heading out of the competition. Then fate moved its giant hand, and fog started swirling around the ground like something out of a Stephen King horror tale. Referee Hill took the teams off for twenty-five minutes and resumed for a short while before eventually abandoning the match with only six minutes of normal time left to play. I would like to tell you a happy ending to this episode, but in the replay Chelsea went down by one goal, 3–0 overall. Cup defeats hurt the most. We knew in our hearts that we used to eat sides like Norwich for breakfast. But I had lost my appetite for the game. When I won the ball and created goals, I had tremendous confidence which carried over into my personal life. Now I became very withdrawn. I used to love to talk to the fans in the street, but I found myself avoiding them. I even found it hard to communicate with my father on the phone.

All that was left open to us was the FA Cup. In the third round we were drawn away to Brighton. Ron was sent off early in the game for jobbing someone. We held out under some pressure and broke out twice for Os to score. In the next round we were at home to Ipswich. Webb did not play in goal, though it was mooted by me. Hutch was out again; although his twice-broken left leg had mended, his right knee needed yet another operation. I was at a low ebb. Hutch's replacement, Garner, scored both goals, but I played wide and never saw the ball all game. It was very unsatisfactory, especially as Sir Alf was watching. I realised then that unless I went back into midfield, I was finished. I felt so angry. I just wanted to get away from the ground as soon as possible and gather my thoughts. That must have been the first time that I thought seriously about quitting Chelsea. Brian Mears came into the dressing-room, smiling like a Cheshire cat: 'Great game, Alan.' I replied that he must have been watching a different match.

The draw for the next round took us to Hillsborough. Messrs Smith and Coleman were not playing. John Sissons, the ex-West Ham 'wonderkid', was. A brilliant but erratic player, he was a contemporary of Bobby Moore. Sexton bought him for Chelsea after I left, but he was past his best by then. That day he played particularly well and set up Wednesday's goal after twenty-five minutes. His pin-point cross was deflected to Coyle, who blazed it first time over Phillips into the roof of the net. Bill Garner equalized just on half-time, when Os hooked the ball across the face of the goal and Peter Houseman returned it immediately for Bill to smack it in. Osgood grabbed the winner in the second half with a spectacular header from Hollins's dipping free-kick. He threw himself full-tilt at the ball to give the Wednesday keeper no hope. Chelsea wore a strange away strip of red, white and green that day. Compared to the migraine-inducing strips of the nineties, though, it would look very staid. Wednesday pushed up near the end, and only some smart saves from Phillips avoided a replay. Near the end, Garner and the Wednesday skipper had a row and both walked.

I saw that my only way out was to ask for a transfer. This was festering in my mind. In the sixth round we drew Arsenal at home. To draw on Eric Hall's tired vocabulary, we had two 'monster' battles against them but floundered on the iceberg of their sheer professionalism. The first game was a cracker. Even Frank Carson would have said so. Os scored another wonder goal. His form was superb; he carried us to some extent that season. Gary Locke crossed, Kember knocked it down and Peter bulleted a shot past Bob Wilson. The Derby goal was, I think, struck more savagely, but this was from further out, much further out. A lifetime later, Wilson was presenting TV's *Football Focus* and Peter was guesting. They re-ran the goal and Os cracked, 'You are still no nearer to it, Bob.' It won the BBC 'Goal of the Season' competition and he also

won the ITV *Big Match* equivalent for a goal against Derby
(another one) in the League. This effort came on New Year's Eve,
when he sent two defenders the wrong way and scored from 25
yards with his left foot. Little Ian Britton, making his debut as
substitute, supplied the pass. If satellite TV had been in existence,
he would have swept the board there also. Mind you, I could give
you a five-minute dissertation on some Hudson goals that should
have been contenders. My free-kick at Tottenham, or even the
phantom Ipswich goal.

Arsenal were amazingly resilient, though. They got up off the
canvas to hammer in two goals in ninety seconds. First Ball's ginger
head flicked in Armstrong's corner, and then Charlie George put
them ahead. Phillips lost the ball on the edge of his six-yard box,
Kennedy turned the ball back in and Charlie crashed it home. Our
defence was weakened by the absence of Ron Harris through
suspension. Dempsey and McCreadie were carrying knocks and
Houseman was unfit. We battled back to equalize, Os heading on
Locke's cross for Hollins to score. That is how it finished, and on
the Tuesday we went to Highbury for the replay.

This proved to be my last Cup game for Chelsea.

11

Someone Left a Cake Out in the Rain

'I had four managers in five years at Chelsea and none seemed to want me. I had no confidence, lost faith in my ability and could see no way out.' Graeme Le Saux, 1995

'Football is our history. It's the people's game. It should give us our hopes and our idols. I have always loved it. It has just been interrupted by school and things like that.' Terry Venables, 1995

Richard Harris, the actor, used to arm-wrestle Tommy Baldwin in nightclubs after a night of solid drinking. Harris, along with Richard Burton and Peter O'Toole, was one of the original hell-raisers. Tremendous guy! He could drink like Cooke and fight like Baldwin. Like the 'Chaps', he had a consummate talent that he never abused. He had a huge hit record on both sides of the Atlantic with a Jimmy Webb song, *'McArthur Park'*. The title of this chapter is a line from that song. Le Saux must have felt like me, a cake out in the rain.

At Highbury, the other R Harris, Chelsea's very own Man called Horse, was still suspended. Sexton gambled, pushing doughboy Hollins to right-back; Kember wore the number four shirt, and Bill Garner came in up front. The game started off like a rocket and got faster. In the opening seconds, Charlie George went through the middle like one of Jack Berry's two-year-old sprinters and put the ball away, but Norman Burtenshaw, one of the most controversial refs of all time, had blown as young Charlie started his run. George made the ball talk that night, for like Os and Cooke he was a big-match player. Garland was booked for lunging in on Charlie. Bedlam! The noise was overwhelming. I looked up at the sky, it was a weird watermelon colour.

After twenty minutes, we went in front. Bill Garner's selection paid off. In typical Hutch style, he got his head to Hollins's cross and Houseman headed in what was to be his last Cup goal for Chelsea. For the first half-hour we played easily our best football of that mediocre season. Arsenal were rattled. I started to boss the midfield. Highbury was another good ground for me, I always felt comfortable there. I started playing the angles, prompting and probing. I was doing glide dummies, approaching a pass across its line of play. The nearest foot glides over the ball and the further foot plays the ball with the inside surface in the direction of the glide. The Arsenal players started to look at one another. The Chelsea players started to feed me in a way they had not done for a long time. Just on half-time, the Gunners had an amazing piece of good fortune. Orient had scored at the same juncture. The night became dark with something more than night.

Kember brought down George Armstrong outside the box. It was an obvious free-kick and Burtenshaw awarded it. Arsenal protested en masse. The ethics of this have already been touched on. Coerced by the players and the crowd, he consulted a linesman before changing his decision to a penalty. This was a puerile act by the North Londoners. Had they been cheated of a penalty, you could have understood the vehemence of their protests, but to 'create' a penalty was sickening. It was an indictment of the way the game was moving. In those days the media interest was intense, but the increased TV coverage today has concentrated the pressure and hype even more, money being the root of it all. In a popular song of the day, Steve Harley sang, 'You spoilt the game, no matter what they say.' Ball stepped up to take the penalty. All of London wanted to see the game, and it seemed that most of them had crammed into Highbury; 62,746 inside, with the gates closed twenty minutes before kick-off and an estimated 10,000 locked out! The city must have shut down early that evening.

Ball combined the temperament of a vampire with the nerves of Senna. He had seen it all, done it all, been there and back on the bus. A World Cup winner barely out of his teens, what could faze him? He smashed the kick high, past Phillips. You could have bet your house on him scoring from a situation like that. I once saw him take a penalty for Arsenal at Anfield in a vital League game. Those sporting lads in the Kop booed him continuously, gobbed at him and pelted him with orange peel and rubbish, but his kick almost tore the net down and he celebrated by collecting the ball from the back of the net.

Stan Bowles was another one. At Newcastle he faced a torrent of abuse and went up to the crowd and pointed to the exact spot where he placed the kick. He stared back at them without expression or comment. Chelsea's recent shoot-out win, also at Newcastle, showed similar style.

I felt the scurry of rats' feet up my spine. Just as Ray Goddard had put a nail in our coffin, now Ball hammered down the lid. We lost it then, really. I could see it all slipping away. It was like finding a £50 note in the street, then going into Corals and putting it on a losing bet. That was your luck for the day. Thirteen minutes into the second half, Kennedy rose to meet Bob McNab's floated centre and smashed in the winner. Poor old Ray! I do not recall a game against Chelsea when he did not score against us. Later, he joined Liverpool to play in midfield and won another stack of honours.

Chelsea were the Worcester in the sauce of the seventies, but maybe the vodka was mixing too much. The football intelligentsia were writing us off as a power in the game. Someone in the press said we were uninspired. The season petered out. After the Cup defeat we had a run of five straight beatings in which we scored only one goal. The last game of the season was against Man United and turned out to be Bobby Charlton's last League game. He had an inauspicious, colourless farewell: Os scored the only goal of the game. He deservedly won the Player of the Year award for Chelsea.

Money reared its ugly head, as it has a way of doing. I went to see Sexton about a new contract. I still had it in my mind to quit Chelsea, even football as Best had done, for a little while. I asked the Chelsea manager for a substantial pay rise. My timing on this occasion was bad. Rumours were already circulating about the drain on the club's resources the new stand was proving. The economy was in crisis and a strike was looming in the building trade which was to devastate construction plans. I was told to put six England caps on the table before I asked for more.

Was Bobby Moore right, I asked myself, about putting country before club? Ask not what you can do for your club, but what you can do for your country. I think most fans would prefer players to perform better for their club than country. Tony Waddington confirmed to me later in my career that it was better to play consistently for your club week in, week out. After all, it is your club that pays the mortgage with bread-and-butter football.

Sexton's words grated on me. I had obviously given too much to him and not enough to Sir Alf. Can you imagine what it must have been like for a young player like me, who, having brought great Cup success to the club, is now informed he has to bring half-a-dozen England caps to the bargaining table? Sexton had lost it as far as I could see. I came away even more confused. I had a sense of incompleteness. It was the old club v country scenario. When he was manager of Chelsea, Tommy Docherty said that he hated it when his players received international recognition. They started to reserve their best form for that stage and their League form would suffer as a result. Players at the England matches would mix and compare notes about wages, bonus payments and perks. This would inevitably lead to transfer requests when disparities came to light.

The situation at Chelsea was corroding quicker than the East Stand did! It was designed so that the rust made it stronger. The Shed used to say that some of the players went rusty before the structure. I was told that I was paid less than Osgood because he had signed a new two-year contract. Thinking about it now, that is when I should have pushed hard for a transfer. I should have sat down with Os and discussed the wage structure (two heads and all that stuff), but a lot of our friendship was unspoken and certain subjects were never broached.

I met him outside Sexton's office. It was contract time, and players were going to and fro. Dave looked grim, as when Eastham scored at Wembley. I joked to Os that at least he would not be adding to the management's woes in that he still had another year to run on his contract.

'What do you mean?' Os replied. 'Mine is the same as yours, just a year.'

A year! Sometimes you can be a right innocent, Hudson, I mumbled to myself.

Laughs were harder to find as the atmosphere became more intense, but the spirit between the lads was still good. Webb, in particular, came in for a lot of stick. He was going through some sort of identity crisis. Today it would be called a mid-life crisis, but Dave was still in his twenties. He could never work out if he wanted to be a Mafia-type gang leader or a Hanson/Branson tycoon. He was seen at the Kray funeral a few weeks before the Silver Jubilee of the FA Cup win, the John Gotti of Griffin Park. When he arrived for training, in the old days, he looked like a city slicker with his briefcase and *Financial Times*. John Dempsey used to quiz Webb about how many property transactions he had closed on the way to work. Demps also asked him about the contents of his briefcase. It had been suggested that the case had slowed him up at Wembley when Eddie Gray had melted him. To complete his corporate image, he owned a white Rolls-Royce for a while. I do not know what happened to it, perhaps Moon drove it into a swimming pool.

When I first broke into the team, my King's Road image and reputation as a young man about town spread around the club. One morning after training, Webb challenged me as to where I was going. Perhaps he had no pressing board-meetings that day. I told him that I was starting off at the Markham for a few swift ones, followed by a spot of lunch at Alexandres. Webb was up for that and threw me his keys for the white Roller.

'OK son, take me there,' he commanded.

So off we went. I drove slowly and carefully along the King's Road, with Webby sitting in the back with his *FT* and briefcase. I parked near the Markham, where Marks & Spencer have their store now. As I tossed the keys back, he asked the budding Damon Hill if he had ever driven a Roller before. I shook my head, impressed.

'As a matter of fact, Dave, I have not driven before.'

You should have seen his face! I only ever saw him more disgruntled when he scored an own goal at Highbury. His beautiful Roller, piloted around the King's Road by the upstart midfielder! Strange, do you know, he never asked me to chauffeur him again.

Cars figured in Tommy Baldwin's history. He featured in a high-speed car chase with the police in which a vodka bottle was thrown. George Best asked me to point out that it was empty at the time. Later, a fight broke out in the cells of the police station. It was even more heated than the debate at Arsenal over the Kember/Armstrong penalty.

Tom was a great pal of Charlie Cooke. Charlie was always aloof and very withdrawn. We never really got on, different characters altogether. To this day I am in awe of his massive talent. Re-reading this manuscript, I can see just how crucial he was to Chelsea. He gave me a hard time when I first broke into the side. Sometimes in the game, when he called for the ball, I would whack it back as hard as I could, the attitude being, 'You wanted it, here it is.' Such was his first touch and instant control that I never recall him losing it. It was instant, no matter at what angle or pace it arrived.

A further indictment of the modern game is the longevity of players like Ray Wilkins and Gordon Strachan, who played in the Premiership as the big 40 loomed. By progression, George Foreman was a world heavyweight boxing champion at forty-six. Why is it that players can carry on for so long? Less training was done in my era. The truth is that no ball-players have broken through to oust their older counterparts. When I discussed the current game with Cooke at the anniversary dinner I made the point that, on the basis of Wilkins's performance, even at the age of fifty Charlie could have made a contribution. He went away with a thoughtful look on his face.

The season died on its feet. Chelsea finished mid-table. Injuries restricted me to only twenty-six League appearances. I stopped caring around then. Ob-la-di, ob-la-da, life goes on!

12

The Long Goodbye

'Though it must be said that every species of bird has a manner peculiar to itself, yet there is somewhere in most genera at least that at first sight discriminates them, and enables a judicious observer to pronounce on them with some certainty.' Gilbert White, 1778

Season 1973–74 started badly for Chelsea. It was to get worse, much worse. To this day Chelsea have still not recovered from the sale of Osgood and Hudson. The knock-on effect was so damaging to the finances of the club that they have not won a major trophy since. The constant stream of brilliant youngsters that Chelsea produced over the years were snapped up by other grateful clubs. Recently the two 'Grahams', Le Saux and Stuart, have won Championship and Cup medals with their respective clubs, whilst Chelsea struggled. However, the era of Glenn Hoddle, followed swiftly by Ruud Gullit's succession, has demonstrated that Chelsea are at last striving to play the football the fans were used to. This is the way I wanted to play when I returned to Chelsea from America, but the incumbent management team had other ideas. The world-class signings of the last couple of years at last showed the supporters that the club meant business. Ken Bates's part in all this cannot be underestimated.

Soon I was to cross a line with Chelsea that I was never able to cross again. Years later, after my wanderlust was cured, I went back to the club I loved. Chelsea had a stronger leader in Bates, but it was too late for me to make my mark. I was never given a chance by the manager. Oscar Wilde said that each man kills the thing he loves. A bit of both Chelsea and me died that season. I found the whole atmosphere disagreeable. I became burned out on the whole situation and started behaving badly; longer lunches, even more to drink, if possible. The tension mounted. Even when I was injured I was hauled before Sexton for having a long lunch. I was with Garner and Kember, we were all carrying knocks and were not playing. I only had a couple of pints and shepherd's pie for lunch. I recall the pie more than the drinks, but Dave carped on and it really annoyed me, it was so petty. Things like that make you more defensive in your attitude, which does not help the matter. I was repelled. Dave suggested we were letting our club-mates down by going down the pub. Well, I ask you!

Would it have been different if Bates had run the club rather than Mears? He stuck by Hollins too long, I always thought. Loyalty, perhaps. But I think he would have been quicker to see the damage to Chelsea long-term in the 1970s situation. Lampooned by the media, Bates has one of the sharpest minds in the business. Think of the mess Jimmy Hill has got Fulham into compared to Bates, an out-of-towner who took over CFC for a £1 note.

The 'team talks' in the Markham after the away games became more heated. Sexton was never there, and must have felt excluded. I guess he was very isolated. It was like a bad marriage, with two partners drifting further apart rather than talking to each other. The only two players at that strange, unreal time with a real line on Sexton were McCreadie and Webb. The rest of the team urged them to fix up a meeting where we could clear the air, thrash out our problems and differences; a forum where our views could be heard. The joke was that all the concerned parties had Chelsea at heart. Not only did we want to further our careers, we wanted to keep on being winners, especially for our marvellous fans. We hated seeing Chelsea being beaten by inferior teams.

The showdown never happened. Clandestine meetings between Sexton and Mears were being held. The financial pressures on the club must have been more severe than we imagined at the time. All the while, the East Stand was emerging like a phoenix from the rubble. In essence, it was a vulture picking the flesh off the club and leaving a carcass. I withdrew more into my own head, as withdrawn as I was from central midfield. The 'mod' look developed into the King's Road Dandy/Brummel heritage: velvet jackets, cashmere polo-neck jumpers and exquisite bouffant razor cuts; all very *fin-de-siècle*.

The summer tour took us to Iran. We played three games in Tehran. Os really had a go at me. He said that unless I started playing, Chelsea had no chance of taking the League. He said that I should forget everything and just concentrate on football.

I finally put my transfer request in writing. Sexton turned it down. I asked to see Mears, but was refused a meeting. I was told that Sexton ran the team and did not want me to go. The team was in decline. Cooke had joined Palace and Hutch was being worn down by further injuries. The team that had confronted the League with the greatest array of gifts it had ever seen, struggled to score goals in my last months. The fragile pyramid of our talent was collapsing like a magician's box, inwardly. I was left out of the first game of the season, away to Derby, where we lost to a McGovern goal. Manchester United made an offer of £200,000 for me. Sunderland came in with a bid after their deal for Alan West collapsed. They had just won the Cup and were anxious to consolidate. Other reports claimed that QPR were ready to offer Gerry Francis plus cash for me. I went along to see Venners, who was still pulling the strings there, because I would have loved to play alongside him and Stanley.

I was back in the side for the second match, another single-goal defeat by Burnley. Later, I scored the first goal at Birmingham in an exciting 4-2 win, but our form remained patchy. Before the game in Brum we went to see Ali v Frazier at the Odeon, Leicester Square. One of those nights you did not want to end, ever. We burned down the darkness. Stoke beat us 1–0 in the League Cup, the first time we had gone out at the first hurdle in that competition since 1967. If I knew then! On the evening of the Stoke match,

Sexton and Osgood had another huge bust-up. This time Sexton
blamed Os for the defeat and the row ended with Peter storming
out and swearing at Dave. I finally caught up with him at a Stoke
night-spot called 'The Place'. Os was consoling himself with
champagne, but was very annoyed. I sensed that the situation could
not continue much longer.

On a trip to Charterhouse School I was struck in the left eye by
the ball. I visited a specialist and was ordered to rest. I missed a 0–0
draw at Arsenal. Ray Wilkins, at 17, made his debut as sub one
Friday night against Norwich in the autumn of 1973. We had
rearranged the game to avoid a clash with QPR, who were playing
Arsenal. Rangers were already starting to steal some of our thunder
in West London. My old mate Stan Bowles had superseded Marsh
and was starting to weave his magical spells. Bowles was far more of
a team player than Marsh, and Rodney was never in the same class
anyway. For a short while, Roy Wegerle was touted as the new
'Stan'. Wegerle was described once, by Marsh of all people, as the
best player since George Best. Roy never really established himself
as a major player in our game. He had an all-too-brief stint at
Chelsea, who sold him for buttons. Less than a year after leaving
the Bridge, he was sold for a million pounds, a huge capital loss by
Chelsea. Wegerle had some nice tricks; the Johnny Rep back-spin
with the ball circling outside his foot was one, I saw him use it a lot.
We beat Norwich 3–0. I set up the first from a Tommy free-kick.
The same player hit the third after my shot had been beaten out by
Kevin Keelan. Even in that short spell on the field, Wilkins stood
out as a player of promise. I think it was a pity that I never got to
play with Ray. I am sure that our styles would have complemented
each other. I always was puzzled why managers always saw an
emerging talent as a *replacement* for an existing one. Docherty
admitted that the metamorphus of my talent was one of the reasons
for the removal of Venables (another talent I would love to have
blended with). He never saw it as Venables *and* Hudson, in the same
way that Sexton never attempted to harness Wilkins and Hudson.
Economics dictated, as always; trading up, as they say in the City.
What they would tell you in the City, though, is that the first rule
is: never sell your main assets.

Chelsea had some major midfield talent over the years that was

England-class. Mick Fillery was a London lad who could chip and curl the ball like a Brazilian. He was very inventive and strong. After I returned to Chelsea from my sojourn in the States, I found that Fillery was on the verge of quitting the club. I begged him to reconsider. I had a vision that an axis of Hudson and Fillery in midfield might have taken a few people by surprise. The management opted to build the midfield around an artisan like Spackman, an honest work-horse. One obsession led to another. Where had I seen that before?

Coming up to Christmas, Leeds visited the Bridge. They had learnt from Old Trafford and were accumulating honours. Their 2-1 win completed what was then this century's record start of twenty First Division matches undefeated (they went on to make it 29, which is still a record). Os scored a nice header and Tommy hit the post, but they won easily. The thought crossed my mind that the gulf between them and us had widened. They still had hunger, we just had anger. The problem was, the anger was being channelled internally. The night of the Leeds defeat, I had a steak dinner and a bottle of red wine before retiring to bed. The wine helped me to sleep, but I didn't stay there. I woke at four and lay awake. I thought, disjointedly, until dawn.

On Boxing Day, West Ham were the visitors. It was our Armageddon. At half-time we were 2–0 up and strolling in a winter wonderland. The Hammers were having a dreadful season and were bottom of the First Division. Ian Britton shot us ahead from my pass. Just on half-time, I beat three men and scored off the post. Happy Christmas! In the second half, though, our defence fell to pieces. West Ham threw everything into attack and the hill of beans was blown apart. The marking was shambolic. Lampard, Bobby Moore's big mate, went through on the left to score. Then fate moved against us once more. On the hour, Os smashed a volley against the bar less than ten yards out. That would have made it 3-1 and probably would have been 'Goodnight Vienna' for West Ham. Perhaps things would have been different. Instead, straight from the rebound, the Eastenders broke away to equalize through Bobby Gould, who would later manage Chelsea.

Clyde Best, a huge Bermudan forward, one of the first black players to make an impact, was giving Webb a torrid time. He scored two headers to transform the game: 4–2. A joke result, a bigger pantomime than anything showing in the West End! Sexton cracked. Our limitations, exposed against Leeds, were magnified by this little lot. The defence looked as if it had been mortar-bombed in the second half, but amazingly he reserved his fury for me and Os. We should have given it more to Nobby, was the refrain. He was Sexton's favourite. I didn't mind, he was one of mine too. Funny, it was his 300th first-team game and his birthday. He just shook his head and counted the tiles around the shower. Happy Birthday, Peter. Happy New Year, Dave!

Rumours abounded after the furore. Ron was to lose the captaincy to Os. Ron was struggling too, and his influence on the team was waning. I wanted the Chelsea captaincy as I had never wanted anything else. Shortly after the Wembley Final against Leeds, Sexton had assured me of my long-term future at Chelsea and promised that I would captain the club one day. Now I was being made the scapegoat for defensive errors and Os was being heralded as the next captain. Things like that crushed my spirit. Most Geminis are cynics. Do not ask me why. I suppose all cynics are hopeless romantics. You get more disappointed. It was a hideous time of my life. My congenital insomnia was fuelled by my anger at the situation and how the whole thing was moving out of control. Sometimes, when it rained, my ankle would hurt like hell. No star power at Chelsea soon!

On the Thursday I went out drinking with Eddie McCreadie, my best mate at the club – maybe in the world at the time, alongside Mick Carter and Tony Davis, now that Les had gone. The next few days were going to be very bad, I said to myself, with Liverpool coming to the Bridge. All the time that I was indulging in this behaviour, I was thinking, 'What is it all about? Where is it all leading?' It seemed to me that one defeat (on and off the field) led inexorably to another. The next day, Sexton cornered me. He said my breath stank of booze and this was the main reason Chelsea were losing. Not a word was said to Eddie. The manager had recently brought in a rule that any player watching the game should not be consuming any alcohol – he had once caught two of the lads spectating with bottles in their hands. (We got round this by drinking spirits out of a tea cup.) Stung by this, I countered by saying that my consumption was no greater than when we were winning trophies. I added that it was not drink that was costing us points, it was lack of confidence and new ideas. Peter Osgood sprang to my defence, stating that I had been the best player all season. It was the wrong remark to make to the anguished Sexton, and added fuel to his contention that Hudson and Osgood were the root of all his problems.

Liverpool beat us 1–0 the next day in the last match I ever played in the first team for Chelsea. I scarcely remember the game. Cormack, the clever midfielder, headed home from Toshack's cross. We never had a shot. I had given away a penalty at Anfield earlier in the season, but Bonetti made a great save from Keegan. The defence played badly again. It was like the auto-immune phenomenon, in which the immune system becomes so confused it self-destructs. That was to spill over to the whole club.

On New Year's Day 1974, Chelsea were away to Sheffield United. Os and myself were dropped, along with Bonetti. Tommy was sub. As so often happens in football, the players selected out of a crisis responded and Chelsea won 2–1. Kember lobbed a rare goal with the keeper off his line, and Hollins scored the winner after another error. It was a result as damaging in its repercussions as the Stoke, Orient, and Arsenal defeats.

Maybe Sexton thought he could do without us long-term. If he had built a better Chelsea and replaced us with improved versions, I would have admired his courage. History proved that he did not. Chelsea barely survived the season and perished as a force in the game for decades. Years later, I see it differently, a little. Only a little! I think Sexton wanted us to go to him and apologise, reject our lifestyles and become who he wanted us to be. Of course, we did not. Unlike in the movies, no last-minute reprieve or reconciliation took place. For years I wanted Sexton to ring me and say he was wrong. Part of us hated what he saw in the other, part loved the other because of the talent he saw. It was a weird relationship, the crux of the whole business. Do I miss Chelsea? The good times; the buzz. Always!

Os and I were training with the reserves. We did not expect to get back in the side for the Cup game against QPR. Dario Gradi called Os over and said he was wanted by Sexton over on the first-team pitch – condescending, like a South East Counties League player being called over to make up the number in a Combination game. The finest centre-forward in the history of Chelsea declined the invitation; Os had had a gutful. Nobody pushed him around on the field. He announced that as he was playing for the reserves, he would train with them. He did not want to play for Sexton any more. While he was saying these words, which would result in Chelsea becoming a death camp, I was getting a mental image of him scoring at Old Trafford, when we walked in fields of gold. I was nearby, juggling with a ball. As Os stormed away, I added my support (as Os had done for me). I told Gradi I wanted out also. Sexton arrived on the scene. He was livid and shouted that we could both leave Chelsea. I had been asking for a move for months, but was always told 'over my dead body'. That January day, he told me that I was trouble and that he had been trying to get me out of the club for ages. Then he told me to fuck off.

It could have been engineered, the whole thing. The club was desperate for cash to pay for the East Stand. What better way to raise funds than to sell us? The duplicitous games at board level in football sickened me. Perhaps the management, blinded by the victory at Sheffield, thought the club was bigger than the stars. I am keeping out of the argument. I have a vested interest. But ask any fan what they think. Ask any Manchester United fan after their defeat by Everton at Wembley and the loss of their title by a point: would they have liked to have Cantona in their side? The situation worsened in the summer, as their stars departed. To the fans, the stars *are* bigger than the club. To this day, the older Chelsea fans are bitter about how the matter was handled. A lot of people stopped going and never went back.

Brian Mears, the chairman at the time, was part of a dying breed of Englishmen: educated to exert authority and expect respect. Today, such men find themselves completely at odds with the rapidly changing game. Men like Sugar, Bates and Walker would not have allowed their clubs to almost die because of what were little more than personality clashes. In subsequent years, Ken Bates's personality dominated the club. Dixon, Nevin, Speedie and Hazard, all names on a par with the seventies stars, were all ultimately submerged by events.

We walked out of Chelsea. Bill Garner drove us to a pub at the back of Sloane Square called the Duke of Wellington. It did the best shepherd's pie in London. It still does. There, we planned our future away from the Bridge.

13

Fire Escape in the Sky

'Show me a hero and I will show you a tragedy.' F Scott
Fitzgerald

'A manager has got to be able to hold the respect of his players.'
The late, great Bob Paisley

In the end I joined Stoke, managed by a fellow called Waddington.
My father advised me to go there. Stoke was the complete antithesis
of the King's Road. I had reservations when Tony Waddington met
me in Russell Square. I loved the man, and every memory of him is
a fond one. Those were the days when managers signed you, not
chairmen or agents. Researching this book, I observed how the
transfer listing of Os and myself blew the market apart at the time.
Numerous exchange deals were mooted, involving Brian Kidd and
even George Best. Spurs and Arsenal were quoted as being
prepared to unload Martin Chivers and Kennedy to land us. Even
Leeds were preparing a bid for me, it was reported. Are you sure? I
never did hear from Revie. QPR were interested and chairman
Gregory, advised by Terry Venables, was weighing up a bid.

I was a restless soul, brimming with insecurities, needing to be reassured. Sitting on a park bench in Russell Square, Tony advised me to escape the bright lights of the big city. QPR would be no change for me. I think Rangers were a bit worried about my reputation. I do not give credence to tittle-tattle about other people's private lives and never did. The prospect of playing with Venables and Bowles appealed. Later, Sexton was to manage QPR – I wonder how that would have turned out.

Looking back, I never expected too much of Chelsea. I feel nostalgia and loss sometimes. I lived for playing. I was never an ego-maniac like some of them. They filtered their own selves out. I never played the role of Alan Hudson – I never had to. People always thought more of my presence than my achievements. Bowles gave the game more than it gave him. What he left behind was a wasted nobility and some wonderful memories. Therein lies the paradox. Did the same thing ultimately break us all? Bowles, Best, Hudson, Currie, George, Osgood, Worthington ... the list goes on to Cantona, Ginola, Collymore and Gazza, as the spotlight shines on them with a glare even more penetrative than we experienced. Were we heroic failures with impossible aspirations? Yes. To dream the impossible dream, yes, but if you wanted to understand it, you had to be there. Only the talentless waste their talent. We had a special kind of talent that promised more than it could ever fulfil.

Bernard Shaw (not the Sheffield United full-back) said, 'We learn from history that men never learn anything from history.' The history of Chelsea is one of conflict. Docherty/Venables to Osgood and Hudson/Sexton to Hollins/Bates to Speedie/Bates to Bates/ Harding. Sexton's victory over the dissidents was short-lived; a rather hollow victory. Unsatisfactory on all counts! Osgood left to join Southampton a few weeks after my departure. At one time it looked as though he would unseat the manager, but the party line won. It normally does.

Os never really set Southampton alight the way he did Stamford Bridge. He won another Cup winner's medal against Docherty's Man United, but never managed to get back into the England set-up. Like me, he was to cross the Atlantic and then return to Chelsea. Sexton was eventually sacked as they crashed down the League like a juggernaut out of control. It was out of control after the Orient game. Nobody won; we all lost, especially the fans. The late Matthew Harding made a good quote at the height of his problems with the Chelsea chairman. He called the fans 'emotional shareholders'.

Waddington met me off the train. They said I was the first young star from the 'Smoke' to come north. I wore a Prince of Wales check sports-jacket and a Take Six polo-necked jumper. The Football League did not sanction the five per cent payment on the basic £200,000 fee. I never did get it.* The ruling was that a spoken request carries as much weight as an official one. They referred to my heated exchanges with Sexton. Rumpole of the Bailey would have been out-manoeuvred. By a quirk of fate, Stoke met Chelsea twice in the closing months of the season. We did the double over them. In only my second game for Stoke, I figured in the incident that led to a controversial penalty being scored. It was the first Sunday match ever played in the First Division. Geoff Hurst scored after I went down under a Gary Locke challenge. Chelsea maintained that Locke had played the ball. At Stamford Bridge in the last game of the season, I scored the only goal of the game. It was the strangest feeling of my life. Throughout the game I received a lot of abuse from the crowd. My family were there and were shocked by the extent of the vitriol. The usual 'Judas' chants and boos were commonplace, but some of this was plain nasty. The real fans cheered me though, because in a way it was a vindication of my style and beliefs. A fight broke out in the West Stand between some (should I say fundamentalist?) Chelsea fans and some troublemakers who just liked to bad-mouth players. I was born with blue blood in my veins. I scored the goal for *my* Chelsea. Since my day, there have been a few 100 per cent men – Micky Droy and John Bumstead for example – but the majority were mercenaries passing through.

I only discovered recently that Johan Cruyff was born in the next street to Ajax's ground. Like me, he was raised in the shadow of the club he grew up to play for. His circumstances were poor. His mother was a cleaner at the club, scraping along on a widow's pension to bring up her family. The great Dutch club used to assist her in making ends meet, never dreaming that one of her family would grow up to be its greatest ever player. It was said that Johan

9 COOPER STREET · MANCHESTER · TEL:061 236 8020 / 236 6752(Office)

O S C A R S

Mr. A. Hudson,
Stock City Football Club,
Victoria Ground,
Stoke.

1 September 1975.

Dear Alan,

You are still the best player in the country by a mile.

Ram it down their throats where we know it matters -
on the pitch.

       Your pal,

       George Best

never forgot the kindness extended to his mother and played with such a passion for them he became an immortal. Lovely story!

That is the greatest gift I could pass on; playing with passion for a club. I dream of a major talent taking the football world by storm, a young player exploding on to the scene as Best did; another Pele with the skill of a Bowles and the charisma of Moore! Is it too much to ask? Could anyone overcome the pressures today? The tabloids and the TV coverage? It would be nice to think so. Perhaps he is out there now in a park, practising, waiting. I would love to be involved enough in football to nurture such a talent.

When I came back from America and rejoined Chelsea, I tried to get them to play football from the back. Hoddle believes in building from the defence, and in Gullit, Chelsea at last found a player who could create from the sweeper's role, a player who could attack from any position. When Holland destroyed the Irish Euro Championship dreams, we saw again football triumphing over forces of lesser skills.

In the movie *Scarface*, there is a scene where Al Pacino causes mayhem in a fancy bourgeois restaurant. Swaying drunkenly in the doorway, he shouts at the embarrassed diners, 'You don't have the guts to be what you want to be! You need people like me. You need people like me so you can point your finger and say, that's the bad guy. You think that makes you good? So take a look at the bad guy!'

My *Sporting Life* form at Chelsea Football Club would read: Broke quickly start, winning top prizes including FA Cup, European Cup Winners' Cup, League Cup runners-up, Selected World Cup squad (Mexico) 1970, Missed break through injury, Banned from international football for three years 1971, 'Fell out' with manager 71-72, Loss of form 72-73 through injury and unrest, No chance with management, Moved yard for record £240,000 to Stoke City.

14

Clowns to the Left,
Jokers to the Right

'That was the finest ninety minutes of football I've ever seen. I thought Peter Doherty's performance could not be surpassed, but you just did it ' Bill Shankly

I'd played at the Victoria Ground two, maybe three, times. Now I was pulling into Stoke-on-Trent railway station for the first time as a Stoke City player. It was, as I was to find out over a number of years, raining as usual; not just rain but that depressing drizzle that the Potteries seem to have made their very own. As I sat on the train, I recall seeing a paper stuck in a litter bin, with a picture of Peter Osgood on the back page. The story told of the speculation about his move to Southampton, only forty-eight hours after shaking hands with my new manager on a move to join me in a deal which would have really stunned the whole of football. The tabloid soaked up the rain like a sponge (no, not Tommy Baldwin) until it started to drift away from itself, much like Ossie's move to Stoke City. Tony Waddington had been close to pulling off a near-miracle

161

which would have seen Peter Osgood become the biggest thing in the area since Sir Stanley Matthews. However, I had to go it alone. My new team were third from bottom of the old First Division and it was January already, with mighty Liverpool the next game and my debut awaiting.

On the Saturday evening, I was sitting in the Lord Palmerston in Merton Road, Wimbledon, watching the results come up with my uncle George, when it suddenly hit me that, having drawn their match at Ipswich, my new team-mates were very much in the mire.

'What have I done, signing for this lot?' I asked both George and Tommy Hunter, the proprietor, who was a man with a very fine wit.

'I didn't think you could go much lower,' replied Tommy, knowing of my recent months of uncertainty and unhappiness at the Bridge. To which George, always the one with great faith in his young nephew responded: 'Just wait and see at the end of the season.' He did not know how right he could be.

Like most ex-Chelsea players I had a tendency to step into sinking ships! I was looking forward, though, to a get-away period, trying to rebuild my career. I was also looking forward to the peace and tranquil surroundings of the Staffordshire countryside. Who was I kidding? The expected stay at the North Staffs Hotel was soon dismissed by my new boss and I was invited to move into the luxurious bungalow of Geoff and Judith Hurst. This was against my wishes, for I have always liked my own company and space. However, the deal was done and now I was a lodger of the only man to score a hat-trick in a World Cup Final, now playing for Stoke. Hursty, whose home was set back in five acres of beautiful countryside, was quick to make use of yours truly for his nights out. The bungalow was called 'Crosswinds' but was swiftly renamed 'Crossroads', such were the comings and goings of guests. My family would visit on match days, my agent Ken Adam and Kathy Peters, the charming wife of the second third of those famous Hammers, Martin. It was all very different for the boy from the King's Road, with the girls getting up in the morning to go horse-riding while we trained. The nearest I got to 'London life' was popping into Ladbrokes after training, and the only horses I'd ever seen in the King's Road were the ones with the men in blue on!

I was looking forward to my first week's training and the build-up to that great first match which was much more exciting than my Chelsea debut. I thought a quiet dinner and an early night would start my new career off just dandy. After dinner, though, I was informed by my new team-mate that it was a Monday night ritual in Stoke that we had to be at a nightclub in Hanley. The Place, which I was already familiar with, became my new watering-hole. It was a very famous club for its live music in the sixties, and was now my new Cromwellian. Well, it was quite fitting that I should be introduced to all my new team-mates in such an environment after everything they had heard about me, and they were not slow with the wise-cracks.

The Thursday morning training session was when Tony Waddington really put me under the most intense pressure, and had me in a situation that caused a little animosity amongst a few in the dressing-room. In a full-scale match against the second team, he put a different colour top on me and told our players not to pass to any other colour but mine. Straight away our left-back Micky Pejic was my number one enemy, and he would do the very opposite when in possession of the ball. I took it as a great compliment from my new boss but did not thank him for it. The likes of John Ritchie, Jimmy Greenhoff and Jimmy Robertson were all experienced players and did not like being told to give the ball to a twenty-two-year-old troublemaker from the Smoke. But I got through my second test of the week and had no idea what was in store for me that evening, only forty-eight hours before the big match, a match that was either going to win over the fans or lose them straight away. The phone rang at about seven o'clock and Hursty answered it. 'Hello, Os, how are you?' was all I heard, and within twenty minutes we were in The Place's sister bar, The Placemate. Ossie had come up to watch my debut and had decided to celebrate with me before the match instead of afterwards, just like at the Athens Hilton!

Another 2am touch, the second in four days, and the daunting task of playing against the best team in Europe without knowing whether some of the players I would be lining up with were going to pass to me or not. Not the best preparation by any means, but there was one thing for sure: I was prepared to go it alone once again, *demand* the ball to the extent of taking it off my own team-mates or going back to knock it out of our goalkeeper's hands to start our moves off. This became my trademark at Stoke City, to be able to go beyond our back four and work my way upfield playing one-twos, mainly with the brilliant Jimmy Greenhoff.

That Saturday was one of the most exciting and rewarding of my career. It is still talked about to this day in terms of the best performance ever seen at a ground already famous for so many Matthews virtuoso displays. If I had failed that day, I would have been called a burnt-out, overrated superstar from the Smoke who, in his first four days in town, had spent more hours in The Place than on the training ground. Well, the only way to do it is to take the bull by the horns, as I said before, and on this occasion it worked out. My debut was spectacular, with everybody – as I've seen so many times – jumping on the bandwagon to sing my praises, the same people who had their knives already fresh off the sharpener. My first couple of passes were into the front players' feet so that I could pace myself, always staying behind the ball, never having to chase back. The pitch was heavy, but it was my pitch, and I was starting to hear the buzz around the ground get louder and louder. I knew this was going to be my day, the day I won them over. Waddo gave me the freedom of the Victoria Ground and always did, just letting me go wherever I wanted, whenever I wanted. How could I fail?

It was quite a contrast to my latter days at the Bridge, when Dave Sexton would keep swapping and changing things tactically, forever disrupting things to suit his temperament, using me as a right-sided player to fit somebody else in. That was not my game. Waddington gave me my head, allowing me to play to my strengths of controlling the pace of the game – much like a Cauthen, Piggott, Eddery or today Frankie dictating the pace from the front – and always bringing people into the game. Slowing it down and then quickening it up, something I could do all day long. At Stoke we had this down to a fine art, with the likes of John Mahoney battling, grafting and biting on my right, and the sublime skills and educated left foot of my great buddy Geoff Salmons on my left. We had the blend, the blend that Sexton could not get if he and all his cronies spent the rest of their entire life at Lilleshall, for Waddington had

insight and imagination to such an extent that 'coaching' went well
and truly out the window and down the Trent!

The game ended 1-1 after our keeper John Farmer dropped one
at Tommy Smith's feet in the dying seconds. This was probably the
only mistake he made while we played together, and it just had to
be that day. We had totally outplayed the champions, and
Waddington's gamble in bringing me to the Potteries now looked
like a bargain: a record £240,000 fee which made the £3,500 paid
for Sir Stan in the early sixties look ridiculous (and in today's
market, quite laughable). Sir Stan was forty-six at the time, but the
return of the prodigal Matthews sent the gates soaring and set the
framework for the team that was eventually to beat Chelsea in the
League Cup Final, claiming their first ever major trophy and
paving the way for my record-breaking transfer.

Chelsea and Stoke City had crossed each other's paths over the
years. When Matthews inspired Stoke to win the 1962–63 Second
Division title, they had narrowly edged out the Blues. City won a
vital match at the Bridge over Easter to clinch the title. My father
was one of the 70,000 who packed into the ground, to witness a
game which was remembered for the Chelsea crowd booing their
very own Eddie McCreadie after one of his 'specials' on the great
man. Ron Harris, playing one of his first matches, was also giving
Sir Stan some treatment, which was to become Ronnie's trademark.

Chelsea, being Chelsea, led the table by a mile nearly all season
only to blow it as only they could. But amazing results in the last
two matches put them in a position which was to change the whole
outlook at Stamford Bridge. A 1–0 win at Roker Park was enough to
rob Sunderland of second spot and set up a dramatic last match at
the Bridge. The Wearsiders only had to draw that memorable
evening at Roker, but Tommy Docherty had very different ideas,
packing his team with defenders and playing the match like a
European tie. In goal, a young Peter Bonetti was showing very early
signs that he would become the greatest keeper in the history of
Chelsea Football Club. It was reminiscent of his Cup Final show
years later against Leeds; he seemed unbeatable. 'Catty' was not
only simply the best but 'Simply Blue', something that the late
Matthew Harding was so proud to be, and admired in the likes of
the Cat. My old youth team coach scored the only goal that evening,

scrambling home a corner in what seemed Chelsea's only worthwhile attack. Tommy 'The Charmer' Harmer was one of the last great inside-forwards, a ball-playing artist who could make the ball talk and always stressed to me that you must work so hard on your first touch and control. The record books say the ball went in off his stomach, but it really flew in off a lower part of his anatomy, so to speak!

The Doc played Frank Upton and Derek Kevan up front, probably about as nice a duo as Ossie and Hutch. Upton was later coach at the club and was a real sergeant-major type who became Chelsea manager for the day. In this time, he told me in a little club in Gloucester Road that if I signed, I would have to knock the Frank on the head and call him Boss. He also told Duncan McKenzie, who was then a Blue, and all the rest of the players that they would too. Later in the day, he had to go back and tell them that it was still all right to call him Frank because Danny Blanchflower was taking over. I've heard of being 'King for a Day', but that takes the biscuit!

Kevan was another old pro who could look after himself and the younger ones around him. Along with Frank, he dished out leather all game, which stopped Sunderland from ever working up any rhythm. If a club is to win anything, they must have aggression up front. Mark Hughes reminds us of this today, for it was he who led the line at Man United for so long to begin their success story under Alex Ferguson. Leeds United had Clarke and Jones in our day and Liverpool Toshack; since then, the likes of Joe Jordan have filled this role at both Old Trafford and Elland Road. They were throwbacks to the good old days when I was a kid watching at White Hart Lane and Bobby Smith would hit any target in a green shirt that came his way – and he'd take the number five along with him if need be. Another real handful in those days was Andy Lochead, who was like a real gladiator, not one of the TV ones which Fashanu deals with.

Hughes wears the shirt that our own Ian Hutchinson made famous, if only for his long throw. A player who trod a very fine line between being courageous and off his head. A player who would put his head where devils, let alone angels, would fear to tread, and nine times out of ten get the better of his opposite number, with his knock-downs and flick-ons to his partner. Shearer is another who leads the line with courage, power, aggression and unselfish running, chasing lost causes which have rewarded him so richly. A centre-forward of the old type who would have got in any of the great teams in any era, Shearer is a player who does not have to rely on service. He creates his own chances and takes them at an incredible rate.

Kevan scored early on in the last game of the season, a match that Chelsea had to win by five goals to be promoted alongside Stoke. Now they showed the other side of a coin which Tommy Doc was soon to show how to toss. Bobby Tambling, 'Jumbo' as we knew him, hit four as the Doc's Diamonds began a new era, under the man whose influence would produce two of football's most well-known and talked about managers of our time, Terry Venables and George Graham. I still firmly believe that the Chelsea side which Tommy developed was potentially the greatest in the history of the club. OK, I was not around before the fifties, but this squad of players could have gone on to the kind of glory that Shankly brought to Liverpool. With the likes of Venners, Graham, McCreadie, Bonetti, Hinton and Tambling as a base, he then had the insight to buy well (Charlie Cooke) and have a youth system that would be worth the crown jewels in today's crazy market.

Venables and Graham are two proven great managers and must rank alongside the best of the rest, two of whom were at the match that cold afternoon of my Stoke debut: Shanks, the main man, and Stan Cullis, who had brought such fantastic success to a now-forgotten Wolverhampton Wanderers. Cullis was reporting on the radio and was quoted as saying that this was the finest debut he had seen in all his years in the game. Mr Shankly and Mr Waddington did not disagree!

I wore the number ten shirt. Arsenal's Paul Merson wore the same shirt for eight years before Dennis Bergkamp joined the Gunners and insisted on having the number which was a tribute to whoever wore it all over the world. As my good friend Mick Carter says, there are only four shirts you wear if you can play the game: four, six, eight or ten, and for me ten tops the lot. Pele made it extra special, and all my favourites, beginning with Haynes, would insist on wearing it. There was the great Spaniard Suarez, who caught my eye at a very early age, and let's not forget Michel Platini and Bogicevic. Only Johan Cruyff could better it by changing the rules, adding the four to the ten and becoming the first player – and how magnificently he wore it – to wear fourteen.

My form against Liverpool was to launch me into a new phase of playing the game. I had proved at Chelsea that I could play in a system that suited Dave Sexton, where I would be the general dogsbody doing all the fetching and carrying for my elders. Now this life was more like it, for I was the one who called the shots in a side that depended on my controlling things. I had done my apprenticeship in the big time, and now I wanted to prove that I was not just another player who came through the Chelsea ranks. As happened at Liverpool over the years, so many players that leave the great club are soon forgotten.

My debut performance against the might of Liverpool was to be bettered some time later, when Shanks paid me my finest compliment – and he was never a man to praise the opposition; he was a one-colour man, simply red! I remember Chelsea going to Anfield once and giving one of Docherty's famous defensive performances that he had off to an art. A 0–0 stalemate had the great Shankly muttering that his team had had so much of the play they had 'worn out the pitch'. His one-liners became clichés. On another occasion, his Liverpool side were torn limb from limb by a Johan Cruyff orchestration in which Ajax wiped the floor with them 5–0. At the press conference after the match, Shanks just shook his head and said that his team 'could nae play against defensive teams'.

Peter Doherty and Tom Finney were Shankly's heroes and he would always use them as comparisons or yardsticks for a performance, with Finney his main man. He once said of England's possibly greatest ever player that he was able to beat his full-back 'with his overcoat on' – and he meant the wartime maxi-length type, not the lightweight cashmere beautifully worn by George Graham and Kenny Dalglish today. Shankly was once asked who was better, Best or Finney. After a brief pause, he declared that Tom just had the edge over the Irishman. 'Mind you, Finney is nearly fifty now,' he added.

Ossie later recycled this story in best Oscar Wilde fashion. Ken

Bates had asked him how the team of the seventies would have fared against the Chelsea team of today, and was told: 'Our team would have just about won.' The Chelsea chairman to this day is envious of the mystique and glamour of our Cup-winning escapades. He shot Peter an old-fashioned look and asked what he based his opinion on. Ossie quickly answered, 'The obvious skill factor and all-round strength – but then again, some of our boys are fifty now.' How can you come back at that!

Let me clear up any confusion here about Shankly's praise. The following season we beat Liverpool 2–0 in an important League match over that always gruelling Easter period. I cannot believe it when I read today about the likes of Ruud Gullit wanting a rest period over Christmas and New Year. This has become the most important and exciting time of the English game. All of a sudden we are letting the likes of the great Dutchman talk such nonsense; the sooner someone explains that he is in England and playing it our way the better. He may be one of the greatest talents our game has ever seen, but he must realise that if we dug Mr Shankly up from his shrine, he would tear the dreadlocked Dutchman to bits for suggesting that it is more important to be with our families over such times. We all know what Shanks said about the game, don't we? And how his wife said to him one day that 'I think you love Liverpool Football Club more than me,' to which he replied: 'Dear, I love Everton Football Club more also' – such was his passion for the game of football. So the new Chelsea manager had better just get on with what he does best and entertain those crowds that pay good, hard-earned money, not just over the season but during those very hard times at Christmas when people – unlike him – struggle to put food on their loved-ones' table. This Bank Holiday Monday match followed a trip to London where we played on the Good Friday (talk about the Long Good Friday) at West Ham and the Saturday at Highbury. This was regarded as the most critical period of the season, when titles were won and lost and the stragglers down at the bottom sealed their fate. Too many of today's players complain just like Gullit, getting fortunes for what is part-time work in comparison to us.

The matches in London took their toll on my ankle, which was now chronic, with the combination of two games in successive days and the grounds hardening with the advent of spring. As John Francome would say, 'The going's changed from soft to firm.' Or in my case, from 'good to bad'. On the Saturday, travelling back, I told the boss of my predicament. He told me not to get off the train thinking that I would not be playing on Monday, but to have a few drinks, relax, prepare for Monday and pray for rain. He called me first thing on Sunday morning, on a delightful day with absolutely no sign of even an April shower. 'You'll be fine tomorrow, Alan. I've just spoken to the weatherman and he assures me of rain, rain and more rain, so you'll be fine.' Perhaps Tony had a line on an Apache Indian rainmaker in the Potteries.

The following morning, I woke early and immediately checked my garden but found it as dry as Dave Sexton's drinks cabinet. That's me out, I thought straight away. I felt such disappointment at missing so crucial a match at such a vital time.

I got to the ground for treatment earlier than usual to find, to my amazement, a Victoria Ground pitch absolutely saturated. It was as if a miracle had happened – or had Tony been in touch with the Pope again? The Liverpool players arrived and went straight down our tunnel to check out which footwear they would need. The look on the faces of Keegan, Toshack, Clemence and all was a sight to behold. Keegan came off with his Church brogues caked in mud. 'What's been going on here, Huddy? We haven't had an inch up the road.' I shrugged my shoulders and just could not tell him that the local rainmaker was really the local firechief, a lifelong Stoke City fan and a very good friend of Mr Waddington. They had spent the previous day making an artificial lake on the pitch, which was like a scene from the *Towering Inferno*, the 'in' movie of that time.

The stage was set for me to play my finest-ever match in a red-and-white-striped shirt. Tony had done his bit by showing me how much he wanted me out there; now I had to justify his having called out the fire brigade. We overwhelmed the men from Anfield with a display which was usually dished out the other way around, by them against teams at Anfield: the complete runaround! I finished the match by nutmegging the tough-tackling Tommy Smith, right in front of the directors' box. 'That's for the guvnor,' I thought. Liverpool had received some of their own medicine. From the time they inspected the pitch to the final whistle, they just did not know what to expect next.

As I sat at my locker, covered in mud – what a wonderful feeling – there was a knock on our door. A head popped round it and it belonged to Shanks.

'Can I come in, Tony?' Tony, as always the gentleman: 'Our pleasure, Bill.'

As I took off my right boot, Shankly was standing over me with his hand out. This was when he paid me the finest tribute that any footballer can have paid to them.

'Son, I'd thought Peter Doherty's performance would never be surpassed, but you've just done it,' he said, and he could not have done it in a better place, right in front of all my team-mates, including the ones who were a little jealous. It was the sweetest sound my ears have ever heard, and don't forget I am a Frank Sinatra freak.

The key to Liverpool's domination of the English game was their strength in midfield, Graeme Souness being probably the best of the lot with his incredible strength of leadership. There was quality in everything he did – apart from when he was going over the top, that is – and he had that wonderful shooting ability to go with all his other marvellous attributes. Bill Shankly's last signing was Ray Kennedy, whom he converted from being an out-and-out front man into a great midfield player. I often wondered how it would have turned out if Bill had signed me or Osgood, or if the transfer of Frank Worthington had not fallen through. Liverpool were a wonderful team, but I often wondered what extra dimension a 'maverick' would have given them, albeit a rehabilitated one!

One last story about Shanks concerns the time when one of his players limped off at half-time. This was in the days of no substitutes, and the physio was just about to pull his boot off to see the extent of the damage. The Anfield boss screamed at him, 'No, don't take it off, he'll never get it back on again,' such was the swelling. The problem with writing about Bill Shankly is that you could go on all day long. The complete legend!

Tony Waddington insisted, as I do today, that a team had to have class in midfield to have any chance of becoming a great one. What won me over at the transfer discussions was the catalogue of class individuals that he trotted out as players of Stoke City Football

Club. I followed the likes of Jackie Mudie, Roy Vernon, Jimmy McIlroy, Peter Dobing and George Eastham, and struck up as great a midfield–frontman partnership with Jimmy Greenhoff as there had ever been. These were all great artists, great craftsmen every one of them.

It would be impossible to pick out the greatest goal in Greenhoff's collection of gems, just as it is with Osgood, Worthington and Le Tissier today, all players who had, and have, that magnificent timing. I would watch Jimmy in training and purr at that wonderful touch of his. A touch like silk and an uncanny awareness. He was once quoted as saying that the pair of us were like twins, telepathic in fact, such was the uncanny way that we found each other in any situation. We could actually have played blindfolded and still known where the other one was, which was a quite fantastic feeling. Jimmy was probably the best volleyer of a moving ball I have ever seen. His volley at Birmingham over Christmas that year was, I think, 'Goal of the Season', but he would hit them like that all the time. The only problem with playing for a club like Stoke was that we never got the television coverage, and therefore the wider recognition, that the bigger clubs did. That was one of the reasons why the country never got to see him leave so many goalkeepers stranded, and why players such as Greenhoff, Salmons, Bloor and Dodd never made it into the England squad.

Last season I was involved in a little fracas outside the Chelsea players' tunnel with Kevin Keegan and Terry McDermott, a case of egos getting in the way – theirs, that is – and it was followed by a newspaper article in which the ex-Liverpool player talked about 'putting your medals on the table'. All I've got to say is, that does not determine how good a player is, or what he knows about the game, or even whether he is qualified to manage one of the richest clubs in the country. All I do know is that these two did not exactly fill the trophy cabinet up at St James's Park – in fact, it was more a case of Old Mother Hubbard – but what Newcastle have done is not only spent a fortune but spent it while making a million and one excuses.

When I think back to how close I came to winning a League Championship, it becomes a little hazy. You could say that I played for what I call 'nearly teams', like some players are 'nearly players'.

The three clubs that I played for in this country were all potentially Championship material. At Chelsea, Sexton broke up a squad that managers today would cut off their right arm for. Stoke City, in my second season, took over at the top around Christmas and looked to have it very much under control. Not like today, when you hear people talk of pressure. We really were playing like a team worthy of taking the Championship in front of all the big boys: Liverpool, Everton, both Manchester sides, Arsenal, Spurs, Leeds, Derby County and all the rest, with the kind of background that people in the Potteries only read about.

Peter Shilton once wrote a newspaper article and mentioned my name, saying that I was a moody character, an inconsistent performer and did not live up to my potential. I must remind him that I played seventy-odd consecutive matches for Stoke City before breaking my leg at Derby, and in two-thirds of those was the star player. That does not rank as inconsistency in my book. Not only would Peter Shilton not know a player if he changed next to him, he was also the reason why I cannot boast of winning that honour, and I wrote to him and explained this. For it was in that season at Stoke City that he decided to go AWOL. I believe we would have won the Championship if Tony Waddington had not listened to Alex Humphreys and had kept John Farmer between the goalposts at the Victoria Ground. To this day, I can see Shilton waving his arms around like one of those creatures out of *The Planet of the Apes*, a little similar to Peter Schmeichel today. I can also picture him kicking the floor against Newcastle in the last minute of the match, when confronted by Alan Gowling. The people leaving the ground could only look around in amazement, seeing him lying on the floor as the lanky striker waltzed the ball into our net. It was one of the most bizarre incidents I have ever witnessed on the football field. We only just had time to kick-off before the referee blew for time, and were all back in the dressing-room while Shilts was still lying face down in the Victoria Ground mud.

That, as so many other times, cost us very important points which finally spewed our chances down the Trent. Yet it was not his mistakes that were the most painful thing but his attitude. He would try to con people, his own players, by telling our centre-halves to push forward more and get out of his way. You see, he hated crosses and would have been more at home in one of Christopher Lee's *Dracula* movies. One of our strengths in that Stoke side was the uncanny defensive structure built around a chap called Dennis Smith, who had to play deep because on the turn he was the opposite of Linford Christie. But Smithy facing the play was a sight to behold. He was first to everything that moved and hardly ever missed a challenge. It gave everybody around him the opportunity to pick up the pieces (which more often than not was the opposition's number nine), and Jackie Marsh, Alan Bloor and Micky Pejic had this off to a fine art.

However, Shilton wanted to change all that because he wanted the box for himself, and would constantly scream at Smithy to push out. The moment Dennis pushed out, it was the opportunity for the other team to get it over his head, which was one of the reasons that led to Shilton kicking the floor. I once heard him say to Smithy, in our own North Staffs Hotel, that 'You will play for England if you listen to me and push up about twenty yards.' This was the last straw for me and I let him know it, and from that day on it was Shilton against Hudson. What I did not like about these kind of snide, behind-the-back-of-the-manager team meetings was that it was personal. As I said before, the Championship would have been resting proudly on Mr Waddington's drinks cabinet if only he had not signed this goalkeeper. I know the reaction of ninety-nine percent of people reading this book will be one of total disbelief, but you would only have to conduct a survey in the backstreets of Stoke-on-Trent to know that I would not be far off from the truth – and I did help with the rumour!

I will not go on too much about the ex-England keeper, but must tell of how he was the target for all the dressing-room jokes, especially the old 'weights-in-the bag' trick. The two main assassins here were the Irishman Terry Conroy and his sidekick John 'Josh' Mahoney. Stoke at that time must have been the only club in the First Division that could not afford a washing lady. To my astonishment on my first day, we had to take our kit home and have it washed, which was something of a culture shock compared to Highbury and Stamford Bridge. It turned out that our goalkeeper's wife refused to do such chores, so he had to go to the laundry room after training to wash his own kit, while all the chaps were lying soaking in their bathtubs. Well, that was apart from Terry and Josh, who would fetch the weights from the gym and put them at the bottom of his bag. The boys would not go home until Shilts had picked his bag up and headed for the dressing-room door. This would happen on a regular basis, and Shilton would rant and rave when reaching the exit, not having a clue who the culprits were. Someone once said *that* was why his arms were so long!

You may have guessed that Conroy and Mahoney were our dressing-room jokers, while their pal Micky Pejic was the dressing-room moaner. In between there came the others, including Geoff Salmons, Jack Marsh, Sean Hazlegrave and yours truly. Sean was a player who was very talented but never really reached the heights that he could and should have. He was let go by Waddo after a match in Amsterdam when, after Tony had substituted him for Jimmy Robertson, he approached the bench and kicked the manager in his 'Niagaras'. Sitting next to Tony that evening was Mr Brian Clough. On reaching the players' lounge, Sean was taken by the hand and complimented by old Cloughie! I stood there in disbelief, as Clough said, 'That is the way to react when being pulled off.' I immediately thought out loud, 'I could just see him doing it to *you* and getting a handshake.' Brian followed this up by signing Sean for Nottingham Forest and promising him the captaincy, which was the end of his career – need I say more!

One of the most bizarre transfer deals I had ever seen done was the signing of my room-mate Geoff Salmons. It was on a tour of Cyprus, in the lovely surroundings of Famagusta. Sheffield United were there playing the locals, and Tony asked me to go to the match with him. I said to Tony that I had better things to do than watch Sheffield United in Cyprus! He explained that it was very important for me to join him, as he needed my approval on a player he wanted for the following season. Salmons was that player, and after half an hour, for I was in a rush to get to our local nightspot, I agreed with Tony that he would be a great addition to our 'nearly team', but also pointed out that the way he was playing might not complement me. The manager assured me that 'Sammy' would be our 'outlet' on the left side, that player with the magic left peg. And he did not disappoint anyone with it. His ability to cross the ball at full speed

was in the Alan Hinton class, and that, I can tell you, is the best
compliment I could pay my old drinking partner. In the early hours
of the following morning, Waddington had Sammy up against the
hotel bar, telling him what a fantastic place Stoke-on-Trent was.
But Sammy was sold not on the area but on the manager, just like I
was after our first meeting on the park bench in Russell Square. (I
would much rather it had been on that fabulous island in
Famagusta though.) Also on that trip, Tony almost pulled off
another coup when he tried – and very nearly succeeded – to lure
Franny Lee into his plans for the following season. Tony simply
could not be in the company of great players without trying, or at
least dreaming of them running out with a red-and-white-striped
shirt on. It was another of our manager's 3am signing sprees, but
Franny was not as easy as Sammy to catch. Sammy had to sort out
the most important part of his deal, though, and that was to explain
that this tour was not a one-off for him, that he drank like that all
the time in Sheffield. Waddington's reply was short and sweet, and
without hesitation: 'If you have been playing like that while
drinking, do not stop.'

This was the trip when war broke out between Greek Cypriots
and the Turks, and we were nearly caught in the crossfire. On our
last evening there, Jimmy Robertson, Tony and myself had been
having a lovely time throwing plates all over the dance floor at a
local nightclub when the first bomb fell. We were sitting on the
pavement outside, waiting for a cab, when suddenly the whole
place shook. As luck would have it, we were leaving the following
morning, otherwise our first few matches of the season would have
had to be rearranged. Chelsea's David Hay was not so lucky. He
was held up there and did actually miss the start of the new season.

Our manager was a great believer in travelling, and we were
never disappointed with the stamps on our passports. He was also a
firm believer in taking a couple of the young players whenever we
went abroad, for he would say, 'They will leave home boys and
come back men.' One evening in Cyprus, Tony was sitting at the
hotel bar, drinking with the captain of our aeroplane, when he
spotted two young players by the names of Kevin Lewis (an
ex-Busby babe) and Danny Bowers creeping up the stairs to their
bedrooms. Tony caught them out of the corner of his eye and called

them over to see what they were up to. These two were trying to creep past him, thinking they were late, but Tony gave them a very different sort of dressing-down: 'I have not dragged you halfway around the world so you can have an early night. You can have plenty of those in Stoke-on-Trent. Now get yourselves out the front door and enjoy yourselves.'

What a wonderful approach this man had. This was one of the reasons why he had so many successful youngsters come through under his management, because he would have the blend of experience and youth both at home and on tour, where young players would go away with their idols and watch and learn not only the playing side but how to behave and also enjoy themselves.

15

The Best Is Yet To Come

'Out of the tree of life I picked me a plum,
You came along and everything started to hum,
Still it's a good bet, the best is yet to come.'
        Tony Bennett (from that famous San Francisco album).

There were not many players who went 'North of Watford' and made an impact in those days. The first was Dave Mackay, who was finishing as I started, and the only other one who made such an impact in the Midlands was Charlie George, back to Charlie again, another 'maverick' who features in Rob Steen's book of that name, along with those other greats of our time. The one disaster of this 'maverick' tribe was QPR's Rodney Marsh, who went to Manchester City and, along with Malcolm Allison, promised so much but delivered so little. The result was disastrous, with both men not only losing City the title but arrogantly walking away, thinking it was everybody else that was wrong. I don't think so!

One of the reasons Tony Waddington was so adamant about getting my signature on the Stoke City-headed contract was because of a conversation he had with 'Big Mal', when Malcolm had a player

178

on loan from Tony and agreed a price for him which was about three times the amount Tony wanted. It went something like this.

'What are you going to do with the money, Tony?'

'I'm putting it towards buying a kid from Chelsea.'

A little pause from Mal, as he remembered Tony's passion for inside-forwards, as I always like to call us.

'You do not believe that Hudson would leave the bright lights and come to Stoke.'

The bet was struck between the two men and the rest is history. Two-nil to Waddington.

My time in Staffordshire was memorable both on and off the field – not only enjoying the success of my first season there (the best in the club's history, just like Chelsea's) but making many friends and becoming notorious for driving over two roundabouts in Newcastle-under-Lyme. I could have sworn they moved the second one, which was situated just by the golf club where that great old winger Jimmy Robertson lived. Robbo was quite instrumental, later on, in my leaving Stoke for Highbury, just as Mooro was in my going to Seattle. Jimmy has a lot to answer for!

Probably the biggest match that Stoke City had ever played was in the UEFA Cup, the season after I joined them, in Amsterdam against the might of Ajax. Could anyone have foreseen this fixture a year ago, sitting in a pub in Merton Road, when Stoke were third from the bottom of the League? The first leg took place just a few days after my second car crash, following a night out with Mr Waddington – whom I had just dropped off – and Geoff Hurst at Tony's beloved local in Crewe. Can you imagine, Geoff Hurst and Alan Hudson socialising on a Saturday at the end of the railway line! We had just beaten Carlisle, after they had come up and topped the old First Division, with a vintage Stoke display of pure football, and on the Wednesday we had to face the team who were known for 'Total Football'. I ended up playing with stitches in my face and a broken hand. We drew 1-1 after Rudi Krol beat Farmer with a thunderous 25-yarder. I was effectively an innocent bystander on that particular evening, but by the time we got to Amsterdam things were different. We had recovered from being totally outplayed and overawed, and I had recovered from my accident and was now ready to carry on from a memorable performance at Carlisle (football, that is). England's assistant manager John Gorman played left-back for Carlisle that day, and always mentions it when ever we meet. He wasn't a bad player for them, or for Spurs and Tampa Bay Rowdies. Like most full-backs, he could tell a midfield player when he saw one. Then again, he played with Glenn, just like Eddie Mac played with Baxter and Cooke.

George Eastham and Gordon Banks had been on a scouting mission for the club before the first leg. Their team-talk frightened the life out of our less experienced players, and it showed in our performance. On the trip to Amsterdam, I told the lads that we had nothing to fear from what we had seen in the first match, especially as they had carried me for the ninety minutes. I repeated this to both George and Gordon as we left the hotel for the ground. My attitude was that if we could take on Liverpool, we could take on anyone.

Also on this trip with us was Brian Clough, who had just been sacked from his position at Leeds United. 'Old Big Head' was a great friend and colleague to our manager – they shared a mutual respect – and had invited Tony on several of his own teams' trips into Europe. It was the first time I ever met the man whom I had so much respect for – and that went out of the window instantly. At Manchester airport, he sat there like Terry Waite waiting to be brought home, with his book in one hand and his, as always, arrogant attitude in the other. I was asked to have a photo taken with him and said it would be a pleasure, as you would, but he just had to shatter an illusion that I had built up of this 'one-off ' of a manager. Don't forget, I had been in the company of Sir Matt Busby, Bill Shankly, and played under Sir Alf Ramsey by the time I had reached twenty, not to mention Elton John, Peter Wyngarde, Jack Jones, that great American singer, and of course the greatest of all time having had cocktails with Pele, so I wasn't really new to this 'meeting famous people' game.

I later found out from one of his ex-players and my boss in Seattle that he had slagged me off about my behaviour after the match. He had come to the conclusion that I fell off a bar stool at the airport. I wrote to him after hearing this story, stating how disappointed I was with his comments. I said, 'If you cannot say something nice

Touchdown from Australia after a run-in with Terry Neill in 1977. Malcolm 'Super' Macdonald was right behind me. *(Press Association)*

Hiding from the manager at London Colney with George Armstrong after the calamity of Australia in 1977.

Out of work after walking out of Highbury but still had time to catch up on some long distance stuff. Yes, it was tea! *(Daily Mirror)*

With my dad, Bill, after signing
for Stoke, second time round.

Boxing guru and football nut
Frank Maloney and I just before
Lennox Lewis's latest fight.

Only Sinatra was superior to the great Tony Bennett who Ray Evans and
I met at the Kingdome, Seattle, before one of our matches in 1982.

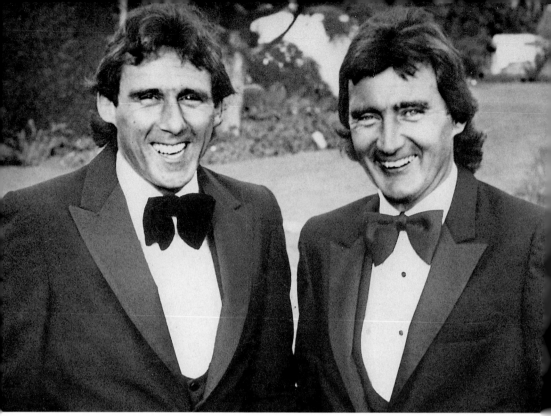

Night out with Ray Evans before the 1981 Soccerbowl in San Diego.

One of our many visits to North Staffs Hospital in 1983 with director
Geoff Manning, Peter Hampton and manager Bill Asprey.

My favourite DJ Mel Scholes, Signal Radio, and my all-time favourite racehorse, Red Rum, at Uttoxeter during a charity bash in 1986.

Pinch me! With my hero Viv Richards, a truly great guy, also Chris Garland, Dave English, Bill Wyman, Neil Foulds and Chris Willsmore.

The most talented player in the country, Matt Le Tissier and I discussing our caps – or lack of them – before a match at the Bridge in '95.

A picture to treasure, in the tunnel with Matthew Harding at that same Southampton game of 1995.

Down Scribes with three ex-QPR players, Terry Venables, Stan Bowles and David Webb in 1996.

In Terry Neill's Sports Bar in Holborn before last season's 1996 Final. How times have changed!

Mark Abery's 'Stars Cup' brings Joe Elliott and his Def Leppard band together with me and Frank Worthington.

Lucky at last! My gorgeous Ann accepts my proposal for a June '97 wedding.

about someone, don't say anything at all.' The reason this really upset me was Cloughie's first match in charge of Leeds was at the Victoria Ground, and I was instrumental in making it a nightmare start for him, making all three goals. Please don't get me wrong in reading this book, thinking that all my games were magnificent. I just had the knack of doing it in front of the right people, in 'big matches'. Nobody talks about their bad moments, do they? Does Francis Albert talk about his bad songs? That is something that is a guide for us lesser mortals, to search for perfection! I explained the incident to Clough in the letter I sent to him, and also pointed out that I did not think this was the way a man like him should react, speaking behind people's backs. If he had anything to tell my boss, it should have been about my performance against his new club, which sent him down that very short, bumpy road which ended in the Leeds United players threatening a boycott unless they got rid of this bloke who just waltzed in and tried to uproot all that Revie had laid. After all, 'Those in glass houses should not throw stones', should they?

I was to be in his Nottingham office not long after, for our second confrontation. He poured me a glass of champagne and brandy in front of Hinton and several others of his cronies, saying 'I got your letter, young man, and you're getting the first glass, because you have got balls.' That was after I had stood up in front of his chums and assured him that Alan Hinton had not been talking out of school, this was between the two of us. (I had obviously told Alan about my letter.) My respect for the man was restored, but what would have happened had I not gone back that night and seen him in a different light, a man who went on to do the most remarkable job at the City Ground that has ever been achieved anywhere in Great Britain? Was this why he admired Mr Waddington so much, with his having done so much for a similar small club, a club which, under a lesser mortal, would never have reached those great heights alongside the élite clubs like Manchester United, Liverpool, Glasgow Celtic and Arsenal?

Forest are now finding out just how amazing the man was, and after the way he was treated – no matter what his attitude – they deserve the position they are in right now: as I write this, placed firmly at the bottom of the Premiership and looking doomed.

Greatness does not come along too often, no matter in what shape or form, and Clough brought – not bought, like today's nearly men who couldn't even put a deposit down on the European Cup – Forest the kind of success that only a man with his uncanny ability could. I doubt whether it will ever be seen again at places like the City Ground. It would be easy for me to talk about 'Old Big Head' in the same way he spoke of me, for I, like so many, have heard stories that should not be told. That is why I write about him in the right context: greatness!

My days at Stoke were numbered after the roof blew off the stand before a Cup tie against Tottenham – and they were not insured, nothing had changed! The whole situation, like all good relationships, was slowly coming to an end. Most of the problems came from one or other of the directors. One, in particular, was a man who was so powerful in the Stoke-on-Trent area that he once said to Tony that if we were struggling, 'I'd play in goal.' This was why Tony was forced into buying Peter Shilton, because 'The Big Bear' was a goalkeeping guru. If he thought that Elvis – and I don't mean Frank Worthington – was still alive he would have told our boss to sign him, if only he played in goal.

Alex Humphries – his son is now his mouthpiece there – was the man behind the club's downfall. When you talk about someone being egotistical, call in to see him and get a lesson. He was behind the firing of the Waddingtons, Hudsons and Greenhoffs of Stoke City's world, and then sailed the ocean waves on his yacht boasting that he bought Matthews. This particular man, with his supermarket chain, would not know the difference between Stanley and Jessie. I remember getting off the team bus one evening at Goodison Park and witnessing one of the most embarrassing and bizarre sights of my life, as our kids carried the kit off the bus in his supermarket 'hand baskets'. This in front of a crowded audience who must have thought it was an edition of *Beadle's About* or Noel's 'Gotcha'. We then had to enter the dressing-room and take our kit out of his baskets. That was not really an incentive to play for the club any more, and it gave me the first real notion that I would not be there much longer. Humphries was in the same class as our very own Ken Bates and Alan Sugar, always putting the people who really cared about the club second. Another nail in my coffin in this town that I had really come to love, mainly through the likes of my boss and his friendship with Mr George Byatt. Oh, what sweet times we had! Then there was the Stoke Conservative Club and the Richmond Club, which many Londoners would visit and could not wait to return to, with Brian Shenton, one of my first friends there and still so today, doing the FA Cup draw out of the ice bucket with Jackie Marsh. Better than we have ever seen it done on the pathetic BBC by the goons at Lancaster Gate, the people who have done so much damage to our game through knowing so little, yet having so much power!

The best thing about my stay at the Victoria Ground was that, while I was proving all my critics wrong, I actually, after six years in and out of the squad, got my first England cap. It seemed such a long time ago that I was being hailed by Ramsey and picked for the Mexico World Cup, yet here I was, still uncapped. My selection came at a time when Tony Waddington went public, saying, 'Alan Hudson will get picked for the World XI before he does for his country,' such was my form at the time. I was selected in Don Revie's squad for the match against the world champions, West Germany, a team who had not been beaten since winning that tournament. This was to become the best week of football in my life. It began at the Victoria Ground, where we beat Manchester City 4–0 and I gave a performance that hit all the headlines, with television highlights showing me scoring a great goal and setting up two others. A gentle knock to the England manager. To this day, I do not think that mattered, for I believe he would have picked me anyway for England's toughest match since he took over the reins, but for all the wrong reasons: to fail. He had had plenty of opportunities to play me beforehand, but chose one that I'm convinced he thought I could not live up to, so that I would fall flat on my face. Sorry, Don! Then he could leave me out and continue to pick the likes of Trevor Cherry who served him so well at Leeds United.

Revie did not like Chelsea players, or those who were ex-Chelsea, and I was no exception. I had a couple of falling-outs with him, including one when I was an over-age player in an Under-23 match in Hungary and he tore off a strip of both Jimmy Greenhoff and me for not coming down for lunch one day before the match. Jimmy and I were in our room when Revie's right-hand man and spy, Les Cocker, called.

'Get yourselves down here. "The Don" is not very happy with the pair of you.'

Yes, it sounded like 'The Don' really believed he was that famous one played by Marlon Brando. We reached the bottom of the lift, and Revie was there to give us the third-degree, why we must sit and eat with the rest of the squad. There was no point in arguing with a man like this, because once he had made up his mind that 'if you did not play for Leeds, you did not know the rules', that was your lot. I was picked for the Germany match and never wished good luck by the man in charge; but that only helped me to prepare for the biggest match of my life with more determination than ever before. If I had not been up to the test, or played badly, I would have been cast off and labelled as not being up to international football by Revie, and all the buzzards who had been waiting to swoop. Even to this day I know it would have stuck, but instead, the question most asked of me is, 'Why did you only get one more cap after such an incredible debut?' I was playing against West Germany and Leeds United rolled into one. How many people could have made their England debut under such circumstances? Oh, how sweet success can be! Not only did I put one over on the Germans, but Revie as well. Two birds with one stone, so to speak, and not the ones Besty speaks of.

As I left the England dressing-room on that memorable night, my first sight was of one of my all-time heroes, the great Franz Beckenbauer. We had left our dressing-room to Revie's final briefing on the Germans, which was, 'Remember what they did to our homes in the war.' For a moment I thought my good old pal Stan Boardman had crept in, but I looked back and, sure enough, the words were coming from 'The Don'. I knew that I had to take my chance in this match because it was more than likely to be my last, so I had absolutely nothing to lose. That night we had two other newcomers in the side, and luckily for me they were at full-back. Both Ian Gillard and Steve Whitworth were very useful players, and this was my opportunity to get the ball early, and plenty of it. I said to them, just as Baxter said to Eddie Mac, 'Just get it into me, and I'll do the rest.' It worked a treat, and the three of us all enjoyed terrific England debuts. We have a lot to thank each other for on that brilliant night in March 1975. I know it was March, for the simple reason that I fell asleep in my hotel room watching the Cheltenham Festival in the afternoon. That was when I woke up and found that my room-mate Gerry Francis had gone home. Not even a 'Good Luck' note!

The match itself could not have gone any better for me. Like Cheltenham, I had my favourite ground, soft (that uphill finish in the heavy would have suited me fine), and this time we did not need the fire brigade. It lashed down all day and all night, which was just the way I liked it. A lovely cushion for an ankle that was truly appreciative. The plaudits came in afterwards, like on so many Alan Hudson debuts, from Beckenbauer, the one and only Gunter Netzer and Helmut Schoen himself: 'England finally have a world-class player,' was the main one. We were quickly running out of those, although I sometimes wonder how many we ever had. Maybe Gordon Banks, Bobby Moore and Alan Ball were the three whom I could really put in that category. The obvious one would be Bobby Charlton, but my illusions were shattered after my first two matches against him. Alan Ball, on the other hand, was the opposite: he grew in my estimation after I played against him, the best one-touch player I've ever come across anywhere in the world. In Bobby's defence, he was a spent force by then and I should not judge him on his last season when he finished up a grumpy old has-been. I could see why he and George Best never hit it off. (Then again, who did hit it off with him? Not even his brother, I am led to believe.) I suppose it was a little like me playing against Bryan Robson in my last season, when my legs were gone. It was at Old Trafford, and I knew that it was time to call it a day, but at least I did not go around moaning for the entire ninety minutes. Robbo was a player whom I admired immensely, and would have been a revelation in the high-flying sixties and seventies with his great ability to play with the best and socialise with the élite. Certainly England's last class act and true hero.

My first ninety minutes for my country were over, and had been well worth the wait. I could not wait to get up to the Long Bar, where I had first gone with Mooro some six years ago, to throw my mud-splattered shirt at my old man. I would not have swapped this one even for the Kaiser's. Recalling those words before we left the dressing-room – 'Remember what these bastards did to your families in the war' – well, I didn't. I just saw this as an opportunity to show the English public that I had been overlooked for too long, and to let the 'knockers' know that they were way out of line. The war didn't ever enter my mind when the news came of my selection. Such was the manager's way of motivating his football teams. I often wonder how he motivated his Leeds team before a real 'war', at that Old Trafford Cup Final replay. They, like our players, I know did not need any.

Revie had caught Alan Ball and myself out, or his spies had, on one of his England get-togethers. Ball, Frank Worthington and I would spend our afternoons down the road from our Cockfosters Hotel at friends' homes, having a few 'tasters'. First, it would be a few gin and tonics at Bernie Winters's place; then on to another of Bally's pals', where we would have a little sing-and-dance while the other members of the squad were playing carpet bowls and bingo. On another occasion, the little fella and I went out for the evening the night before a match against Czechoslovakia. Bally was one of Revie's subs, while I was not needed once again. Alan said, 'Come on, Al, I'll take you down my local,' which was the White Hart in Southgate. We left the hotel on foot to the nearest pub and called a cab. Bally gave the cab-driver the fare and fifty quid on top for starters, just to take us anywhere we wanted to go. We left the White Hart at around 11.30pm and headed for our beloved La Val Bonne in Kingly Street. On returning to the pub at about 2.30am we were now into the swing of things, joking about if Bally was brought on in the first minute. We arrived back at the hotel at about 4am and dived through the back entrance. Nothing was ever said until the next squad got together. As soon as both Bally and I had arrived, we were summoned into the lounge. Revie did not pull any punches.

'I have been informed that on the last meeting here, you two were out all night clubbing it in the West End. Is this true or not?'

For the first time ever, I did not know what to say, because I did not want to drop Bally in it. So I just sat and waited for Alan to answer; whether 'yes' or 'no', I would happily go along with it. The silence of the pause seemed like an eternity before Bally said, 'Absolute rubbish, Don.' That was all that was said, apart from when we asked where on earth he had got such an incredible story. 'A cab driver phoned me to tell me,' was his reply. That's nice, we agreed, maybe the 'nifty' wasn't enough!

My second and last cap under Revie was in a European Championship match against Cyprus, which was something of a panto. I was being followed, man-marked, by one of my greatest fans, a waiter from Fulham. He told me this after about twenty minutes, when there was a stoppage for an injury. I realised he spoke like a Londoner, and asked him why he was following me around when he should really be enjoying the occasion and trying to get the ball for himself. His answer was obvious, and so I had to contend with this for the entire match. It wasn't like the usual marking job though, where you could run your man off by taking him deep into your half and then deep into his, because there was no space in his. It seemed as if the whole stadium was parked inside the Cyprus half. Apart from Malcolm Macdonald scoring all five goals, this was a fiasco. Supermac told me how after he'd scored his fifth, Kevin Keegan rushed into the net to get the ball out and said to lay one on for him. Now we know Malcolm, and we know that once in that box he has tunnel vision, but I was surprised to hear how the ex-Newcastle manager asked him to share the glory. I can't imagine Shearer saying that to Ferdinand, can you?

This was to be my last ever international, at the age of twenty-four. As for why, I can only say it was a combination of several things. My sensational debut, which really hurt Revie and rebounded on him; our trip into town; our mishap in Hungary; our afternoons missing from bingo and carpet bowls; and Chelsea knocking the hell out of his beloved Leeds United in the Cup Final. On top of that, I had played a great part in one of the most dramatic matches ever seen at Stoke City, some say the best ever seen there. It was the day Revie's team arrived having gone thirty-odd matches unbeaten from the start of the season to equal the all-time record. They needed to stay unbeaten that day to break it, and it turned out to be an afternoon to remember. A packed house had just settled in to their seats when Leeds went one in front with a goal from Peter Lorimer. This was followed by a bizarre goal from their brilliant skipper Billy Bremner, who cheekily put a free-kick down and chipped our keeper John Farmer before Paul Daniels could have got his pack out of his pocket. Only a player of Bremner's vision could have done such a thing. This caused pandemonium, as the referee let the goal stand. Two-nil up, and the record safely in their hands – or so they thought. Little did they know that we had our very own fighting spirit in the Potteries, and it was time to use it. We were now incensed, and they were trying to put on that great show of keep-ball and take the proverbial at the same time.

After about half an hour, I came up with our first goal, which put us right back into a match they had thought was 'in the bag'. A right-footer into David Harvey's right-hand corner, and the scene was set for one of the all-time great comebacks. Just before half-time, we were awarded a free-kick just outside their box. I remember thinking how the stadium was buzzing as I picked up the ball and had a look at the situation. Their wall was being organized, with Hunter, Bremner, Giles, Lorimer and Gray, I think it was. Not a bad line-up here, I thought to myself, and my mind flashed back to the wall Chelsea set up in that 1967 semi-final at Villa Park, when Peter Lorimer hit one of the hardest free-kicks I've ever seen past Peter Bonetti, only for it to be disallowed. That was in the final minute, and if it had not been Leeds I could have felt sorry for them. As I was weighing this up, our left-back Micky Pejic came storming up and grabbed my arm. 'Let me give it a go,' was his way of telling me that he would not take no for an answer. How pleased I was that he felt that way, for he truly lashed a left-footed shot out of the reach of the Scottish international keeper once again. This really was now, Game on!

The second half started like a real Cup-tie, with a little bit more added to it. This was truly the best of English football, with two teams fully committed to victory. The 'big boys' who had thought they had it won and now had to win it again, and the 'underdogs' who had come back from two down against the best team in the land and were now sniffing the blood of victory. Our half-time team talk was one of 'let's finish the job' and get at them, while theirs must have been one of 'what the hell went wrong?' Their plans were being torn apart by a team who, fully wound-up, could compete with any team, anywhere. They had their players in Giles,

Bremner, Gray and Lorimer; and we had ours: Greenhoff, Mahoney, Salmons and yours truly. They had their kickers in Hunter, Charlton, Reaney and Giles once more; and we had ours in the shape of Smith, Bloor, Marsh and Pejic. So this would never be a one-sided affair, whichever way they wanted to play it.

That second half was nothing short of thunderous, with both sides flat-out at each other's throats. Like any other game against Leeds, there was no love lost and no quarter given. We now had the advantage for two reasons: we did not want them to break that record, and having come from behind we had the bit between our teeth. They had tried it on in the first half, the way only Leeds could do, but now it was our turn. The atmosphere at the Victoria Ground that day was electric, and the whole country was by now getting the news that this game was becoming a classic. They had seen the score go 0–1, 0–2, 1–2 and now 2–2. I knew deep down, leaving the tunnel for the second half, that it was going to be us who would stop Revie's team from breaking that record. For me, it was going to be a little like the Cup Final replay where they had led Chelsea on three occasions but, once pegged back, did not like it.

They were not liking this too much either, as Mahoney, Salmons and Hudson were now the masters in the middle of the field instead of Giles, Bremner and Gray. We had taken the initiative, and it was soon to pay dividends. A right-wing corner was swung in by Geoff Salmons's sweet left foot to find the head of Geoff Hurst, who in turn headed it across the face of the Boothen End goalmouth where, diving in between all those flying Leeds boots, was the figure of our very own 'Captain Marvel', Denis Smith: 3-2. The whole ground erupted, as the Leeds bench jumped up with fists flying everywhere. Jimmy Robertson was now showing the Leeds defenders a clean pair of heels, and also his fiery Scottish temperament. He and 'Wee Billy' were about to have it out in the tunnel at the final whistle. Jack Charlton was to smash our visitors' dressing-room windows in, but that was not the only thing smashed on that wonderful afternoon of pulsating football. We had given the best team in the country a two-goal start then a right pasting, a day that started as a nightmare and finished jubilantly. Not only the victory but the way it was achieved is what I always take great satisfaction in, and there could be no greater satisfaction than when putting one over on Don Revie and his not-so-merry men.

This was the last time I had come face-to-face with Revie before he left his beloved club to take the national job. Not really a happy memory for him. He later went on to abscond from the country and coach abroad, and has now left us. His Leeds players still speak of him as the 'Messiah', as I found out just recently on the TV show *There's Only One Brian Moore*. Allan 'Sniffer' Clarke was on the programme with me, and tried to dedicate the entire hour to Don Revie and Leeds United. Needless to say, I just sat taking the 'hit and miss', as he deserved. The old Leeds school really do believe they had a divine right to dominate. But the Old Trafford replay and that 3–2 blockbuster at the Victoria Ground were just two reminders that we others had our say in what they were going to win and what they were not!

My time at Stoke City ended in sorrow and left my boss in tears at the entrance of our ground, something I could never ever imagine happening. The final straw came when I received a tax bill for about five grand which I never had. This was money that we were supposed to have earned at Chelsea in our Cup-winning days. I called Tony straight away, explained the situation and asked if he could sort me out a new extended contract and have the club pay the bill for me. The answer was, 'Alan, we are absolutely skint,' thanks to the roof falling off and all. Can you imagine, when I read of £42,000 a week in today's game and all the money available, how I feel? We were getting that amount over three years, not one week. However, no sour grapes from this quarter – just saying how and why players moved in those days under such crazy circumstances. Today they move for more millions; we moved to survive! Stoke City holds my greatest football memories because of the sheer pleasure and delight it was to come off the field, having performed to the best of your ability, knowing that it was appreciated by a manager who in my eyes was as good as you'll ever get – and I've had a few, and top ones at that. Waddington was the master; just ask Sir Stanley!

My *Sporting Life* form at Stoke City would read as follows:
Quickly away into stride, Consistent performer, Some exceptional performances including international debut against World Champions, Hampered by broken leg, Never recovered, Needs more give, Moved on to new yard, Arsenal for £200,000.

16

Highbury Fields Forever

'I wander into town/Just like a sacred cow, visions of swastikas in my head, plans for everyone.' 'China Girl', David Bowie.

'The best thing about the future is that it comes just one day at a time.' Abraham Lincoln.

It seemed I was destined to get back down to the Smoke, but Arsenal was never in my mind until Jimmy Robertson called me, early one Saturday evening, after he had just played in a match down at Ipswich. I was out with a stomach injury. Jimmy said he had been talking to the Arsenal manager after the match, and was asked if I was available. The following evening, both Terry Neill and Ken Friar were sitting in my front-room in Barlaston. (One of the great things about writing your memoirs is that it reminds you of the 'coincidentals' – in this case, Stoke were playing at Ipswich on the day I was to leave, just as they had played there the day I signed. Just a little something you could take massive odds on with your local bookie.)

From my first day at Arsenal to my last, it was like the opposite

191

of your greatest dream. Don't get me wrong, I loved every minute of it; but things just continually went the opposite way of my time at Stoke. I arrived with the injury, and it seemed that everybody thought I was 'at it'. Pictures taken at the time had me wearing a Mexican cardigan, the type sported by Starsky and Hutch – as opposed to Ossie and Hutch – who were all the rage then, with their red-and-white sports car and Huggy Bear (no, not David Webb). My relationship with the manager is now laughed at by both of us. I go regularly to Terry Neill's Sports Bar in Holborn, where now we can actually both agree that our run-ins were very humorous. I just see it as if through a kind of misty screen, something that was not really happening, but actually *was* happening so very quickly.

My strength has always been having the ability to set my sights and go for it, whether it is a cross-country run or a three-day binge (which are very similar, actually). What one must remember is that the game of football then was just that, 'a game', whereas now it is totally and strictly business. If our careers had spanned our entire lives we still would not have paid off the mortgage. By the time we had paid the bills and had a couple of nights out – or in my case, three or four – we were 'brasic' the following Friday. The reason I mention this is because it perhaps explains why we could not take the whole thing so seriously. Just look at the fine given by Bryan Robson to his Brazilian signing Emerson, of £96,000. That works out at six years' wages in my playing days at Highbury. Forget trying to work it out in real terms, but a good bottle of wine then was still only about a fiver different from what you pay today; and remember, we were playing in front of fifty thousand every week where he plays in front of about thirty on Teesside. When I say about taking the game seriously, I do mean that in a sense today it really does not compare. If you screwed up then, you might get left out or transferred. If you mess up today, it could cost you the chance of becoming a millionaire overnight. Quite a difference, wouldn't you say?

I recall being told that when Dean Saunders left Derby County he and Mark Wright were summoned into the office of the club secretary, Mr Stuart Webb, and told that they must go. Strictly financial. Because of this situation, Webby asked the Welsh international if he had any preference as to which club he wanted to talk to. To which Dean replied, 'Any club that will put a million pounds into my bank account before I set foot outside the Baseball Ground. He added that Liverpool were his preference, though. Two other clubs agreed to this, along with Liverpool, and the rest is history. What I did find, though, was that after that Saunders was never quite the same player again. Before he became one of the 'football millionaires', he had to earn his money by 'busting a gut' to get on the end of passes. This is one of the reasons why the game is poorer for the big money in it. Deano used to turn bad balls into good balls with his enthusiasm to 'get there'. Now he doesn't need to, because he already has!

My first match at Highbury was against Chelsea in front of just 1,644 fans on a rainy Wednesday afternoon. A reserve match was not the way I had planned to mark my return to the Smoke, especially at a club where I was so determined to succeed. I teed up the winner for Wilfie Rostron after giving a performance that the manager was delighted with. So were the rest of the lads there to watch, for by now they must have thought I had come to their club just to lounge around, having only ever seen me on Fred Street's treatment table. My much-vaunted link-up with Alan Ball was now a thing of the past. How I would have loved to wear the Gunners shirt alongside this player! I could have reignited his Highbury career by using my younger legs while he was instrumenting the play, even though that was my job too. Such was my respect for him. Our manager thought that he was burnt out (or that was his excuse), that his powers had diminished, and saw him as merely a peripheral figure in his midfield. Maybe I might just have changed that, but once again another dream was shattered. That midfield would have been the equivalent of the 70s 'Brady Bunch', with Chippy our outlet on the left, dropping his shoulders and rolling defenders as he did so nonchalantly, a little like Charlie Cooke himself but on the opposite side of the pitch. And as we all know, all left-sided players look better players than us right-sided ones, don't they? Take Baxter, John Barnes, a wonderful ball-player, John Robertson, that Nottingham Forest stroller who beat people just for fun, and Everton's Kevin Sheedy, who gave the Scousers and Ireland that wonderful option when things were tight. Sheedy is often talked about as the man behind that very successful side of

Howard Kendall's, and that is because he had that very rare ability, just like the others just mentioned. Left-sided players, class ones that is, come along once in a blue moon, and those mentioned were all particularly special.

Graham Rix played in this Combination match and impressed immediately, so it was no surprise that he went on to be a very good player, although I thought that if he had played alongside Ball and me, he would have been a more complete player. Rixy would try the hard things too much, a little like Chippy, whereas if he had taken a leaf out of Bally's book, he would not have been in the shadow of Brady so much. Rix, like Chippy, as Don Howe explained, did not know when to mix his game up, not knowing the right time to take his man on, or play one-touch or hit the long one. These two players were like the coach stated, 'predictable'. Rixy now is Ruud Gullit's right-hand man at Stamford Bridge, and I sometimes wonder how he coaches players when he still would need coaching himself, especially when he has been responsible for bringing the Chelsea youngsters through under Glenn Hoddle. I am sure I would not let the likes of Graham Rix coach any of my young kids.

I still had to wait for my first-team debut – doesn't this sound stupid? – for several reasons. First, the team were playing exceptionally well, George Armstrong in particular I remember, and secondly my stomach strain was a constant pain, just like my relationship with the manager was to become. My first game was an evening match against Leeds United, usually a fixture I looked forward to, but this time I was struggling for match fitness and practice, and it showed. I was disappointed that my first performance in a red Gunners shirt did not come anywhere near the standards I had set myself, especially for debuts. That evening, my old pal and fellow 'maverick' Tony Currie gave a performance of sheer quality. Not only that, he did it from a position up front. Although TC was one of my all-time favourite players, as far as I was concerned this was not the night to show the Highbury faithful what a truly great player he was. For there were two things I never liked, and that was to be number one, upstaged and number two, outclassed. Tony definitely did both this particular evening, but then again I wasn't the first, and I wasn't fit either.

The last time this had happened to me was in the match at Goodison when Ball himself, along with Harvey and Kendall, chose to use us as a punch-bag, buzzing around playing one-touch for fun while we were 5–0 down with still half an hour left on the clock. Of course, it was later found out that our two centre-halves had been seen arriving back at our Merseyside hotel later than I had got home from the Val Bonne before going on to lick Arsenal. However, I did not have to go out on the field against Joe Royle the next day, and face the 'Big Man' in full cry. David Webb and John Dempsey were captured by one of Dave Sexton's spies, who sat at the hotel entrance, and that was just another nail in the coffin for the 'social team'. I don't know what Dave would have done had we got a result, but he disciplined Dempsey by immediately putting him in the reserves for a couple of matches. I cannot remember what happened to Webby ... but then again, there was only Eddie and Webby that Dave could talk to.

My most treasured memory of my days at Highbury is that fantastic trip to Singapore and Australia, which ended with my pal Terry sending both me and Malcolm 'Super' Macdonald home, from a tour which should have been, as I said, a dream! It was here that I had the pleasure of spending time with another all-time favourite of mine, Mr Jock Stein, and of playing for the first time against one of the finest players of our day, the great Bogicevic, the Yugoslav who could run a game just the way 'Slim Jim' Baxter would. I had seen him play about five years earlier for Red Star Belgrade and never forgot him. This was while I was touring Tehran, or somewhere like that, and I went along to see a match with this 6ft 2in giant of an inside-forward or left-half, or whatever you want to call them today. Oh, how I hate the new names for players, especially hearing Trevor Brooking going on about 'wing-backs'. Bogicevic and I were to pit our wits against each other several times later on, in New York, Seattle and California.

Malcolm, Georgie Armstrong and I seemed to be the target of our boss on this trip, and it turned out that two of us had to go. We were like the Marx Brothers, and Terry could not control or break the three of us, however hard he tried – even to the extent of, one morning after we broke a curfew, subjecting us to a running session which would have broken Daley Thompson. However, wee Geordie and I saw this coming and, in the ninety-degree heat of Singapore, broke his back as he attempted to run us into the

ground. I remember whispering to George on our last lap that we
would keep going when the others had stopped. Well, they fell to
the ground clutching the nearest bottle of mineral water, or any
other drink they could lay their hands on, while we set off on
another lap, like a lap of honour. This did not go down well with
the boss. Armstrong was a superb athlete, which Terry knew, but
that day he also realised that a fit Alan Hudson could not be broken.
It always gave me great pleasure to enjoy the good things in life, and
there was and still is no better life than playing football for a living.
Being able to go out training every morning, working to improve
your skills while everybody else is in their office; travelling the
world while keeping fit; and, the icing on the cake, waking on a
Saturday morning knowing you will be playing in front of fifty-odd
thousand people. The reward was far more than money: it was
coming off the field after a performance, something that no money
could buy! But remembering our old chums, the sixteenth-century
swordsmen, it was all about, 'Whatever state of mind you are in,
ignore it, think only of the cut.'

OK, at times it seemed we were out of line, but we actually could
burn the candle at both ends, especially on such a marvellous tour.
Was Terry Neill such an angel while playing for this same club?
Not to mention the likes of George Graham in his playing days.
Why is it that when they go on the 'other side', they spend more
time chasing around for players who, deep down, really could be
their saviours. It got to the stage where Terry was paranoid about
the 'Likely Lads', and I sometimes had to check under the beds and
behind the curtains to see if he was about – yes, Beadle again. After
a couple of laughable instances one when we were left behind at the
stadium after a Celtic Red Star match, plus the one of the running
session, I was then given a telling-off by my boss for taking Jock
Stein up to the first-class lounge on our flight from Singapore to
Sydney. He said I had been up there already so to go back down, to
which I replied, 'Terry, do you know I'm with one of the greatest
managers of all time?' It was funny because the great man himself
had asked me to take him up there, for we were now getting on
famously after our daily visits to the swimming pool, where we
would sit and listen to the 'Big Man'. Uncannily, he reminded me
so much of Mr Waddington. Jock could not understand the

relationship between the manager and myself, and asked me why he always seemed to be hunting for me. I think he was right – I felt hunted, and what made it even worse was that I could not understand the reason why!

In Sydney, we lodged at the famous Rushcutter's Bay Hotel, a place which is frequented by visiting cricket teams, and one where Ian Botham and his playmates have enjoyed plenty of good times. Strange, isn't it, how all great players have such a good time! I have some wonderful memories of Sydney, and in particular of the Boon family, who are big football fans. They took Malcolm, Geordie and myself into their homes, and showed us all the best spots in this most wonderful city. I was to become very friendly with the youngest Boon of them all, Johnny, and hope that this book reaches him there to send my sincere thanks once again. Such is the wonderment of our great game and the opportunity to play it: we would not be able to visit such fantastic parts of the world had it not been for our ability to play this most marvellous sport, as it was then, yes sport. What perks!

By the time we reached Melbourne it had become one hell of a fiasco, with every player commenting on who they thought would crack first. There was no way it would be us, because we were having a ball, and if you cannot go away on tour and really 'let it go' after a long hard English season, when could you? We were not exactly up to the tricks of the Euro 96 boys coming home from the Far East, were we? Well, the inevitable happened when we reached our hotel at about four in the morning to find that it was the closest thing to Fawlty Towers that you'd ever come across. Malcolm and I got to our room and I opened the door to find two beds, one of which I threw my bag on as the other was made up ready for Ronnie Corbett. I know Malcolm was bandy, but this was ridiculous. I turned straight to him and said that I thought the manager was really taking the 'ultimate' out of the one and only 'Supermac'. Before the door had closed, Malcolm was steaming down the corridor looking for Terry. As I unpacked, he returned, shaking, because he could not find him. All he found was someone who got us a room with beds capable of sleeping two adults. If Malcolm had found Mr Neill, I think we would have got an even earlier flight home, but that was still to come.

That afternoon it was showdown time as we walked into the dining-room. With everybody sitting around, looking as if we had just been around the world three times and without sleep, Terry announced that there would be a training session. I turned to Malcolm and said, 'Not me, mate' – saying it long before Harry Enfield did – explaining that he was really taking it out of us now, and that I was going to take a couple of sleeping tablets and catch up on some much needed shut-eye. We ordered two gin and tonics and four sleepers – two each, off Fred Street – and planned the rest of the day. My theory was always that players need rest at the right times, and this was one of those times. We had played matches in Singapore, and well, and been run off our feet in training; all this after a long, hard English League programme. Brian Clough won the European Cup by training three days a week at Forest. Here we were being treated like a bunch of entrants for the next Olympics. After such a horrendous last day and a half, we should sleep through the afternoon, get up, have some dinner and have a few nightcaps before retiring, was my train of thought. I knew it would not turn out this way; nothing was ever simple with Terry. Our drinks arrived, and before you could say 'Terry Neill', there he was, standing between us, offering us a swift return back to London. Well, I must admit it was a bit rash, but everything that seemed to be happening was no surprise, and whatever happened next was certainly not out of Cilla Black's show. So we were now the devils who were 'carrying the can' for all that had gone on, and believe me I could tell stories about what went on in Singapore (which did not involve us 'Three Musketeers') that would make this book a best-seller – only on a different shelf, not the sports one!

Later that afternoon, Geordie came to our room fuming, telling us that he had been to see Terry and pleaded with him to send him home as well, explaining that everything that we had done while away, he had done too. But the manager was too shrewd for this one. He knew that the folks back home would question the sending-home of one of Arsenal's most popular players of all time. Hudson and Macdonald, though, were hung, drawn and quartered without a fair trial, in fact none at all. We had been successfully hunted. I have toyed with the idea of not telling this story because of the stir it could cause, but after some deliberation and careful thought, I feel it is something that should not be swept under the carpet like so many other things at Highbury over the years. The situation 'down under' got very heated, there were many skeletons coming out of the Marble Hall cupboard, and one, in particular, some friends of ours did not take kindly to. Of course there were people who wanted to see the back of our Arsenal boss – 'Whacked Out', as Jimmy Smitts says in *NYPD Blue*.

Let's put it this way; perhaps the tour had been badly botched and mismanaged. I will give you another analogy. In the 1960s, Brian Jones of the Stones was hounded for drugs, and the public would say, 'Oh yeah, him again.' But if Bill Wyman or Charlie Watts had received the same attention, would there have been the same reaction? The powers that be always have to be seen to be doing their jobs. Thus the bigger the target, the more the publicity, and the more they felt they could justify it with such drastic action. Run that, if you like, Keith Richard to Eric Cantona. I always thought that people were sent to Australia years ago, and here we were getting a plane ticket the other way! Recently, while playing in a charity match – oh! I guess you don't get to read about all the charity matches we 'mavericks' give up our spare time for, to help raise money for sick children, the homeless and the needy – at Millwall, I was approached, in front of several famous people including my good pal Frank Maloney, by a chap who was a passenger on that infamous flight home. He thanked me, not only for the pleasure I had given him whilst playing the game, but also for the entertainment value both Malcolm and I had added to the in-flight attractions, adding that we mavericks must have some wonderful memories if this trip was anything to go by. He sure was right!

Back to Jimmy Smitts! On that trip, we were having cocktails with some friends when they were told some of the stories from the Arsenal camp. We had just eaten a dinner in their palatial home which would have fed a whole wing of Wormwood Scrubs. Malcolm asked where one of their associates was – he had been a frequent visitor to one of the Arsenal team's watering-holes, but had not been seen for a while. 'He is on tour with the National,' was the reply. I later found out that this was a colloquialism for an inmate being moved around the prison system. One particular family member was getting rather agitated, listening to the three of us going on about being hunted and many other quite remarkable stories. The lights seemed to dim in the living-room, and an eerie feeling came over the whole conversation as a voice said, just like when, in *Godfather II*, Al Pacino was gnawing on a satsuma and planning a hit on a key witness – 'Do you want your manager to leave this country? Just give me the nod.'

In complete silence, the three of us looked at each other, not knowing whether to laugh, nod or even move a muscle. In just about a couple of minutes, which seemed like an eternity, we all realised that this fella meant it. 'If history has taught us one thing,' Pacino said, 'then it is you can kill anyone.' This scene went whizzing through my head. I had never imagined that I could or would ever be in such a situation, which you thought only happened on the silver screen of Hollywood. We looked at each other in horror, as Malcolm and I sipped our gin and tonics and Geordie his beer. Bill Shankly's most famous quote about football being more important than life and death now took a completely different meaning. The 'hit' was never mentioned again, and as I said, Terry now runs his very successful wine bar in Holborn. There are many times, while standing drinking with him, that I have a little smile to myself, knowing that he never had an inkling about this conversation. I often wonder what would have happened if one of the three of us, or even all of us, had nodded instead of shaking our heads so very slowly. Maybe I would have finished my career at Highbury after all, or even been the host of a watering-hole by Holborn Viaduct. You must remember that these were the good old days when there was hardly any money about. Nowadays, with the multi-million-pound contracts and underhand dealings, I could see the picture a little more realistically. Imagine, with the kind of money flying around today, if someone cut your career short. It could cost a player millions – and a heavy comes along saying, give me ten per cent of whatever and consider the job done. As they say in *The Godfather*, 'Now this is different, it's BUSINESS.'

The following weekend, on our return to England, George came around to my home, and we told our wives this unbelievable story. Malcolm and I would tell people on a Thursday afternoon in the Town House before our Cup matches, knowing it would be OK because nobody would believe such an incredible tale.

In Terry Neill's book – what do you mean, you haven't read it! –

he explains that he gained entry into our room, found both Malcolm and I unfit to train, and told us to pack our bags for London. Actually, my total recall – and as you must have gathered by now, I have a wonderful memory – of this particular incident was that it was George Armstrong who came to the room and not Terry at all. As for being in no fit state to train, he was absolutely correct, and that went for the rest of the lads as well. Having played sixty-odd matches back home, travelled halfway round the world and found ourselves playing and training in mid June, who on earth would have been? Ken Friar waves us goodbye with that wry smile that only he has when he knows the score, knowing that Highbury secret: to cover it up. Well, the days of the players carrying the can at this great club have gone. They have been the ones, for a change, who have got some credit, and deservedly so, for carrying both directors and management so well in these latest times of lunacy. With Terry Neill, George Graham and Bruce Rioch and now the dirt starting to be dished on new man Arsene Wenger, they are now, I'm pleased to say, 'The Hunted'.

Our flight home was one of pure magic and hilarity. The last of the eight-hour legs was one big party in the sky; to this day, the best I've witnessed. We drank on the first leg which took us to where we held a press conference, slept through the second and brought the bubbly out all the way through the flight into Heathrow. We had some elderly ladies coming back from holiday 'rocking and rolling' in the aisles, one of the women toasting the pair of us for being quite the opposite of what our manager had sent us home for. Raising her champers, she said happily, 'You two have been sent home for being naughty boys. You are wonderful, and have finished our trip off in the most fantastic way possible. Cheers!' Such was our ability to mix with the best and the rest. We represented Arsenal in the way that it should be done. Not tearing up seats and smashing TV screens aboard planes, but with the class that reflected the respect we had for the club. It was not our fault that we did not feel the same way about the manager. I can honestly say that in all my time in the game, I have never abused anybody while travelling and representing any of my clubs. In fact, quite the opposite!

I have said in the past that the reason people in the game have to

cause a problem with the likes of myself is as follows: I could go out
and enjoy myself to the full, come in training the next morning, run
them off their feet and do 'extra' while they were showering, then
turn in consistent performances on a Saturday afternoon. The
element of jealousy was obvious. They seemed disturbed that they
never had the ability to do such a thing, for they were all lesser
mortals who talked a good game and hid behind that word 'professionalism'. My recipe is a simple one: 'Work hard, play hard!'

Just recently I have got to know some of the top men in National
Hunt racing, and can only say that they would have fitted in very well
in our world, and we in theirs, for they have the self-same attitude.
People do not see the hard, and in their case dangerous, work put
into the job behind the scenes, only the adulation that goes with
coming into the winners' enclosure at Cheltenham, Newbury, Sand-
own or Ascot after riding such wonderful finishes in those big races.
The likes of Steve Smith-Eccles, Graham Bradley, Graham
McCourt, John Francome and Peter Scudamore, and they have won
enough between them, risk life and limb every time they get out of
their beds each morning, and this gives them all the more reason to
live life to the full and enjoy themselves and the moments that go
with them. To celebrate great times and maybe commiserate at the
not-so-great ones, just like we footballers did. 'The Eck' would have
fitted in quite nicely on our tours, as would 'Brad' and all, for they
would have been all right sleeping in Malcolm's bed in Melbourne –
that would have been no problem at all! While on the subject of sleep,
Brad ended up winning last year's Champion Hurdle because of his
inability to hear the alarm clock. It is one of life's wonderful stories,
and one which turns out right for the 'good guy' for a change. He
failed to get up one morning to 'ride out' on what they all thought to
be the only possible winner, Alderbrook, and was 'jocked off ', only
to show them what a marvellous horseman he is by looking over his
shoulder up the Cheltenham hill to see the red-hot favourite following him home.

'The Eck' was the pilot for my biggest ever win in racing, when
partnering Alone Success in the Triumph Hurdle. I was in Don
Shanks's indoor coaching school, in Tampa Bay, when Don told me
that his pal Smith Eccles really fancied his chances in this
prestigious race. I relayed the message to Mr George Byatt back in

Stoke-on-Trent, and returned home to a handsome pay-out of over five figures. Maybe not quite Jim McGrath, but enough to keep George, Mr Waddington and myself in lunches at the Poacher's Cottage and Federation House for quite some time. Steve went on to win three Champion Hurdles on the great See You Then for Nicky Henderson, and in doing so showed what a remarkable jockey he was. I was also fortunate, whilst writing this, to meet a great pal of his, the great Peter Scudamore, and can see between these brilliant sportsmen so much of the camaraderie that we had in our day. 'Scu' smashed records for fun, and fits in nicely with the great people I have had the pleasure to meet along the way. It is amazing that the greater the personality, the nicer the person. The epitome of this is the cricketer Viv Richards, whom I have met several times through my great pal Chris Garland. I can only say that Viv carries that familiar style and grace throughout his life, and would have been 'Pele' had he made it in the game he loves so much, football.

It was while playing for Arsenal that I was to meet yet another wonderfully famous character. One night, out with my great old pal and Chelsea nut, Alan Phillips and Peter Shepherd, at the time the chauffeur of the mustard man Ben Coleman, I found myself in the company of April Ashley. He, or she, was running her own restaurant in Knightsbridge. It was a candle-lit affair and both Allan and I were sitting in disbelief at the presence of such an attractive woman. I found this first sex-change queen an absolute delight and it was not long before both Alan and I were spellbound. You had to keep reminding yourself just exactly who you were sitting opposite, although it became very difficult after a few glasses of vino. Allan was our Maurice Keston, that Tottenham entrepreneur, who would invite the whole side to his table at the London Hilton at every given opportunity. A wonderful gentleman who is sadly missed by us all. I was very fortunate at the end of his life to become very good friends with this warm and charming man, who would now be enjoying the rebirth of this new Chelsea team, with Zola being the first player since Charlie Cooke to capture the hearts of the fans with his extraordinary dribbling skills, so reminiscent of the 'Prince' himself.

17

Season of the Witch

'To be popular, one must be mediocrity.' Oscar Wilde.

The writer Primo Levi, who saw such terrible things happen at Auschwitz and eventually committed suicide, said that it is not possible to be one hundred per cent happy. Equally, it is not possible to be one hundred per cent unhappy. In my last season at Highbury, I felt that mixture of emotions, for my career at this great and most famous club was winding down like a child's mechanical toy.

I fell in love with the club at the tender age of thirteen, whilst playing for West London Boys against Islington. She was to be an unkind mistress! My first impression, which I was later to take for granted, was the underfloor heating on this terribly cold and wet evening. Under the aegis of my father, we travelled over to North London in the team bus, Tom Tranter and all. I remember the raindrops running down the window, blurring it like an impressionist painting. Such were the dreams we youngsters went through on evenings such as this. My immediate opponent that night was none other than Charlie George, a player who, as you'll have gathered by now, should have been, in fact was, a giant in our game. Probably the most popular player ever to wear the red shirt with the cannon on, just like me Charlie was the 'local boy made good'. And how we did it in style, with him scoring that glorious winner against Liverpool at Wembley to clinch their famous Double, while on the other side of London I was winning the FA Cup and the Cup Winners' Cup, with both of us still in our teens. Charlie assumed an added dimension, gaining those layers of pathos and enigma that the public and press find so becoming.

That night, we were just two schoolboys trying to claw our way out of the environment we found ourselves in. (Strange, this christian name/surname reverse that you also find in pop music with Elton John – we know it's Reggie – and George Michael. The Arsenal forward-line of that season included George Graham and Charlie. Linked together in the programme, it read GEORGE (Charlie) and GRAHAM (George). Was this prophetic or what? Heralding the era of the most successful team ever at Highbury.) Now here I was another thirteen years on and, after the calamity of Australia, looking to be on my way out of this club that kids would give their right arm to play for. However, I returned for the pre-season to give it another go. This was the only club for me, but I was always thinking of what might have been. Meaning, if only Arsenal had the kind of manager I had left behind at Stoke City, or even the Terry Neill I know now!

The season started with Terry pulling the greatest stroke of his time at Highbury – and he pulled a few, believe me – by getting Don Howe to return as first-team coach. This really was his salvation, and a move which saw the team go from the lower depths of the First Division to three consecutive Cup Finals. Don was the master planner, the man who brought discipline and organisation to this very rocky ship – one that was very close to sinking, in fact. He won me over straight away, and I realised that there could still be a future for me at this great club, if only I was left to play instead of being watched as closely by my manager as I was by the opposition. I still found it hard to recapture my Stoke form, the form I had lost since breaking my leg, the kind that would have won over the Highbury crowd in an instant.

The last time I had played well at Highbury was in fact in a

match for Stoke City about a year earlier, one I became famous
for at the club. I really am not one for drinking the night before a
match, but this particular evening was very out of character and, I
say it myself, out of order. My great pal and roomie Geoff Salmons
and I arrived at the Russell Hotel to find our manager, Mr
Waddington, at the Champagne Bar, his first stop on our Friday
night stay in London. I suggested that we had better eat out this
particular evening, and so both Sammy and I, and Eric Skeels, that
great old Stokie, headed for my all-time favourite eaterie,
Alexandres. This was about six-thirty and they did not open till
seven, so we made our way to Camilla's flat which was situated next
to Chelsea Town Hall, at the top of the street where George Best
lives now. After a couple of bottles of Mateus Rosé, we went on to
the Royal Table, which was so often used by the boys in blue –
Chelsea that is, but now those days were behind me. The
atmosphere in this place was something the likes of both Sammy
and Skeelsy had never witnessed before, with all those gay waiters
flying around, flirting with the two new 'good-looking' footballers
amongst them. Needless to say, the service was that little bit extra
special after I told the boys that one of the lads was
'Stoke-on-Trent'. The waiter, in fact, was the outrageous Miquela,
and so we got the full treatment. After leaving there, Eric Skeels,
who was not playing the next day, said that it was ten o'clock and
time to return to the hotel. At the top of the restaurant steps was the
sound of my old pub's music blaring out. Yes, the Markham Arms
was still alive and kicking, and that was where we were heading. By
eleven-thirty, we were hailing a black cab – not the one Dennis
Wise got – and looking to be back within twenty minutes, or so
Skeelsy thought. On our route back to our hotel, we just happened
to pass Kingly Street, the scene of so many England celebrations
and any others you care to think about, and La Val Bonne. The
older and wiser member of this trio decided to take the cab home,
leaving Sam and me to face the music alone. At three-thirty we
staggered back to our room after nearly drinking London dry; you
see, my mate Sammy is a seasoned pro at this drinking game.

I remember this being about the third game of the new season
and, having personally just had two dodgy ones, therefore deciding
to change tactics. The following morning, before our pre-match

lunch, I had to shower my room-mate and get him into some kind of state so that he could face Arsenal. This I was always good at, getting the best out of my room-mates, lecturing them on how we could not let the boss down. Some might say we already had; others so what, the damage was done. At two o'clock, I was outside the Marble Hall sorting my tickets out with my ticket-man, uncle George, when he said to me, 'You smell like a brewery.' I replied that so I should, I'd just drunk one. On giving him the dozen or so tickets for the family – always a big following, the Hudsons – I whispered to my uncle, 'George, don't worry about a thing. I'll beat this lot on my own.' To which he replied, as usual, 'Al, you are a lad. This is Highbury.' Even better I thought, how I love a challenge!

In the dressing-room, Eric Skeels came over and told me that Sammy could not do his boots up, and he had had to do them up for him. This was the time to take him in to the shower area for a briefing. 'Don't worry, just hug the line and I'll cover inside you,' was my advice to my midfield partner. The word had now reached the home dressing-room that half our team had been out on the tiles all night, and this would be a non-event. I recall having the ball for about eighty minutes, or so it seemed, watching a new superstar come on as sub for them in the shape of Liam 'Chippy' Brady, and eventually hitting the winner after a mix-up between Sammy Nelson and Jimmy Greenhoff left me with the opportunity to shrug off Sammy before drilling a shot into Jimmy Rimmer's right-hand corner. It was an amazing performance that I was regularly reminded of in my days there. Our manager came in and said that one or two players looked as if they were not quite fit, and we had better step up our training schedule – but we were only three games into the season! Lifting his head gradually, he glanced at both Sammy and me. He obviously knew, but also realised that it was a one-off and that we could still do the business for him.

I think in my first year at Stoke we were unbeaten in London for about ten matches, also winning at White Hart Lane for the first time in the club's history. Another time before a match in London, after a few drinks on the Friday I found I could not sleep, for the simple reason that I was very excited at coming back to play there. So I took two sleepers at about midnight. At three o'clock I was still wide-awake playing the game through my mind and took two more, and at six-thirty took my tally to six. By mid-day at the lunch table, I looked as if I had just reprised the previous visit to London, when in fact it was the opposite. By the time we kicked-off at Loftus Road, I'd had two showers and several coffees to keep me awake. The match had been going for about a quarter of an hour when Rangers got a corner on the left at their famous end, where I used to stand through all those great League Cup ties of the late sixties. I was positioned on the near post and Shilton was bouncing about behind me. The next thing I knew, I was being woken up by the roar of the crowd behind the goal as the ball whizzed across our six-yard box. I had finally dropped off!

My best performance in an Arsenal shirt was against Manchester City in a League Cup replay at Highbury, albeit only forty-five minutes. Pat Jennings had put in one of his superlative displays up at Maine Road to bring them back to our place. I was at home that night watching the great man perform the kind of miracles that only he could. I knew I was in good form, although the boss was not picking me now. I had been injured, but had regained my confidence thanks to getting over my stomach injury and being able to train somewhere near my best. This evening I was substitute, and we were being run ragged by the midfield play of Asa Hartford and front-running of Mick Channon. All I could do was sit and listen to Don Howe telling Terry Neill to make a change.

'We are getting murdered in the middle of the field,' he kept echoing, constantly nudging the boss. After about twenty-five minutes Terry said he would give it another five, to which Don replied, 'Could be too late. Do it now.' Five minutes went by, and he turned to me and pointed a finger.

'You're going on.'

I'm not, was my instant reply, my feet are freezing (missing out a word). I turned to Tony Donnelly, our kit man, and said, 'Come on, Tony, come with me.' We walked up the tunnel and into the dressing-room, with the roar of the crowd behind us.

'Polish them up, mate. I'm getting warmed-up, and then I'm gonna come on and win you the game, pal.'

Tony just gave me that little smile of his and shook his head. Two minutes later, the dressing-room door flew open and the lads all came in and sat down as if the game was all over and out of our reach. I just looked at 'Big Pat' and winked. He winked back, as if he knew.

'Huddy, you're on. John, you're off.' (Matthews, that is.)

I was ready for this, thinking to myself: I will just take complete control of the whole situation. We were performing like a team who had never played together before, and had nobody in the middle to grab hold of the game by the scruff of the neck. This was my game, and my big chance to show how it was done. The perfect stage, after seeing the first forty-five minutes of sheer torture. We would now turn it around.

I came on, and from the word go got the ball from every part of the field. Off the full-backs, centre-backs and front men, bringing all the players into the game where they had been starved in the first forty-five minutes. Steve Williams and Asa Hartford were now like I was in the first half, spectators. I nearly crowned a great second-half performance with a great goal, but the shot curled just inches wide of 'Big Joe' Corrigan's far post, after a couple of one-twos with our front men. We won the match with a penalty from 'Chippy' and went through to the next round. The following day, the headline on the back of the *Evening Standard* was 'Masterstroke by Arsenal Boss'. The following Saturday, I was back on the bench for the trip to Leicester. So much for your performance on Wednesday, I thought, but this only told me that nothing had changed. It was Singapore and Australia all over again, nothing new!

Don Howe was the key to Arsenal's sudden change, as I said before. He was responsible for getting the very best out of Liam Brady, because before Don arrived, 'Chippy' was allowed to get away with anything he wanted – on the field, that is – and therefore would not be told. He thought all you had to do was get the ball and dribble. Don wasn't having it, and rightly so. After a match at Villa Park in the early part of the Cup Final season of 1977-78, Don tried to explain to Brady that he should study Stanley Matthews and realise that you have to mix your game up, by trying to outfox your opponent and make the game easier for yourself. 'Chippy' would not have it, and told our coach that he was living in the past. I don't think so! Don told of how Matthews would lay the ball off first-time whenever the full-back closed in, and play 'cat and mouse' with him until he gave him that little extra space to turn and face him. The rest, as we say, was history! He tried to make the point to Brady that he was far too predictable to become the truly great player his magnificent ability deserved, but Chippy would not listen until a few years later – although funnily enough, I read some years afterwards that he'd said that he learned so much from his time playing alongside me. If I helped Liam Brady one little bit to become the player he did, I'm flattered!

Don also had a problem with Malcolm. After one match against Everton, he pulled him up for cheating. 'Supermac' was not a happy man at this, obviously, but Don just went on to explain that while he was gesturing to the crowd behind the goal, every time he lost possession, we were playing with ten men. The centre-half would come across and sweep the ball away, and Malcolm would just keep on running to the touchline, with his hands either on his head or his hips. 'We are now a player short, Malcolm, while you're prancing in front of your beloved fans,' Howe would tell him – and on the following Monday at London Colney, we would go through the routine of hitting balls into the corners for defenders to pick them up, and Malcolm would have to 'spin' quickly and get back into the game. Very simple, and we all knew it, but Don was the one to sort these little problems out, problems he could spot in an instant. He is a master tactician, and if I had played my whole career under him, I would have had more to show for it. He had my utmost respect and co-operation. What a team that would have made at Highbury: Tony Waddington as manager, Don Howe as coach, and Matthew Harding as the 'King of the Castle'. Dreams, oh dreams!

I was to have one falling-out with Howe, and it was a situation I did not like for the very reason that this was the man I respected – and I wanted his in return. It was the week of the Cup Final against Ipswich, and I received a call from Bob Driscoll, who was then working on the *Sun*. He was phoning to wish me good luck for the Saturday, 'if you're playing, that is'. I replied that Don had pulled me aside in the Wembley tunnel that morning and told me that I would be in the team. He said he thought I looked worried about something, and was it about my being selected? I told him it wasn't, because I had come to expect anything at Highbury by now. 'Well, don't worry, you've been our best player recently and you'll definitely be in the side,' were his words. I thanked him for taking time out, and also said how much I appreciated the job he had done since returning.

The next morning, when getting my paper, I was horrified to see that my old pal Bob had dropped me right in it. 'I'm in, says Hudson,' it read. I could have dropped. I had never been worried about facing up to anything, in my days playing, but this was totally different, I was going to face a terrible situation, and one I deserved. On arriving at Highbury, I was quickly dragged into Fred Street's medical room by Terry Neill, who began to give me a dressing-down. Only half-listening, I explained to him that I did not owe him an apology but Don, and that it was a misunderstanding and I was sorry for all the trouble it must have caused. I knocked on Don's door and was confronted by a mean-looking man who was at boiling point – and I could understand why, he felt betrayed. There he was, taking time out for me, and I go and spout off to the newspapers. He could not have been further from the truth, but I was prepared for the worst. Usually I have a magnificent memory, but this conversation, very one-sided, was one that had me dazed. He called me everything possible, and told me that he was finished with me and could not trust me any more. My reply on leaving was that I apologised for my mistake, I was sorry it should end this way, and that I would feel the same way as he did. I had lost his respect, which left me shattered.

That evening, I called my man from the *Sun* and told him of the terrible situation that he had put me in. Driscoll told me how sorry he was, and said he would call Don and explain. 'It's too late for that,' I said, and put down the receiver, feeling totally gutted and let down. I will not take up any space making excuses for our performance in that terrible Final, a match we would have won nine times out of ten, and my second last in an Arsenal shirt. The only consolation was that Don called me to one side in the Wembley dressing-room and said that he thought I was our best player, that Bob Driscoll had called him and cleared the whole thing up, and I was forgiven. If I had left Arsenal without such forgiveness it would have been a terrible blow to me, for the simple reason that I can count on one hand the number of people whom I truly respect and have time for in this game, and the ex-England coach is most certainly one of them.

My final say at Highbury was at our post-mortem on that horrific Wembley defeat, and I did it in style. Don chaired the meeting, and asked for a response from all the players, starting in the corner of the room with 'Big Pat', who as usual was a man of very few words. I was about tenth in line, and Don got to me after about half an hour. I was ready to say my piece. After all, I had been made the scapegoat for almost everything else that had gone on since I arrived, and it really didn't matter much now – the damage had been done.

'I blame him,' I said, pointing my finger over Don's right shoulder and straight at Terry, who looked absolutely dumbfounded, 'for not picking the right team.'

'You're a disgrace, Huddy,' was Terry's response, as usual.

'I know I am,' I said, 'but you picked the wrong team, and Don asked *me* to speak, not you.'

I went on to explain that he should have picked Graham Rix, and had only left him out because he was the youngest. Rixy had done really well in the run-up to the Final, including the semis. I turned to Alan Sunderland and said that it was with no disrespect to him, but Rixy was the man in form and should have played. 'That is my view, and I was asked for it.'

Well, this was it. The hunter had been hunted, and in his own class-room for all to see. I was on my way! At least I can say I played in a Cup Final with this great club. When you think of my idol Johnny Haynes never walking out for such a match, and even George Best, in that golden era at Old Trafford, never getting the opportunity either, you realise what a privilege it was. The closest George got was in that famous season of 1969-70, when we waited for the winners of Manchester United versus Leeds United in the other semi-final. It was finally settled when Billy Bremner got another of his precious winning goals. My final memory of Wembley was just after leaving the dressing-room and entering the tunnel, when I looked on to the team bus and saw my old pal Tony Davis sitting in the front seat, looking as if he had just won the lottery but was too late to collect it. TD was our groupie, according to our skipper Pat Rice, who would shake his head in disbelief before away matches when he found that my man was on the pitch before we were. Even waving to the crowd that day, Ricey just looked over and asked him what studs he should wear. TD finally went over to the bench and told the commissionaire to hold him six seats for the chaps who did not have tickets, all first-team players. (The reason being that Flashman had them all. There was even a story going around that 'Fat Stan' also had the directors' seats for this match in his possession, and that they had to be bought back at a considerable gain for the notorious ticket tout!)

So for a third time, Ken Friar was around as I prepared for another departure. At my home in Barlaston to watch me sign for Arsenal; at the airport 'down under' policing Malcolm and I; and now – they say it happens in threes – at Heathrow airport to get me packed off to Seattle. He did all three jobs brilliantly, smoothly and in a way that makes me always think of him as not only a credit but a saviour – and how many times – to Arsenal Football Club. A genuinely nice man, whom they would be totally lost without.

My *Sporting Life* form at Arsenal would read as follows:
Slowly away due to injury, Fell out with manager, Sent home from tour, Off the rails again, Improved form mid-season, Failed and tired when fell at last.

18

Breakfast in America

One of my all-time favourite groups
were very much hot at the time of my move;
little did I know we'd meet up in Seattle.

So I was accompanied to the airport yet again by Mr Friar only this time on my terms, although he did all the negotiating on my behalf. Ken knew my contract, obviously, and was looking to get the best deal possible for me, which under the circumstances made him a real winner with me. I am not, and never was, the best in these kind of matters, because all I wanted to do was play. I really do not know how I would have coped in today's world of gold pots. Anyway, Ken asked me if I would like him to do the deal and I was delighted to say yes, for it showed that he cared and also meant that Mr Jack Daley, the general manager at Seattle, felt that I was leaving with no bad feelings between club and player. Little did he know!

The deal was struck and I shook Friar's hand, now for the last time, and left the meeting. Mr Daley seemed delighted that he had bought a 27-year-old current international for a mere £100,000, and turned and got back on the very next plane to Seattle before any one had the chance to change their minds. I walked outside and bumped into Don Howe, who was flying in or out with the rest of the lads, and he asked me if it was true. I said it was just no good any more, and that there was too much water under the bridge. His reaction was that I was wasting my talent going to a country like that. I just shrugged. 'That's just the way it is, Don,' was how I left it. He shook my hand, wished me all the best, and I was on my merry way.

I had never signed a contract for so much money, earning over twice as much as I did at Arsenal with a roll-over every year of ten thousand dollars. Within the week, I was met at Sea-Tac airport by Daley and driven to a waterfront hotel, which was supposedly famous for Pele catching a shark out of his bedroom window, in the Puget Sound. I had never heard of the Sound, and also never knew that Stan Flashman swam in those waters. This was only a seven-day trip to get a taste of what was to come, but boy, was I excited afterwards, knowing that I could go anywhere and do anything without anybody recognising me and things being blown out of all proportion by the tabloids. That evening, Jack Daley and his wife picked us up and took us to the famous Space Needle, that revolving restaurant in the sky where so many movies have been filmed. It was just like my move: heaven!

He did not really have to try to sell this place to me, for I had heard enough from Bobby Moore about how wonderful it was. And if it was good enough for him ... I bought a house there and then, and promptly returned to London to finalize my business at this end, which was a pleasure. Another new start, only this time with a totally new lifestyle, and one I knew was fitting for me and the way I liked to live. I was home! One of the most important things, though, was that I was going to play for a man I already knew and had respected for many years, Jimmy Gabriel. When I left him in Gloucester Road after our negotiations, he was very jovial after a few drinks to celebrate our deal. Harry Redknapp later told me that Jimmy called him from the station jubilant, and that was about all he could understand.

Twenty-seven years of age is when I feel we footballers reach our peak, and I was to peak thousands of miles away from where it all started for me. Kicked out of both Chelsea and Stoke and walked out

of Arsenal was my club track-record to date, and my international
one wasn't much better. Chosen for the World Cup squad for
Mexico 70, captained the Under-23s, banned for three years by Sir
Alf Ramsey, and then picked to fail against the Germans by Revie,
only to spoil his party. Two caps was the extent of all this, but I
suppose I must have the most impressive record of any
international on earth: Played 2, Won 2, For 7, Against 0.

However, the control is always out of your hands and you must
always try to look at both sides of the coin. At Chelsea it was one-
way traffic, with the Board siding with the manager against the
players, allowing him to get rid of them, and then after finding out
it was the wrong decision, deciding to sack that same manager. At
Stoke City it was Humphreys who wanted to pull the strings, until
such time as it became evident that he was pulling all the wrong
ones; and at Arsenal I was always the 'hunted', as if I was an
apprentice at this game. They could not have been more wrong
about me at Highbury, because players like myself, and the
Osgoods, Worthingtons and Curries of this world, would stand on
our performances, and also turn out on crutches when the
goody-goodies were off-colour. Do clubs ever take into considera-
tion all the terrific things you did for them? How, apart from
entertaining and winning great matches under the most thrilling
circumstances, you would promote the club whenever possible and,
in my case, be a part of the club who put much more in than he took
out? I would be the first out with the younger players in the
mornings and the last one in, but that was something that was
always overlooked. They were worried that you might become too
popular, or that players would realize you knew more than the
manager. I recall Alan Ball telling me once that after a
dressing-room argument – sounds far too familiar – with both Terry
Neill and Wilf Dixon, they said to him, 'If you think you're so
clever, *you* take the training.' He had told them in front of the
players that their training sessions were boring (I can vouch for
that!) and that he could do better. That very morning, Ball took the
training session and the rest is history: he was better, and so
obviously he had to leave Highbury!

Alan once told me a lovely story of how he returned to London
one lunch-time after playing against his favourite opponents,

Scotland, at Hampden Park. It was a Thursday afternoon and he, like most of the chaps then, fancied an afternoon on the town. Having achieved this successfully as usual, he found himself at a new watering-hole in the backstreets of London. Bally had starred once again in this match – a fixture he always played with even more passion than usual, if that was possible – and felt good about himself. He was looking forward to going into the Marble Hall dressing-room the following morning and blowing his fumes over the likes of Frank McLintock, to rub salt into the Scottish wounds once again. It was now about 1.30am, Friday morning, and the man behind the bar asked Alan what he would like to finish off the evening. 'A gin and tonic, young man,' Bally squeaked. While pouring the drink, the bartender informed him that this was the regular club of one Mr Bertie Mee. The last drink was gulped down in one by England's World Cup winner, and as they say in my favourite newspaper, he made his excuses and left, as quick as one of his one-two exchange passes. Later that same Friday morning, he was summoned into the manager's office – how I know the feeling – obviously knowing what for, but not being able to hide the fact that Mee knew he had been out since getting off the aeroplane at lunch-time. So the little midfielder ventured into the inner sanctum of the ex-physio's office, which was like a merchant bank or the premises of a venture capitalist. Mee, as usual, looked immaculate in his suit and highly-polished brogues.

'Come in, Alan, and sit down,' waving towards a chair. 'You have been playing quite superbly for the team, as you did on Wednesday night also, and your attitude is faultless. But please could you keep out of my Pleasure Palaces, do I make myself quite clear?'

The last few words were spoken in a different tone, as he told the little fella to get training for the big game the following day. There are no words to say in those situations and Bally knew that; not like the time of the sergeant-major interrogation from Revie. That was the end of the matter as far as both parties were concerned, and that is the way it should be. A player should be judged and treated on his performances on a Saturday, and Bertie Mee realized that. He knew he was dealing with a player he admired, who had been there and done it, and he wanted Alan to do it for him again and again. Great

man-management. If only the Sextons and Neills had had such, not
so much insight, but logic and downright common-sense. I also
remember Terry's assistant Wilf Dixon telling one of the young
lads that when he was at Everton, he had invented the 'five-a-side'.
These are the kind of people that we had to deal with in this game,
and people wonder why we went out and got drunk! Ball left
Arsenal for Southampton to team up with the likes of Keegan,
Channon, Shilton and Osgood, all household names both on the
football field, on the social scene and on the racetracks of England.
Channon has done remarkably well as a trainer and is right up there
with the top names in the 'Sport of Kings'.

So I was now doing my stuff in the beautiful city of Seattle,
Washington, where I had settled in as if I was born to be there. The
lifestyle was the best I had ever come across on my travels and the
King's Road was miles away. This really was the best experience of
my life so far, with the opportunity to play week in, week out,
against the best players in the world, flying around the United
States playing in all those magnificent stadiums and frequenting the
best bars and restaurants from Portland, Oregon, to Tampa Bay,
Florida. My favourite of all was New York, because I knew that
Sinatra had spent so many hours there 'shooting the stick' with his
old pal, the late, great Dean Martin. My first night there was for a
match where I faced Georgio Chinaglia. He was one of the most
famous footballers in the history of soccer in the USA, a player who
went from Swansea City to New York Cosmos and became a
legend. Also in their line-up were a host of other world-class names,
including Bogie, my pal from Singapore. I scored the all-important
goal which won us the match – the first time I had taken part in a
shoot-out – and was quickly accepted as the rightful captain of the
Seattle Sounders. The night life in the 'Big Apple' was very much
up my street, and I fell in love with the action that came with it. My
first impression was of the Piano Bar, where I could imagine sitting
around listening to 'Old Blue Eyes' at his best. My first request was
for 'One For My Baby', the song that begins, 'It's quarter to three.'
Needless to say, we stayed much later than that.

New York really was 'My Kind of Town'! My overwhelming
feeling was one of relief at knowing I was back doing what I did best
and happiest doing just that. It was great being able to go out and

enjoy myself without the feeling of being 'hunted'. I was to have many happy memories of the Big Apple, and none more so than winning the Transatlantic Challenge Cup which included the hosts, the great Cosmos, Celtic and Southampton. We had beaten both the British teams in our Kingdome in Seattle, which showed that we were a match for anybody, and now needed a draw against the mighty New York to take our first ever trophy back to the North West. The Saints boasted Keegan, Ball, Charlie George and Mick Channon in their line-up, and our victory was quite an achievement for a side containing four Americans who had only read about these superstars in magazines. The Celts' best player was their present manager Tommy Burns.

The final was another dramatic encounter between the best two teams in North America. It ended with us getting the draw we required, in a match that lived up to all expectations and was a credit to the North American Soccer League. The New York Cosmos would, I am convinced, have been a top-three side in the then First Division, maybe even now in our Premier League. Such was the quality not only in their side but throughout their multi-talented squad. Steve Hunt, the ex-Coventry star, was playing for England but could not get in their starting line-up. Need I say more?

Seattle is the home of the aeroplane, and in fact Boeing was our training ground. They would set the engines off in the middle of a training session and we would all look at each other and think of home – not going home, just wondering what was going on there. I had no problems, for my family and friends were frequent visitors and more often than not didn't want to return. I had a delightful surprise on the day I moved into my new home, when there was a knock on the door and, on opening it, I found my next-door neighbour standing there with a beautiful home-made cake. That wasn't the delightful surprise, which came when she introduced herself, welcomed us to the area and wished us a long and successful stay. Bob and Jean Barman were from California and had moved, just like us, because of work. We became great friends in a country where if you did not make friends with the natives you had a definite social problem. Needless to say, with a name like Bob Barman, he and I got on famously. I used to envy him every time I picked my mail up from my pigeon-hole next to his; can you imagine having a name like that in my position? The social life was great, with barbecues and house parties at every given opportunity, and we were very much into that. Our other friends there were the Fukotomis, a wonderful Korean family who would be regulars at all our social get-togethers. Grace would be first there with her home-made lasagne, which she thought helped me play that much better. She must have known that I was an 'Italian' nut, being a lover of their restaurants, singers and gangster movies, which although made in America were really transported from Sicily. To say this was home from home was the biggest understatement of my short life to date. Seattle was another one of the high points in this topsy-turvy football career of mine, and I was to love every single minute!

There were obviously times when I missed home, but things were changing rapidly there, not only in the game of football but socially, too. Violence and muggings were becoming more popular with the kids than playing in the 'Cage' was with us. So this part of the world suited the Hudsons just fine. The weather was a little like over in our homeland, but somehow you didn't take so much notice of it, because there was always so much going on. My son was slower to adapt, but after a little while he was the 'Del Boy' of SE 48th Drive.

19

From Highbury to the Seattle Kingdome

Or 'From Russia With Gloves'

'Miles and years from where I started. The many times I stop and say cheers/or shed a few tears for the pals that have parted.' Alan Anthony Hudson (*Seattle Times*, 1980)

Unlike when I joined Arsenal, I knew exactly what I was walking into with Gabriel at Seattle. It was not easy in a lot of ways for me, because I was the first real big-name player whom they had signed on a permanent basis. They had had many great players before me, like Bobby Moore, Mike England, Geoff Hurst and Jimmy Robertson, who were internationals back home. Now I was to play alongside the likes of Tommy Jenkins, a wizard with the ball at his feet; Tommy Ord, a lad from Victoria who scored many goals for the Chelsea youth and reserve teams; Adrian Webster, who spent some time at Colchester; Mick Cave, a prolific goal-getter at York;

221

Steve Buttle, the best of the lot, who could have been a real star had
it not been for a wonky knee; and several unknown young
Americans. This was a far cry from playing alongside Osgood,
Greenhoff, Cooke, Brady and Ball, wouldn't you say?
Our goalkeeper was quite the opposite of Bonetti, a 6ft 4in
Russian-American called Mike Ivanoe who made Tommy Baldwin
and Charlie Cooke look like teetotallers and Oliver Reed a kitten.
He had spent some time in the slammer for fraud. What's new in
football?

When it comes to goalkeepers, I played in the same team as 'The
Cat', 'Big Pat' Jennings, Clemence, Shilton, Rimmer, Farmer,
John 'Sticks' Phillips, Tommy Hughes and lastly Peter Fox at
Stoke City, who was magnificent in the season I returned to the
Victoria Ground. Ivanoe realised that he had a lot to live up to and
we hit it off straight away, for we loved the same things in life: the
game itself, good company and enjoying ourselves to the full. This
we certainly did in this beautiful city. When I arrived, 'Big Mike'
had just come back into training after his spell inside, though
before they caught him he made sure they were not getting the
money back. He pulled up outside the training ground in Renton,
and was getting his kit out of the car when two of our team mates
pulled up alongside him. As he opened the trunk, the two lads saw
his big box full of US dollars, and before you could say 'Las Vegas'
they were at the Seattle-Tacoma international airport awaiting a
flight. The story goes that they did not leave the hotel room for
three days while enjoying the best service that money could buy. I
will leave to your imagination what the money went on, for like
you, I only heard about this and cannot say I was there, worse luck.
I was joining a team of playboys; just my luck! Here I was, just
about to rebuild my playing career with players who were lesser
known – but only on the field, for they were superstars off it, I can
tell you!

My early days there were quite a fantastic experience, because I
was living in a marvellous home in the hills of Bellevue and could go
anywhere and do anything I wanted without feeling I was being
watched or 'hunted'. My boss 'Gabby' was a joy to work for and a
dream to play under, such was his love of the game and life itself.
He is still going great guns at Everton under the management of Joe

Royle. This was the man who had gone 'over the top' on me in my first ever Football League match at Southampton some ten years earlier, and his story was that he, like George Best, had mistaken me for Ronnie Harris; also, that he was having a bad time sleeping so had taken some kind of pill to give him a lift. He was a player of great character who had seen and done it all in his memorable days at Everton and then finished off doing a great job at Southampton. Off the field, he was the opposite of my previous manager and that suited me just fine. We hit it off straight away – as we had on our only other meeting, in Jamaica, when the Saints and the Blues were touring – and enjoyed a season which was just short of a success, which led to Jimmy being fired at the end of it. It was a bizarre decision to say the least, for in my eyes he was doing a great job, but as always there is forever someone who knows better. I was sitting in a restaurant just off the King's Road when I phoned Seattle to hear of the news, and can tell you I was ready for yet another sharp exit. But Jimmy talked me into staying put and told me just to enjoy the rest of my time there, such was the genuine nature of the man. He was right and I respect him for his advice, for I went on to enjoy some absolutely marvellous times scouring the football pitches and bars of the United States of America. 'The land of hope and opportunity' is an understatement – and don't forget the glory!

Chicago – 'My Kind of Town', Frank sang – Tampa, Fort Lauderdale, LA, Santa Barbara, Tulsa, Atlanta, and everywhere else you care to mention, was a joyride of the highest order. Just one long trip through the streets of the USA, and how I loved it. For the first and only time in my life, I could enjoy the finest things in life and still have money in the bank at the end of the week. A fabulous home with my own proudly-built bar, actually built by an Englishman called Timon Sinclair, which was stocked daily and better than any of your 'locals' here. My music was a mixture of Willie Nelson, Supertramp, Jackson Browne and, in those wee small hours, the 'one and only' Francis Albert Sinatra. He was closely followed by the man he once said was the best singer in the world, Tony Bennett, whom I was to meet a year later before one of our matches. Our picture is still treasured. I cannot begin to think of my life without my experience in Seattle and the way it broadened my mind and outlook on life. It was as if my life before was just one big struggle against the establishment, and now it was miles away and even further from my mind. The only time I felt a tinge of regret and sadness was when hearing of Arsenal reaching their second successive FA Cup Final against Manchester United, knowing that I could not be there, running out of that tunnel with them, to put the record straight for that miserable afternoon a year earlier. I was meant to live and play in America. I truly believed that then, I still do to this day, and I return at every given opportunity. It is not a country for the faint-hearted or the unsociable, so I was OK and was in full training both for the playing side and the social side of this wonderful country. The astroturf at both our training ground and the Kingdome was just the remedy for my ankle, with no bobbles or ruts to turn over on, although at times it would flare up with the jarring. But I could handle that with a few hundredweight of ice cubes both in my bucket and my glass. I would ice my ankle before and after every training session and every match, which would keep it from flaring up. This injury, the ankle which George Best had jumped on that night at Old Trafford, was now eight years of age and showing no signs of leaving me. However, the pain was worth it!

After about a month I was in to the swing of the place, having done my scouting missions with the aid of both Ivanoe and Steve Buttle. Buttle played at Norwich under John Bond and later failed a medical at Ipswich, so was left with no option but to leave Great Britain. Jimmy Gabriel knew of this very talented inside-forward and whisked him over to the Great North-West, and how delighted I was with that. He was to become my playing partner all through my four years there, and I can tell you that, although unheard-of, he was as good as any player mentioned in this book. He had a left foot that I can only imagine God gave him, such was his uncanny ability to do anything with it and actually put the ball anywhere he wanted. If he was writing his own book, I imagine he would tell you about his finest ever performance – when I was around, anyway – and the way he tormented the great Dutch World Cup winner, Johan Neeskens. This was in the match I mentioned earlier when we were taking on the might of New York in their own back yard. Buttle had his more famous opponent in all sorts of trouble with his educated 'left peg', tantalising the Dutchman for the entire ninety minutes, putting him on his backside and 'nutmegging' him all night long. He gave a virtuoso performance, and one which I made sure I told the nation about afterwards as I was handed the 'Man of the Match' award. I explained that they had just seen a lad from Norwich with a gammy leg outclass a world-famous Dutch superstar. It was a performance I would have cherished, and I decided then that he was going to play alongside yours truly if I had any say in the matter. I did not need a say, however, such were his consistent displays of football devilry, as I call it. He defied the odds – another thing I love in a player – with his tiny frame and his limping run, but on the field he was a giant. I can honestly assure you that I am not drunk or going over the top as I write about a player whom ninety-nine point nine per cent of our country have never heard of and never seen. Their loss!

Buttle's big buddy was Micky Cave who tragically committed suicide in his garage, which was another of life's total mysteries. Cave was a good League player in this country who also flew to Seattle looking for a better lifestyle and found it, only for it to end in horror. These two lads were inseparable before I arrived, followed by Bolton's long-serving midfield man Roy Greaves. From then on, it was Ivanoe, Buttle, Greavsie and me who would carry the Seattle Sounders flag around the bars in town. Greaves was a terrific player who gave everything and more in his performances, a manager's dream, so to speak. He moved to the bottom of Bellevue hill and we would throw drinking sessions and dinner parties like confetti. We were the midfield trio, and the big Russian ex-banker, the goalkeeper who made Tommy Lawrence look more like a ballerina than the name he got stuck with (The Flying Pig), was our minder and finder of new watering-holes.

Alan Hinton followed Jimmy into the managerial seat and immediately changed the whole set-up by introducing the 'Brian Clough' style of running a club, with his laid-back and totally relaxed approach to the game. His theory was that whatever it took for a player to perform, 'so be it'. He realised that some played for the money, some for the love of the game, and some for both. He used to come out with some absolute gems, so I instantly named him Clouseau, after that fantastically famous Peter Sellers character. Alan immediately brought in his old Derby contingent

who had done so well under Cloughie and given the Midlands club
its greatest moments. Jeff Bourne, Roger Davies and David Nish
were first, and all was well as we turned from a very good side into a
terrific one. We broke the all-time record number of wins in a
season, beating the great New York Cosmos's long-standing feat.
Bourne was a little bit of a maverick himself, who could make the
ball talk in tight situations and was lethal around the opposing
penalty area. He also joined our gang and was a terrific addition,
with his dry Burton-on-Trent wit and eye for a good time. Davies
came over as an above-average player who took the place by storm.
He later formed a very formidable partnership with Peter Ward,
another of Cloughie's old boys, but this time from Forest. David
Nish was my type of player under any circumstances, with his
stylish touch and swagger which at times was so cool it was scary.

It is the sign of a great player when he always looks as if he has
more time to spare than a rolex. Nish made it look as if he was in a
time-warp. He played left-back all his career yet was all right foot, a
little like West Ham's Frank Lampard, who said he had to have a
great right foot (and he did) to cover Bobby Moore when he went
missing or ducked out on the odd occasion. Frank was only joking,
but I think there was more truth in it than he let on. Frank is now
working with Harry Redknapp, who was also in Seattle under the
management of Gabby. A man who, like Hinton, was part of the
laid-back union, Harry would take the young Americans and have
them wondering what was going on with his East London sense of
humour. After his days-out at Longacres, our local racetrack, he
would have them searching the newspapers for his latest tips from
the course. For months, the likes of Mark Peterson, a very talented
centre-forward, Jeff Stock, a left-back capable of playing in our
Premiership, Eddie Kruger and the rest of our up and coming
Yanks would be looking out for horses like 'Dusty Carpet', which
Harry told them had 'never been beat', and 'Loose Button', which
'must come off'. The rest of the dressing-room would sit around
holding their sides as Harry would continually scour the racing
pages with these young lads, pleading with them to save up all their
money and wait for these two horses to oblige.

Harry was the easiest man in the world to get on with, and if you
could not strike up a friendship with him you must be a chairman of

a football club – which reminds me of Harry's recent outburst, attacking Alan Sugar after the Spurs man tried to belittle West Ham for buying so many overseas players. Harry was right on all counts, and for the very good reason that the other bloke should worry about his own club before he starts trying to put the Hammers right. It was a great shame when Harry left Seattle, for he was the type of man who could lift a dressing-room at all times. His kind of warmth and friendliness, to go along with the great humour, is always needed, not just in bad times but at all times. There can never be enough good people in one dressing-room.

Training sessions both at Renton and the Kingdome were very lighthearted and laid back. The players could bring their kids in to have a kick around and join in our little head-tennis sessions after training. It was here that I got my first sight of a very young Jamie Redknapp. His mum Sandra would cut my hair before matches as the Liverpool super-star toddled around their apartment in the hills of this great city. Harry has been very instrumental in the success of his son by bringing him up with all the Redknapp family values, and I get a run down of his progress by his grandfather, Harry 'Right or Wrong' Redknapp, from time to time when visiting Victoria Park on a Sunday morning.

Our dressing-room was about to greet the arrival of Bruce Rioch, the fourth and last of the Derby tribe, and it was not a happy experience. To say I am not surprised at the trouble he caused at Highbury would be the biggest understatement that I, or any other, had ever made. I was called into the office at *The Sporting Life* by the paper's editor Tom Clarke and asked if I was trying to get him hung, such was the strength of my writing on Rioch's appointment. Well, needless to say, it turned out to be right. Rioch, in trying to bring down the brilliant Ian Wright, showed he had not changed a bit since his days in Seattle. First there was his five-a-side fisticuffs with Davies. Then, when he was not boasting of how he broke my leg with a tackle from behind, he was trying to turn the players against Hinton because he was in for the manager's job. For a very clever man, I could never figure out how he thought that all these instances would never get back to us, for I was coaching the kids then and spent many hours with them. And trying to get me to not try a leg in a match because he had had a falling-out with Hinton was preposterous, because I was probably the manager's closest friend at the club. Was it his way just to try to rub everybody up the wrong way, as Clough had done to his cost at Leeds, or was it just that he wasn't a very nice man? One of the most disappointing things about such a character was that he was one hell of a player for our side. When he moved into the back four, he was as good as you'll get in that position. But that did not seem enough for him. I guess we cannot all be the same. I am just so thankful that he is the minority! Being an Englishman who captained Scotland was his real claim to fame, which just about sums it all up. The other Scottish international in our record-breaking side was the flying Coventry winger Tommy Hutchison, but the two of them were like chalk and cheese. Hutch was everything you need from a player in terms of ability, attitude, athleticism and dressing-room humour – he was our Cat Weasel with his tiny little tash and longish nose. Always one for a laugh and a joke, he was the life and soul of any party anywhere in the country. What an absolute gem of a signing he turned out to be for Hinton, as he ran the left flank for us so expertly. We could just forget about him, for he would go and get the ball himself instead of waiting for the perfect service, another sign of a great player. George Best was the best I'd ever seen at getting the ball back, and that was just one of his remarkable attributes.

That team broke up, and it was time for Clouseau to change things around again as the Derby boys disappeared and in came Ray Evans from Stoke City, Kevin Bond from Bournemouth, and Shaun Elliott and Stan Cummings from Sunderland. They had to follow the tremendous achievements of the previous year and did a very good job, playing a big part in our winning the Transatlantic Cup. Also joining us was Steve Daley – who Manchester City could not get rid of quick enough, another Malcolm Allison howler – and, lastly, the most successful signing of the lot. I had played against the Wolverhampton Wanderers midfielder Kenny Hibbitt several times in my career, but it wasn't until he came to Seattle that I realised what a magnificent player he was. Another underrated star of the seventies, and one who in today's market would command mega-bucks. Hibbitt impressed me enormously, and quickly made an impact on our side with his brilliant one-touch, short and long passing, and wonderful ability to strike at goal from any range, not with just power but delicate, curling shots that had goalkeepers grasping thin air. He was a player I could have played with all my career, and I'm sure we would have ended up almost telepathic, like all great players from the 'engine-room' of the team.

Once again we were a force in the North American Soccer League, only losing in the Final to the one and only New York Cosmos, after an epic semi-final against Fort Lauderdale. In their side were my old Chelsea team-mate Keith Weller – what a talented player 'Sammy' was – and another player who had left our shores for life in the USA, my namesake Ray 'Rocky' Hudson, a superbly talented midfield player from Newcastle United. I had played against him at St James's Park some ten years earlier and thought then that he would be a top player, but he chose the beaches of Florida over the gales of Tyneside. Who can blame him? It would not be the same today, though; had there been the same financial rewards for such talent, I'm sure he would have stayed and been a really big star. But could the Football League really handle two players with the name Hudson? I got the feeling before leaving this country that one was quite enough!

Also at Lauderdale around that time was Brian Kidd, who has done a quite extraordinary job beside Alex Ferguson at Old Trafford and has been linked several times to the England set-up with Glenn Hoddle. Kidd was the youngster who broke into that wonderful Manchester United European Cup-winning side of 1967-68, playing alongside George Best and Co. He will no doubt be the next United manager when his boss decides to take over Sir Matt Busby's seat in the Old Trafford directors' box, and that is the way it should be. It is the way Liverpool used to operate, and United have learned from them: to build your staff from within your club. At Chelsea a few years ago, we could have had the same situation, with the likes of Venables, Graham, Eddie McCreadie – how he was let down – and David Webb all becoming more than a match for the rest.

It was at around this time that I was being linked with a move back to my old hunting-ground of Chelsea Football Club. First I had a call from Tony Waddington asking me to return, and then I received a cable from my old solicitor Brian Levy, trying to lay the seeds for such a move. This was followed by an extraordinary phone call from the present chairman Ken Bates, early one Sunday morning. I had only been in bed some two hours, when the phone rang. Still half boozy, I heard a voice on the other end saying this is long-distance from London and it was the Chelsea chairman. I had now been out of the country for so long that the changes that had taken place were far too much for me to take in. No more Brian Mears and company, just a fella from Oldham Athletic who had saved the club by buying it for a pound. Not a bad investment, eh? And there was my old club Fulham floating down the 'swanee', with good old Jimmy Hill looking over the front of his sinking ship for the anchor!

That was the last time I heard from Mr Bates or saw him until he eventually signed me some twelve months later.

My love affair with the Great North-West was coming to an end, with the change of management and ownership once again. The Coluccio brothers – no, they were not related to Revie – got out and handed over to a person called Bruce Anderson. This really was a turn-around, for the Italians were a real treat, especially Vince (Vinnie to his pals) who would travel with us and treat the lads like his very own sons, throwing dollar bills around as quickly as the 'Crafty Cockney' throws his arrows. They would hand over the reins after our defeat in Soccer Bowl '81 in California, because of the continual loss of money at the Kingdome turnstiles. In 1980 I think we averaged about 28,000, which is astonishing when you look at Wimbledon's rise to the top and their lack of following in doing so. But then again, we had world-class players while they have had to stomach Vinnie Jones. I look back with only the fondest memories of the two brothers who so warmly accepted us Englishmen into their club and hope they still talk in the same terms about the times we shared together. The man taking over from them was nothing by comparison, and turned out to be the reason I turned my back on the city I loved so much.

During the off-season before this last horrendous move, I had the pleasure to join my ex-team-mate and great pal Eddie McCreadie in Cleveland, Ohio, for the Major Indoor Soccer League. Eddie was just taking over there when I was in the process of joining their rivals Pittsburgh. On hearing of my pal's appointment, I cancelled all deals and without hesitation joined up instead with my old drinking buddy from the Town House. It was one of the wisest moves of my life and one I will always cherish, for many reasons. Eddie and I became even closer than we were in our wonderful days going around England enjoying success, and around London enjoying each other's company. He was a joy to be involved with, and an absolute credit to our profession. We shared a similar problem – no, not drink – in that we both suffered from insomnia, but Eddie far worse than I. I remember one Christmas, actually the one when I was to leave the Bridge, he was supposed to come to my house in Sispara Gardens, Southfields, just up from the Park Tavern, with his wife Anne. That evening Anne turned up alone, with the news that her husband had been taken into hospital for this reason.

We used to spend hours in his apartment talking of such times, and of how he would walk the house and peep through the curtains every so often to see if it was light yet. Hence the pills, and booze, and all the other crazy things you do to try to get off for a little while (like falling asleep at the near post at Shepherds Bush). This was something we both had in common, so we were lucky that we had so much more than just that, sharing the most wonderful times together for those six months, in a place where not even Don Revie's taxi-driver would have found us.

'And now, the end is near,' Frank sang, and that was certainly the case for me with the arrival of the two clowns who took over this great Seattle Sounders organisation: Bruce Anderson, and an English coach from San Jose who reckoned he played back home, were the future now, heaven help us! My individual meetings with them were a far cry from the one with Don Howe, a man who pulled no punches and told no lies.

Only a few days before I finished writing this book, I received a phone call from a pal of mine in Vancouver, Canada, who was calling to congratulate me after reading my first column in the super new magazine *Action Replay*. That was Chris Bennett, an old team-mate from Seattle and Cleveland, now the proud coach of the Canadian Under-21 team who, just recently, sensationally qualified for this summer's World Cup Finals in Malaysia. It was on New Year's Day 1997, that Chris called, saying he had just been reading the Christmas edition of *Action Replay* and it had brought back so many happy memories of our times together in London, Seattle and Cleveland, Ohio, where we would sit eating, drinking and laughing over the game we both love. (That's when we weren't training, of course.) With us in Cleveland was West Ham's Clyde 'Bunny' Best, who now is coaching his native Bermuda team, so I cannot see them being fit enough to go too far in world football. Only joking, big man! Clyde was a big cuddly bear, another of life's rarities. I will be trying my hardest to be next to my pal Chris in Malaysia: one, just to be alongside him at such a great event; and two, to check out his players, who he tells me are good enough to make their names over here. He cannot be far off, because one of his boys is now at Barcelona. Chris once told me – and I can't remember it myself – of the time he came to Stamford Bridge, as a youngster of sixteen, for a trial, and how he would never forget how I treated him. It was the time I was just establishing myself in the side on our run towards the FA Cup Final, in those very exciting days when kids could so easily run away with themselves. Ten years later, playing under Eddie Mac, there we were sitting in a downtown bar in Cleveland.

These are the kind of memories I am talking about, and that is why I will waste no more space on the Seattle management that forced me out of my home and the job I loved doing so much, captaining Seattle Sounders. Oh, how the wrong people get such power! Although I must add that the last I heard, they were both flat on their backs. There could be someone up there, after all!

20

On The Road Again

One of my all-time favourite songs by Willie Nelson

This really was becoming my song. Chelsea to Stoke, back down to Arsenal, over to Seattle, and now I was 'on the road again', only this time I didn't like it and that was a completely new experience for me. At the beginning of the book I mentioned a rollercoaster ride. Well, it wasn't until I sat down and started writing and reflecting on my career that I realised it had been even more than that, and that no matter how people judge me, they will never know that a footballer's destiny is at all times out of his own hands. I know that this obviously applies to so many other people in other jobs and walks of life, but it is all the more true when you are travelling with just a pair of boots and your ambition.

I wouldn't change much, because I really have made the utmost out of wherever I ended up. I can honestly say that in my opinion, the only losers were the ones I didn't get on with, because they could not handle me but I could them. It's plain simple, really, and 'simplicity is genius', as Mr Ron Greenwood once said. I have never agreed with a saying more. You see, I could go out and train with

233

the best, play with the best, party with the best and still keep my feet firmly on the ground.

What I cannot stomach are those people in football who have never had that feeling of passion for the game. They have never understood what it takes not only to make it as a player, but to stay up there for so long with all the buzzards lingering overhead – and that's exactly what they are: lingerers. The people who now write and sit on TV panels really talk as if the man in the street has never seen a football before, let alone played it at one level or another, and part of this book is to expose the mugs and impostors I have come across in the game.

Don't get me wrong by thinking I am one of those who knows all the ins-and-outs of every aspect of the game, but I sure as hell am smart enough to know a fraud when I come across one. People who talk a good game! I remember talking for the first time to Dave Bassett at a party given by my old pal Frank Allen, of The Searchers fame, and being very impressed at the way he showed so much passion and know-how; and then I cringed while watching the way he wanted the game played. Talk about being hypocritical! A few years down the line, he had a snidey pop at me on his pal Richard Keys's *Footballers' Football Show* on Sky, saying that just because you've played at the very highest level does not mean you'd be a good manager, with tongue in cheek. Well, whatever he has achieved, there is one thing for sure: I would not walk across the road, or waste my electricity turning on my TV set, to watch!

Still, there I was stepping off a plane at Heathrow one more time, knowing it could be my last. This time it was different from all the others. I was not going back to South East 48th Drive. My nights gargling with Francis Albert over my Crown Royal were over. This was the greatest blow of my very blowy career to date. I was back where it all started, two blocks away from the good old prefab, living with my mother on the Chelsea Embankment. Where would we be without 'good old mum'? Hundreds of matches, thousands and thousands of miles, millions of hours training (or so it seemed, anyway), a few trophies, several homes, and plenty of booze and water under the Bridge that I would run past every morning, in my quest to stay in reasonable shape while looking for another club. This, only a month after captaining my Seattle Sounders side in the

Final against Carlos Alberto, Bogicevic, Chinaglia and all the rest of that multi-talented New York team.

I could have stayed in the US to try to find another team, and nearly did the very first day. It was Fort Lauderdale, a place I would have jumped at, to end my playing days and join up with my namesake Ray, who captained this very good club. It was there one evening that I played one of my finest ever matches against one of the world's great players, the Peruvian Cubillas, one of the stars of Mexico 70. Our Seattle team won 4–0, on the way to our record-breaking season in which we did it with about six matches left. I was also linked with the Vancouver Whitecaps, who were our local rivals and an outfit who at their best were as good as any team in North America. I witnessed two fantastic performances from their players while I was there. One was in my first year at the Kingdome, and it was the last match of the regular season. I had been injured the day before in a freak training incident, when our goalkeeper dived across me in a five-a-side and tweaked my knee ligaments. It was an old injury I had picked up following a challenge from Southampton's Jim Steele which was not too dissimilar to the Rioch challenge, so once again I was sitting a big match out. We had to win this battle of the Great North-West to reach the play-offs. I sat and bit my nails while my old England sparring partner Alan Ball gave a performance of sheer magic, one which should have been shown to the young Americans at least once a week. It was around this time that Bally was going back to manage Blackpool, the beginning of his managerial nightmare, and he spoke to me about following him to Bloomfield Road.

The second wonderful performance was from a player whom I had never heard of, quite the opposite of the great Ball. Peter Beardsley was his name, and I left the field in British Columbia shaking my head in disbelief that this boy had not been snapped up back in England. In fact, I heard he had been discarded by Ron Atkinson at Old Trafford. The youngster ran amok and tore our defence apart, to set Vancouver on their way to a 5–0 win. Not one of my happier nights in North America! So I was not surprised to see Beardsley's subsequent rise to such great heights. In goal that evening for the Canadians was Bruce Grobbelaar. I spoke to Bruce afterwards about his coming to England to play, and he told me that he was going over to join none other than Tony Waddington at Crewe Alexandra. No surprise that my old boss had spotted such talent.

Although my heart was still in Seattle and I wanted to stay, I felt let down once again by the management – there's a shock – and felt I could not hang around to wait for a phone call that might never come. I had a gut feeling that I should have one more try in England, but did not realise how difficult it would be – when would I learn? – getting back into a game which was not the one I had left. The Lilleshall connection had totally taken over and was destroying the kind of 'football upbringing' for youngsters that I once had. Hence the lack of players coming through the ranks, which is why there are so many foreigners here now – these morons from the Football Association had taken our game back more than twenty years. I have been in retirement now for about eleven years, and we have only just started to repair the damage that Charles Hughes and all his cowboys had done.

I once met Hughes at a match in Vancouver with Alan Hinton, and did not know at the time the amount of power this man possessed, or the number of people he had totally brainwashed, from FA coaches to school teachers. Thankfully our nation is emerging from the humiliating era of his 'route one' football, and his 'getting the ball in the box quicker' methods. Can you imagine the likes of Cruyff, Maradona and Best being in our game while he was trying (and succeeding) with such barbaric tactics. It has taken the insight of Glenn Hoddle to see this and change things around. In doing so, there needed to be drastic changes: enter Ruud Gullit. Certain managers who I need not name have had a ride on the back of a bus which has been for people on the edge. These people could not hack it in the real football world, so between them they changed the rules. They stopped people and players from enjoying themselves and expressing themselves, by bringing in robot-type players who would just do as they were told.

Thank goodness the game has got some sanity back. I said on hanging my boots up and watching Channel Four's *Football Italia* that this would be our only way back into football civilization, and so it has proved. Ruud Gullit has introduced the Italians to Stamford Bridge, and now you cannot get near the place. How ironic, as I write of returning to Chelsea from Seattle, that the Blues are now entertaining the fans like we did in the sixties and seventies, and not since have they had such entertainment. Under Ken Bates – and doesn't he know – they have had people managing the club who were living with their heads in the clouds – and most of the time the ball was there too.

Only Eddie McCreadie, and briefly David Webb, have shown any sign of taking Chelsea forward since those great days. Eddie was given a bum deal, getting sacked for asking for a new car. The truth of the matter was, he lifted one of the Mears family off their feet one day, after the director had bad-mouthed one of Eddie's players in the boardroom after a home match. It was a tradition that the manager should show his face there at the end of the game – one Eddie did not agree with, for he knew that this kind of thing would happen. McCreadie at that time had just restored some faith back into the club, after Sexton had got them relegated, by introducing all the young players and mixing them with the left-overs of our side. Micky Droy, Ron Harris and John Dempsey were all that was left. Enter Ray Wilkins, Ian Britton, Clive Walker – how well he's doing at Woking – Garry Stanley, Tommy Langley and Jock Finnieston. After getting promotion, Eddie was sacked. What's new at the circus?

To follow him were Ken Shellito, Geoff Hurst, Danny Blanchflower, Frank Upton for a day, Ian Porterfield, Bobby Campbell, John Neal and my old midfield partner John Hollins, who had gone from being so well-respected to just another of the 'yes men'. On my return, he went down even further in my estimation for the way he sat on that great big 'Stamford Bridge fence'. His coaching was all about fitness and long balls, the 'fiver ball'. I can't remember if that is where I got my stiff neck from, or whether it was going over that roundabout in Stoke-on-Trent. If these are the measure of management at this once great club, it is no wonder they have not put any silverware in the cabinet since that wonderful evening in Athens.

Geoff Hurst was another dead loss in management. The same man I had lived with some eight years earlier was in charge when I almost signed, prior to coming back. He was warned by Peter Osgood not to bring his West Ham attitude – and they do have one

– into our club, but it fell on deaf ears. I telephoned him the day after Danny Blanchflower had been sacked, to tell him that the great Spurs and Ireland captain had agreed to sign me. Hurst's reply was along the lines of, 'If you turn up for training every day this week, on time, I'll sign you.' I had the last words before crashing the phone down, but those are really unprintable.

After a summer of looking for work and gallivanting around the streets of London with my pal Tony Davis, I finally signed for the second time for my local club. At this time I was still a fully-pledged member of Frankie Frazer's Tin Pan Alley afternoon joint, and Doggan Arriff's La Connesseur in the Old Kent Road. Mr Arriff at that time was very much involved in Fisher Athletic and some nights we talked about the prospect of me taking over there, but I had bigger things in mind, once again. This was to become the most frustrating time of my whole life to date! I was to witness three men, Neal, McNeill and Hollins, running a football club with as much idea about the finer points of the game as Frank Bruno. What has always amazed me is that Hollins should have known better after playing alongside Venables, Graham, Cooke and myself in midfield, and Osgood up front. In my experience, every great team – from the Tottenham Double-winning side through to the last truly great Liverpool side, with Souness pulling all the strings – has always had a great 'engine-room', where the brains of the team is. Now Hollins was getting the likes of Colin Pates to bypass his midfield players and hit it as long as possible.

Holly had already gone down in my estimation when one day he advised me to leave the club after an argument with Sexton. After thinking long and hard about this, I knew it was because I would be one less threat to his chances of getting into the side. Now he hit rock-bottom in my book, by the way he talked a good game but was just blind to the fact that young players like Fillery and Jasper wanted to play the game properly. They wanted to play it like I did after watching Johnny Haynes, and Ossie did after watching Jimmy Greaves, but they were told there was no time to fanny about with the ball, and to get it forward. The men in charge have got so much to answer for!

By this time, my return to the club I once adored was quite obviously becoming a nightmare. Night matches at Oxford and

Crystal Palace in front of a few hundred people was not exactly Wembley or the Giants Stadium, and I began hitting the bottle even more, with my marriage now finished and my two little boys over in Seattle. I was alone again and had nothing and nobody to play for, but that would change! In spite of everything, I was still always first out on the training field with Patesy, Jasper, Big Micky, Rhodesy, Clive Walker and Chris Hutchings, practising and enjoying a few moments of skill before training actually began – because there was no skill or thought going into such sessions. The funniest moments in training were when we, the reserve team, played the first team, with the boys rolling their sleeves up as if it was a proper first-team match. I would come back so deep to get the ball from Micky – the only time I ever saw it, really – and the coaches would stop the game, saying 'The opposition will not be playing like that on Saturday, can we have the ball back?' So we had to give them it back. This was surely time to go!

It was a good job the boys in the 'stiffs' were from the old school and were all good lads, so we at least had a laugh to get over the boredom of reserve-team football. One incident always makes me smile, and it came after a reserve match at Oxford. Tony Davis was our driver as we headed for Rocky's in Putney High Street, which was owned by our good friend Rocky Taylor. He had that horrific accident in one of his most dangerous 'stunts', but has now thankfully recovered. However, this evening we were standing chewing the fat about our futures at the Bridge, over a few drinks, when Peter Rhoades-Brown interrupted with a classic.

'I tell you something, I just cannot believe a team like we had out tonight could not beat Oxford,' he said, with glazing eyes. I looked at Micky, as Dale joined the team-talk by asking Rhoadesy what the hell he was talking about. 'We should have never let them back in the game,' Peter explained. 'We should have killed it at 2–1.'

Well, we fell about laughing as we tried desperately to convince Peter that we had been 3–1 up at the time they scored their late second goal. Can you imagine, if he had got home, and his missus had asked him how he had got on, and he said 2–2? She would have wondered the next day, when checking the results, whether her husband had actually gone to Oxford or just been on a night out. It was not until he saw it in the newspaper the following morning that he knew the score. The ironic thing is that Oxford United bought him not long after that match, so he must have been doing something right that evening but it certainly wasn't taking any notice of the game. I can understand wingers feeling left out (I've been there) and ignored as they stand out there waiting to get a touch of the ball, but as for not knowing how many times we had kicked off ... that was taking it to the extreme.

It was moments like this that kept the whole bunch of us from 'losing it'. Another funny episode – and there weren't many, believe me – was when Ken Bates invited several of the older players to lunch in one of Fulham Road's finest restaurants. It was to show his appreciation for our being patient while out of the first team and not creating problems for the management. What the chairman thought was going to be a nice, pleasant 'thank you', turned into something like we used to experience in the old days at Alexandres. In all fairness to 'HRH', his gesture really was appreciated, but there was nothing he could do to keep these players happy. The simple fact was that players like Micky Droy and myself could have run that club better than Neal and Hollins standing on our heads, and with more honesty, style and class – something Chelsea were about in our day.

And now, the end was near ... and it was becoming that way for I am not one to just pick up my money and watch complete fools rearrange the game. I was brought up to play in the proper manner, with a little bit of thought, imagination, style and, like Charlie Cooke always showed, class. The club had now become a footballing circus, and only today do Chelsea fans realise this, through having the opportunity to watch their latest heroes. However, all football fans are fickle, and in all fairness they get carried away, like Matthew Harding, with anyone who puts a blue shirt over their heads.

It was nearing Christmas, and snow was on the ground for a reserve match at Leicester when, through the grapevine, I heard of some interest from Tampa Bay Rowdies. They were sending a representative to check out my fitness in a match, where I had my first glimpse of Gary Lineker. In such conditions, he just looked like any other player with his inability to control a bag of cement on an icy surface. This prospective return to the States was very short-lived, as once again that dreaded knife had come out and a telephone call had warned those Stateside to keep well away.

Following this very dodgy inquiry from Tampa came a call right out of the blue from my long-lost father Mr Tony Waddington, who must have been missing me as a drinking partner. It was an SOS message: 'Save Our Stoke'. It seemed that every time they got to the foot of the First Division, they called for Hudson. I was the 'Red Adair' of the King's Road. Only this time, I too had an SOS message that needed answering, and 'Aye, Aye, Aye' was what Tony was famous for. He picked it up, I found out years later, from a Brazilian singer he met on one of his famous trips. I later found an LP cover in his chalet down in Abersoch that revealed the years of 'Aye, Aye, Aye', which was one of the songs on it.

'Alan, reserve-team football is no good to you. Get yourself up here and get this lot out of trouble,' were his words.

City were something like a dozen points adrift at the foot of the table and were desperate – and if they had seen my lifestyle recently, they must have been desperate. However, better the devil you know! I jumped into the Roller with Jake, the owner of London's famous Browns nightclub, and with Ken Bates's permission whizzed up the M1 and on to the M6. It all seemed light years from my time before, and this time I knew what I was walking into. I met Bill Asprey, the Stoke manager, in the Newcastle-under-Lyme Post House just off Junction 25, and was immediately impressed (but then I had been with Terry Neill on our first date). He talked of a month's loan, which was the new thing in England now, and this seemed like a month away from Colditz; music to my ears. A month back in the First Division, just when I had given up all hope of ever putting on a first-team shirt in the Second. Asprey was more than desperate and had absolutely nothing to lose, so we struck the deal. I would return to London that day, pack my bags and, as Willie sang, 'Just can't wait to get on that road again'.

In all fairness, I have had my disagreements with and still have many doubts about the Chelsea chairman, but he was a different class in the handling of both my moves to and from Chelsea and the days I spent there. This one was no different, for it was best for all parties involved. But I will never, ever forgive him for mentioning money in a press conference on that tragic day of Matthew Harding's death!

So this was to be a loan spell, which I just had to make permanent. It was like someone coming out from 'inside' and saying, 'I'm not going back there.' You have read all about the Hudson debuts – well, this time I was to face Arsenal and Don Howe in my first game back at the Victoria Ground. I had my first training session with the lads on the Friday morning in our gymnasium, where Jimmy Greenhoff and I had perfected a footballing relationship all those years ago. Now I was to come across another great talent who had worn the red of Manchester United and was as skilful as any before him: Sammy McIlroy and I carried on where I had left off with Jimmy – not quite as stunning, though – in that first morning's five-a-side. With our one- and two-touch, and the way we read each other's minds as if we had played together all our lives, both Sammy and I knew we would get through this disastrous situation. I knew that if I could get the ball to the Irishman in positions just in front of their back four, that was part of my job done and he could win us the matches we needed to stay up. When we came out of the gymnasium after that first session, I could see the weight had been lifted off all the players' backs.

'The way we played in the gym this morning is the only way we will get out of trouble,' I said. Looking at the manager, I carried on: 'You have proved that playing your way has been a disaster. So let's enjoy it and play, and if we are going to lose, let's do it by enjoying ourselves.'

How could the manager argue? His track record was not really one you would tout around. Sammy had told me how he'd got a stiff neck watching balls whacked over his head all season, and might as well have been at Manchester airport watching the planes fly over. I promised that he would at least have a month of fun, adding that I would give him so much of the ball he'd be sick of the sight of it. My first move was to make sure I got it, which was quite simple really, because so many of the team were playing without confidence and I was their outlet. Peter Fox was our goalkeeper and in the mould of the greats before him. In this particular second half of the season, he was inspirational. My job was to make sure that every time he got the ball in his hands, he would do nothing else but look for me. He didn't realise until I was almost inside his shirt just how serious I was, pointing to him to drop the ball to the floor. This was the answer, for I could see movement now, with players making different angles instead of standing in the centre-circle and waiting for the goalkeeper to keep directing balls towards the skyline.

I had found my first ally in our left-back Peter Hampton, a very underestimated player from Leeds, whom I could play one-twos off like playing off the wall in the 'Cage'. This would get me nearer to the halfway line, where I could now find the feet of Sammy – funny how in both my spells at Stoke I was to come across a player of the same name – with little dinky passes just around their thirty-yard line. I had told him not to worry about losing it, just take them on and make things happen, and Sammy could do this with his eyes closed. On my right-hand side I had the experience of Robbie James, a laid-back character who could explode now and then, and who always came up with something a little special, too. On the right wing, we had probably one of the biggest wastes of talent seen not only at the Victoria Ground but in the country at this particular time. Mark Chamberlain played on the opposite flank to John Barnes on that memorable night when the Liverpool superstar scored that most glorious goal for England against the Brazilians.

'Chambo', when he put his mind to it, could skin any full-back at any given time, but it was his mind that was the problem. Maybe he would have been OK in today's game, with clubs having big squads and players having to fight for places, but Mark was in the England side while his club were rooted firmly to the bottom of the League. He was the biggest fish in that tiny little bowl, but instead of rolling up his sleeves he would amble around as if 'tomorrow will do'.

At right-back in that side was a lanky full-back who was the target of the Boothen End Paddock. From the moment he ran out of that tunnel, he would be torn limb-from-limb by all the locals he knew so well. It took me quite a long time to get Bill Asprey to move Steve Bould to centre-half, but once he did, that was it – although I still had many battles with every man and his dog as I tried to convince them that this boy was as good as anything we had in the country. At that time, the England shirt was worn by Terry

Butcher, and I recall telling Mr Waddington that this boy Bould was head-and-shoulders above him. Tony, for a change, did not agree with me, and even questioned my knowledge. But in the five-a-sides in our gym, I kept an eager eye on Steve Bould. I love players who have that uncanny knack of doing things right all the time, and yet do not know how well they are doing them.

We had another one a few years before him called Alan Dodd, also a local boy, who could have been a superstar if he had only believed in himself. I remember in my first season there, I was jogging around the pitch with him and asked if he was all right. He told me he was thinking of packing it in, because he was not enjoying it. I told him that he had just marked two of the most feared front-men in the country, Kevin Keegan and Joe Jordan, in the last two matches and given neither of them a kick. He could have given Keegan a yard start. The problem was, he found the game too easy and could not see why everyone would get carried away about the ease with which he did it. He thought I was trying to kid him, telling me I was only saying that because I felt he was inferior to me and was trying to boost his confidence. Believe me, he didn't need Alan Hudson or anybody else. He last played with me in a match at Birmingham for a Don Revie England XI. He was the best player on the field by a mile but typically never got picked again, Revie plumping instead for Paul Madeley whom Dodd made look like a cart-horse, good player though the big Leeds utility-man was.

Steve Bould was a little different in his approach to Doddy, and from an early age I could see he liked a good time and enjoyed himself along with his mucker Billy Parkin, who now manages Mansfield Town. This liking for the good life was a good sign, because it meant that he had to get on, to pay for it! So he worked hard at his game, and has reaped the rewards for all the listening and learning he did along the way. When I finally packed it all in, he would come into my pub, The Merlin Tavern, after matches and would sit for hours talking about the day's game – he would have fitted into our Chelsea side of the seventies. When he told me that Everton had made an offer for him, I made it clear in no uncertain terms that he would be making a big mistake going there, because I knew Arsenal were also interested: I had put two-and-two together after seeing Stewart Houston at Stoke's home matches on several occasions. I am quite proud to say that he listened, went to Highbury and became a monumental success at the heart of their defence. He is the most successful footballer to come from Stoke-on-Trent apart from Sir Stanley Matthews, although Steve has probably won more domestic honours than even the great man himself.

My first forty-five minutes were over and the headlines read 'The Prodigal Son Returns' – I told you there was always something about an Alan Hudson debut. This one was to be my last. We beat the Gunners, with all their big stars including Charlie Nicholas, Tony Woodcock and Kenny Sansom, without too much bother and I was the talk and the toast of the town again. Mr Waddington, the mastermind behind this move, was proudly holding court just like eight years earlier, with his 'G and T' in one hand and his moving patterns in the other, explaining to the Federation House regulars how he had seen me do it all before so many times, and how he was in no doubt that Alan Hudson was the only player to get his beloved club out of the mire once again. That Tony was not on the board of directors, after seventeen years as their manager and messiah, was one of the biggest fiascos I have ever witnessed.

Once again, as on my debut against Liverpool, I had won the fans over. Now I could concentrate on two things. First, getting that contract extended; and then, really having an all-out-assault on catching the teams above us. This was the first time I had been at the wrong end of the table, but it sure beat training with Hollins and playing in Chelsea's reserves. To be back in front of the fans who once sang about 'Walking on Water' was music to my ears again. We were to take a break in Spain before our following match – as if I needed a break – and I found that this set of players was as good at socialising as any before them. Unfortunately, it showed in our following match, at Upton Park, where we looked like a team destined for the drop, losing 3–0. However, a win and a draw from my last two matches on loan earned me that contract, which was the best one, considering my position a month before, that I'd ever signed. This time I moved back out into the countryside and stayed in a cottage owned by a director of the club, Geoff Manning. He was married to the lovely Maggie Crow, who was once the wife of the much-respected surgeon, director and great friend of Mr Waddington in his days as manager. An absolutely charming couple, who opened their home to both me and my family whenever they visited. This being our second time around, my mum and dad were now very well-known in the town and also very popular. Deep down my family, ever since I kicked a ball at the Victoria Ground, had been the most ardent and staunchest of Stoke City supporters, my father mainly because of his incredible respect for Waddo!

My contract was signed, and we went on to pull off one of the greatest escapes ever witnessed. Not only did we survive, we did it by playing just as we had on my first morning in the gymnasium, pure football. The confidence was now there for all to see – what a change in a team. Even our manager started to believe that he was second only to Ron Atkinson, walking through the tunnel jangling his jewellery to the beat of 'And now you're gonna believe us'. Bill Asprey, deep down, was a nice chap who was now getting carried away with how we had got out of trouble. In the final match of the season we had to beat Wolverhampton Wanderers by three goals to stay up. We did so by scoring four, thanks to a wonderful display by our front-man Paul Maguire – and Alan Dodd, who now was a Wolves player. Squire, as we called him, scored all four goals, while Doddy, quite uncharacteristically for him, gave away two penalties. In fact, some said he just would not have been able to live with the thought of helping to get his native Stoke relegated, but that was just Stoke-on-Trent idle gossip (and believe me, I heard plenty of that in my time there).

At the end of the game, while I was sitting in the manager's office with a bottle of champagne, looking out for all the other results, Bill Asprey was standing behind the goal at the Boothen End with his arms aloft, quite a different sight to the one I saw walk into the Post House that first day. As he lifted our scorer's arms up to the crowd to the chant of his name, he whispered in Squire's ear: 'I won us the game today.' in which our striker said 'How do you make that out?'

'Well, if I hadn't picked you …'

Before he could say any more, Maguire told him where to go and flew into the office to give me the news of the biggest 'ball and bat' in town.

Was I surprised at such a response? No. George Byatt, Waddo's sidekick, had told me how the Stoke manager would telephone Tony halfway through one of their extended Friday lunches – at Fed House, where else – and have him on the phone until his lunch was cold. Let's just say that by the time Tony returned to the lunch table, the team for the following day was selected. You know what I mean about managers, and here this one was, standing arms-aloft as if he had just brought Pele through the ranks and won the World Cup on top of it. It was a crying shame because as I say, he was likeable; but he truly believed what he said to our four-goal hero. Bill Asprey had become too big for his massive cigar!

That was certainly the dressing-room verdict after his classic performance behind the famous Boothen End goal – which sadly, as I write this, is in its last season – and his antics-to-come would confirm this. I went into Bill's office to ask about arranging a trip to celebrate our fantastic achievement, only for him to tell me that the club had no money, but if the lads would like to pay for themselves to go to Spain, he would not object. I said that I had a better idea and could fix up a match over in Tampa Bay. Now he was interested. Lighting his 'la-di', he was now all ears, and had a look on him as if it was all his idea. I called a builder friend of mine in the area and he fixed up a week in the Hall of Shame – when we arrived, the hotel was actually called the Hall of Fame – playing one match on the day we arrived and having the rest of the week to get on with the fireworks. I was not able to play, as I had just had an operation on my shoulder after a fall against Southampton, two games before the Wolves match, and entered the country with my arm in a sling. So I had to take over as social secretary, which was ideal. I knew this place like the back of my hand and still had a home there, so I was Tampa street-wise.

I do not really think Tampa was ready for this lot from Stoke-on-Trent. It was a far cry from Waddington's words of taking them away boys and bringing them back men. My old mate Tony Davis was included in our tour party, as our physio could not get away, and TD was to get his first taste of involvement in the dressing-room build-up and the banter that goes with it. For a lad from the Old Kent Road, he was given a hounding by the Stokies. It was a memorable week, the highlight being our trips down to the

Steak and Ale on a daily basis to terrorize the local barmaids, and also to pick our best teams of the previous season. We picked such teams as the 'Ugly Team', 'Boring Team', 'Miserable Team', 'Social Team' and so on, and so on and on again. You name it, we picked it that week. (There was one very big-name player, mentioned in this book, who amazingly got in every one of those teams.) Our lunch-time squad was Brendan O'Callaghan, Tony Davis, Peter Fox, Paul Maguire, and of course the social secretary. Big Brendan, the Eire international, was a big man who could play at both ends of the field with great effect, scoring them and stopping them with his 6ft 3in frame. He was a gem both on and off the field, with his dedicated, will-to-win manner and his incredible wit, which was used at all the most important times. He was a very important part of the dressing-room 'uplift' we had needed to get out of that terrible mess in the season just gone, and he, Foxy, Squire and myself were the social backbone of the side.

One afternoon, on returning to the swimming pool from our team selection meeting, we had a visitor. It was none other than Malcolm Allison, who had come around to chit-chat with the lads on how things were going. Malcolm was training with his mucker Rodney Marsh, and had just been given a job at Tampa as 'supervisor of coaching', or some rubbish name that Marsh had thought up. Fox and I immediately sussed the situation out and put our plan into action, knowing it would work. In no time, therefore, (and we had to do this in style, as always) the ice-buckets were out with the gin, vodka and bourbon, slices of oranges and lemons, tonics, lemonades, and of course Florida orange juice. Now I remember my younger days in the Playboy Club with the likes of 'Big Mal', Venners and Marsh, so I'm sure he would have been impressed. After a nudge, Foxy asked Malcolm if he'd like to join our afternoon 'Happy Hour', to which he replied: 'No thanks. I'm off the booze and we are training this afternoon.' In that case it was strange, I said to the Fox, knowing how professional he was, that he was sitting out sunning it before a training session. 'Maybe someone's sent him,' came our keeper's reply.

After the boys left for London, Tony and I stayed to see the month out. We went to a match at the stadium, where I spoke to the Rowdies' long-time captain and very popular South African defender Mike Connell. He was organising a players' strike if Marsh did not get his pal away from the training ground. I had to laugh, thinking of that afternoon by the pool, as I read how the Rowdies' recent results were the worst in the club's history, losing matches by five, six and even seven goals while Allison was coaching them.

It was during this trip that Asprey decided to break our 'team spirit' up and get rid of a couple of the players, without whom he would have been out of work and on the Stoke-on-Trent dole queue. One was our four-goal hero – I wonder why that was – and the other the ever-reliable and impressive Peter Hampton. I spent hours at the hotel bar that evening trying to persuade the manager to change his mind, and told him that if he sold these players, he would be starting off the season right back where he was when I joined them – not only rock bottom, but with absolutely no chance of surviving. I had gone through this twice already and, with my slowing down by the match, was looking less and less like a Houdini for the club. The manager, as usual, knew it all. He did not listen and the rest is history!

The following season, he was found slumped over his racing paper after a heart-attack, and was told to take it easy. He took it easy all right, but it was too late to avoid the inevitable. This was the time of my biggest regret, and my greatest ever chance to go into management, as I should have gone to him and told him to sit back while I ran things. I was doing that anyway to a certain extent, and Waddo was picking the team from Federation House. This would have been the answer to both our prayers, and also given me the opportunity to get Tony back into the club to help pick the team from his rightful place. I suppose in some ways I was waiting for him to approach me, but it was obvious that he really did think he had been the saviour in that glorious season of '84. We were relegated, and although it had looked a certainty from the start, it could really have been avoided with a little bit of common-sense and understanding of the game and the people in the club; and more importantly, knowing who could play and who could not.

If you think that was a horror story, what followed was a double nightmare, with Mick Mills and Sammy Chung introducing a new kind of management theme into Stoke City. That summer, I was in

Spain with Tony Davis, George Byatt, Paul McCormack and Peter Fox – you must have a goalkeeper with you at all times, and Foxy was ours – when I decided to put in for the vacant managerial post. I did not have long left playing, knew the players well and felt I had the respect of our dressing-room. The pre-season was getting closer, and still nobody had been appointed, when I attended a dinner at London's Lancaster Hotel with Mr Waddington and Mr Byatt. It was a very jovial occasion, with Tony as always holding court and having the time of his life in the city where we won so many matches together – and in which he should have managed, at Chelsea. (I always say that, instead of sending me to Stoke City, Chelsea should have sent Sexton and we could have had their manager, who I'm convinced would have brought a long-awaited Championship to the Bridge.) This particular evening, I was confronted socially by the Stoke City chairman Mr Frank Edwards, who asked me how serious I was about managing his club. My answer was very clear and to the point, as usual: 'With the guidance of Mr Waddington, I am totally convinced I can put Stoke back on the map. I have every confidence to do such a job,' was what I told this perfectly charming old gentleman. He said it sounded great, and that I should call him first thing Monday morning, when he got into the Victoria Ground.

I returned to our table to tell my two muckers of this very interesting news, and we ordered champagne on the strength of what looked a great future for us all. Tony and I would be in charge, while George would make a move to invest at boardroom level. This was on the Friday evening. By the time I arrived back in Stoke-on-Trent, poor Mr Edwards had been dead a matter of hours. To this day I really do not know how I feel about such a double tragedy. Not only the death of a truly wonderful old man, but the opportunity to manage the club I was now so attached to – and had enjoyed so many unbelievable matches with, over the years – was buried with him.

I told you of this truly remarkable rollercoaster ride; and once again, as I write this book, I find myself having a problem believing that all this could happen to anybody, let alone me. Don't get me wrong, I have never been one to feel sorry for myself – but I do sometimes find it hard to take, in circumstances such as these. To say I was double sick was as near as you'll get, but really I had to just think of how lucky it was in the first place that Mr Waddington had called me and asked me to save another sinking ship. Now I was to be confronted by yet another manager of suspect ability. What's new!

There was a time in the previous season when I had one of the worst situations in my playing career – or maybe my life in general – after a caretaker manager called Tony Lacey took over. (Those of you outside the Potteries, don't bother looking for his name in a list of people who achieved something in our game, you'll find zilch!) I was brought up thinking that life should be for living, that smiling is good for you, and that you should help your fellow man, be thankful every day for what we can achieve if we want, and enjoy or commiserate at the consequences. This man was the opposite. He was everything I would not like to be in life with his long face, which was his CV in fact. I cannot put up with people who hide behind what they think is power, and Lacey was typical of this. Like so many others along the way, he was not so much a 'party pooper' but more the kind of character who really should have auditioned for the movie *Halloween*, such was his dislike of seeing people enjoy themselves. So from the word go, that meant that McIlroy, O'Callaghan, Fox and Hudson must be treated like outcasts. As I said earlier, this was nothing new to me after Sexton, Ramsey, Revie, Neill and that so-called coach in Seattle, Calloway, I think it was. This man Lacey really was barking up the wrong tree.

It all came to a head when we played Norwich at home, and he had given his briefing of what he wanted from every Tom, Dick and Harry at the club. He would mark his little blackboard to show in which positions he would want certain players for our free-kicks, obviously leaving me out of the whole set-up. After about twenty-five minutes, we got a free-kick in one of his diagrammed areas and I immediately picked the ball up and took a quick one. The bench nearly went up in the air. I played the rest of the half out, walked into the dressing-room, and before he got in there I had my kit off.

'I'm bringing you off,' he said. 'How dare you take no notice of my instructions on the blackboard? Do you think I do that just to waste people's time?'

While he was pulling me off, I had one foot in the shower. I had beaten him to it. The following day, he called me into his little office

– he was not allowed to use the manager's – and told me I would be playing in the reserves that evening. I answered him very clearly, in a very low tone just like Brando in my favourite movie.

'You can do anything you like, you can think what you like and you can say what you like, but don't you ever talk to me like that again in front of a dressing-room of people, especially youngsters. Because number one, you're ignorant; and two, you come from a different world from me. As regards playing tonight: as my great friend Pat Jennings would say, "I'm injured".'

He threatened to fine me, suspend me, and all the petty things that little people do. I just said go ahead and do it, but keep out of my way. I ended up going to explain the situation to a board member, and put it to him in no uncertain terms that I would not be told what to do by someone of so little importance. After all I had done on and off the field for this club, I would not be spoken to in this way. I would be on the treatment table until the club could find a manager who could do better, much better, and had some insight into the game. Well, I was and they did, but the new one could not see much farther, I'm afraid to say. My days were well and truly numbered, this time it really was the end; as Mick Jagger would sing, 'The Last Time'. Once again I despaired. My legs were no longer any good to me on the place I loved most, the football field!

It was during this period that I got caught up with the brilliance of Phil Collins. After a show at the NEC one evening I realised that he ranked up there alongside many great artists of my time. His rendition of 'Mama' that evening gave me goose bumps on top of goose bumps. I was an instant fan. I had the great pleasure to meet Phil while he was working in a recording studio which backed onto Stamford Bridge. It was two days after the death of my father and I needed lifting. Danny Gillen came over and insisted I get out of the house and come to meet the maestro of the drum-set. I sat in his studio while he toyed with 'A Groovy Kind Of Love'. This was to become another smash for the man who now seems to have become a recluse and has at last started to put his life before music. Danny still stays by his side in Switzerland and is loyal as ever. We met again some time later when I had recovered from my father leaving us. It was at the Royal Albert Hall and in the company of Bobby

Moore who was now looking as if his illness was taking its toll on him. Phil is yet another fan of our great game. Our first meeting felt as if we had known each other all our lives and I still cherish that moment.

21

A Different 'One for the Road'

The perfect duet for Sinatra and Nelson

This really was a combination of a Frank Sinatra and a Willie Nelson duet, with Frank crooning through 'One for my baby, and one more for the road' while Willie would laze through that song which introduced the last chapter. For me the road was coming to an end, and I knew it. I was once asked what happened to footballers when they packed the game in. I answered, 'They Shoot Horses, Don't They?' That could have been the title of this book, and I still believe in those words. Not so much today, with so many things to invest your 'easy money' in, but certainly in our days of playing for twenty years and ending up on the football scrapheap. I was not looking forward to the future. I knew I would have to dig deep into my resources and strength to survive what was to face me outside the game, the game we all thought would never end. They say that everything relates to a song, and that last statement became a very successful one sung by Mary Hopkins. It was written by the brilliant new MBE – about time they got it right – Paul McCartney!

I had first met Mick Mills at the airport on my way to Spain, with Leslie May, after my first season in the game. We spoke then about our mutual friend Ken Adam, that one-time agent of all the young 'mavericks'. I found him charming but not 'one of us', so to speak. He was a really nice guy, but from a totally different upbringing way down there in Ipswich. A little different as well from my old Seattle buddy Steve Buttle, who was at the club at the same time as the ex-England captain. Funnily enough, the first time I met Sammy Chung was in Spain about two days later – was this a coincidence or were they watching me for all these years, knowing they were going to come to my beloved Stoke and turn what had started out in 1973 as a dream, into an ageing footballer's worst nightmare.

Since my return to Stoke – there's a lot of truth in the maxim that you should never go back – I had encountered Asprey, plus a pal of his from West Brom called Albert somebody-or-other; and Lacey, I would have packed it in immediately had I been starting out instead of finishing. Now I had Del and Rodney Trotter. I will never forget the first day Sammy Chung came into the dressing-room and was introduced to the players. Mills immediately asked him to let us know what we were going to achieve in the coming season and how training would work. The players were still sitting there shaking their heads five minutes after Chung left the dressing-room wondering what the hell was going on. This was his talk to the whole playing staff. 'I want one thing from you all, and that is: when you go out training, I want you to wear your running shoes. Change into your boots when we get over to the training pitch.'

Here we go again, I thought, another clown. I had begun my time at the club by helping them into Europe to face the great Ajax under supreme management. Now I sat watching it run like a complete and utter circus. Usually I will have quite a lot to say about players or people in the game but in this instance there is nothing to say really except that I cannot remember one time under these two men that I enjoyed. Heaven only knows what they got up to in the outposts of Suffolk.

In my days in the Under-23s, I was fortunate enough to play with probably Ipswich's greatest ever player, Kevin Beattie. He was as good as you'll see anywhere in the world in that central defender's role. It is a bit of a cliché to say that somebody 'has everything', but even at that early age Kevin not only looked to have it all, he looked the most complete all-round defender we had ever produced. He was only about five-ten but could outjump a giraffe, was in the Linford sprint-class, had the strength of two men, and to go with all that had such a sweet and dynamic left foot. If this sounds like something only Dr Frankenstein could put together, you ask the best judges of players in the game at that time. You will not get any different an opinion.

After one match, I came into the hotel bar and found Kevin and Brian Greenhoff trying to drink the place dry, ordering drinks even I had never heard of. They were giving the top shelf the most almighty hammering I had ever seen, and that really is saying something when I think of Cooke, Baldwin, Osgood and Hutchinson. Not forgetting, even later than that, the great Howard Kendall who, as Sinatra says, 'Could shoot a pretty good stick with that bottle as well.' Howard is now back on the road to success with Sheffield United, and I'm delighted to see one of the great guys in our game overcome his problems. Howard was a tremendous influence on me, as I watched him, Ball and Harvey become the first three-man midfield combination this country had ever seen. Well, if not the first, definitely the greatest!

That day, I knew that Kevin Beattie was my kind of player – not just because of his drinking but his whole attitude. OK, he went off the rails like so many, but I truly believe that in most of such cases it is down to others. The job of a manager and his staff is to keep players focused on doing their job right, and to get the best out of them every Saturday. I recall one time when Mills had a problem at Stoke City with a very talented lad named Tony Kelly, who signed from Wigan and left to play a big part in Bolton's recent success. This boy was one exceptional talent, with his ability to pass the ball like Glenn Hoddle – need I go on? Tony had a weight problem, which is not the end of the world, but Mills and Chung's way of handling this was to weigh him constantly and tell him that if he did not get to a certain weight, he would not get a game. This in a side in which he was the best player! Such is the ignorance of football management.

Tony would come into my pub after matches distraught, asking my advice on what to do. You probably think it strange, young players asking Alan Hudson for advice! I obviously tried to help him, but ultimately it is the people you go in to work with every day who decide your destiny. What it all comes down to is: if the player respects you, he will listen to you and take notice. Tony was 'cattled' by these two men, who thought that getting mud off your shoes before entering the dressing-room was the key to improving players, and that coming back in the afternoons to do work without the ball would improve their technique.

I would have thought the right way to approach Kelly's problems – and let's not forget, it wasn't exactly drink and drugs – would have been to get him involved in the afternoon training-sessions by letting him take those young players who were in awe of his wonderful talent. This would surely have been to the benefit of everybody at the club. The youngsters would learn, you would know where your player was in the afternoons, and at the same time you would be keeping him from the temptations of all those eateries along his way home. Doing it their way instead made him feel as if it was a punishment, which some coaches and managers tend to do. Because they have got nothing to do in the afternoons themselves, they pick on players to come back and train. Don't think I'm not in favour of players coming back in, but it should be for all the right reasons, the constructive ones. It's all about psychology: making players – those who love the game, as this one did – feel important and needed by not only the team but the club too.

Mills and Chung did not have this ability, the insight and the understanding to see such things. So many like them get carried away with their position in the game. As I've said many times before, that word 'power' has so much to answer for, especially when it is handed to lesser mortals to make us all suffer. Well, I was to suffer no more with these two and finally called it a day when I broke my own golden rule. I let Sammy talk me off the treatment table and into a training session which ripped my hamstring. The frustration of being around idiots I had lost all respect for, of seeing the wonderfully-managed times of Waddington turn into something out of 'Fred Carno's', the professionalism turn into worse than amateurism, and the common sense into nonsense – all this was eating away at me every time I set foot inside the Victoria Ground. I have never regained the respect I once had for the way the club was run, and that remains the case today with the training methods and the style of play under Lou Macari. I'm afraid if you have witnessed all the changes that I have – and not just seen them, but lived through them emotionally and mentally – you cannot help thinking it has been nothing short of sinful; sacking Waddington and letting the likes of Lacey destroy what he built. Once again, in writing this I feel sad that I had to go through it, but as they say, 'It's always out of our control.' How different it could have been if dear old Mr Edwards hadn't chosen that time to die on me!

It is amazing, though, that of all the times I dreamed of captaining Stoke City – and I was promised the job many times by Waddington – it was under the management of Mills that I finally did. It just goes to show that right from the start there was no animosity between us, just a vast difference in outlook on how things should be done at a football club. He went on to Coventry, to do another 'marvellous' job with another one from Ipswich Town, Terry Butcher. Inevitably they both got the old 'tin-tac' – now there's a shock!

I had made up my mind that the time had come, and nobody would stop me. I went in to see our club secretary Mike Potts, and once again explained the situation quite clearly. I put my cards on the table and said that it would be in the best interests of the club, more than myself, to cut my contract. I could not have been any fairer or more honest in my approach – honesty being one of my failings – and told him I could sit out the rest of my contract and watch the world go by from the treatment table. But I was in no position to sit and watch the club I once loved become a laughing stock. Had I seen a manager going about the job the right way, showing signs that the club's future was looking good, I would have hung on until they rolled me out of there through the glass doors. But it had all gone, ended in such a sad way. You might say it left a sour taste in a mouth that had been used to tasting champagne at this once great and respected club – and you know who built it!

22

Captain Fantastic and the Brown Dirt Cowboys

This was the album that Elton introduced to the country the day after I had been at a party with him round at David Frost's house. I introduced myself as one of his greatest fans, which I still am. He asked me what was it like to play at Wembley, to which I replied, 'If you're good enough you have no problem – so you'll be OK, and I'll be there tomorrow to make sure.' He walked out on to the Wembley stage, following The Eagles and The Beach Boys, to an already screaming 120,000 crowd, and said, 'Before I start, I'd like to say Happy Birthday to my new friend Alan Hudson, wherever he is in the audience.' I was six rows in front of him, to see him equal my performance against the Germans.

Before I begin the final chapter of the Alan Hudson story, I thought I would take time to sit and reflect on all the great and famous people I have had the pleasure to come across. One of the biggest and most genuine of them all was Reggie Dwight of Pinner, Middlesex. A life-long Watford fan who watched me play in that

259

demolition of his beloved team in the FA Cup semi-final of 1970 at White Hart Lane, he most certainly never held it against me.

It all came about when Alan Ball and I spent the week racing at Royal Ascot in the mid seventies. We were walking through the grandstand when we bumped into David Frost, who was thrilled to see Bally and invited him to his home in Knightsbridge the following evening. Alan asked if it would be OK for young Hudson to tag along, and the man said it would be a pleasure to have two of the country's finest in his home. I suppose it made a change from politicians. Also there that night were Michael Caine and his charming wife. I found him a very nice, down-to-earth chap, which pleased me – but some years later (in fact, just recently) I mentioned it to him in Langan's Brasserie, and it seemed that the years had changed him: shame!

Elton, who was on a par now with my Beatles collection, walked into the kitchen area wearing his tennis whites with a racket under his arm. In the kitchen was Russell Harty, who was hosting a late-night show then and was a huge arbiter of taste. I remember Keith Moon appearing on it once, and his antics were as crazy as ever. I used to see him from time to time in my early days at the La Chasse club in the West End of London. Both Moon and Harty have since gone on to that great swimming-pool in the sky. Also at La Chasse would be Long John Baldry and my great friend of many years Frankie Allen, the one who took over from Mike Pender of 'Needles and Pins' and 'Sweets for My Sweet' fame. Moon's hobby was driving Rolls-Royces into swimming pools, when he wasn't chucking TV sets out of hotel windows twenty-five floors up. And Dave Sexton thought he had problems with us!

Elton was launching his latest album, *Captain Fantastic and the Brown Dirt Cowboy*, at Wembley Stadium the following day. This was, and still is, one of my all-time favourites, with each song of the highest standard, a standard he has never dropped below. If anything he improved that wonderful voice in his duet with Luciano Pavarotti. The cover was quite amazing, with the artwork even more intricate than the paisley shirts worn by Keith Weller circa 1971. I told Elton that if he could match my performance against the Germans he would be OK, and that a group of us would be there to celebrate my birthday. Danny Gillen, my then wife

Maureen, Kenny Adam, brother John and I lunched at Alexandres before heading down Wembley Way. Elton did me proud by dedicating his first song to me on his entrance to the stage, following the exit of the USA's answer to The Beatles, the one and only Beach Boys. If anybody has a tape of that show I would love to hear it, as to my great disappointment they never brought out a 'live' version of this wonderful performance. Just as in football, we like to store the memorable ones.

I was to meet Elton again after a gig at Earls Court which I attended with my Uncle George, Leslie May and Bobby Eyre. This was another fantastic performance from the man who seems like a good wine. I was to go into his dressing-room after this show to give him my congratulations, and on my way to his steps stole a kiss from the legendary Miss Shirley MacLaine, one of Hollywood's longest-lasting screen goddesses. She is an absolutely stunning lady – and I mean lady, not like so many of today's plastic stars – and one who oozed sheer class and charisma.

My favourite singer from a very early age was Sinatra, as you'll have guessed, closely followed by Tony Bennett, whom I would meet while playing in Seattle. This great crooner sang the national anthem before a match we played against the USA. Having got the 'gen' on this secret, I had a plan, along with Ray Evans, the ex-Spurs and Stoke full-back, to snatch a photo. As I was going up to toss the coin in the centre-circle, I noticed Ray edging the great man on to the touchline, trying to ease me out – but Ray forgot I was a midfield player and had to see every part of the field! I told the referee to wait (just like Sky TV do today) and flew over to get one of my prize possessions. Bennett, at an age even older than Jack Charlton – what a marvellous job he has done, and why did the FA not go for him ahead of Wilkinson? – won a grammy for an 'unplugged' album he recorded.

Mentioning 'unplugged' brings me on to Richard Attenborough, another luvvie who hung around the Chelsea board. At the height of my contract wrangles, he invited me and my wife to the film studios to discuss how he could help. They were making *Young Winston*, with his new discovery, Simon Ward, making his big-screen debut. About the only thing I could ever thank 'Dickie' for was bringing the luscious Raquel Welch to Stamford Bridge.

She visited the Bridge one day and walked along the side where they were building the new stand. We were warming-up when everybody stopped and the balls just went everywhere. A certain Mr Osgood was very interested in meeting her, but she was whisked away in a 'limo'. Ossie scored that day and did a lot more running than usual, to impress her. Well, that can be the only reason. He had got his hands on most cups – but not hers, as some people rumoured. I went off 'Dickie' after he called Ossie in and told him that his drinking partner was an AA candidate. Ossie said: 'Don't believe it, Dickie old boy. Huddy doesn't drive.'

Another singer who helped fill my record-cabinet was a smooth, classy chap whom I met while he was dating Susan George. I met him along with 'God' himself, Bobby Moore. Jack Jones was the first real American superstar I'd met, and I could not have been more impressed; what a really nice guy. I saw many of his shows over here and remain a big fan, with my favourite of his being 'Live For Life'.

In my second season at Chelsea, David Webb got quite pally with Michael Crawford, who was then alias Frank Spencer. He would dine with us at Alexandres and travel to away matches like any ordinary fan. Michael always had time for people around him – much like Frank – but he never caused any problems in our favourite restaurant, like going into the kitchen to show Pepe how to cook Webby's steak tartare. On our trip to Bulgaria in the Cup Winners' Cup, he took time out to show concern about a family problem I had at the time. Just chatting away, he said I looked worried and that if he could help in any way, he would be only too pleased. He was quite sincere, but I could just picture him going around my prefab with his brown raincoat and his little beret on, having them all in stitches. I tried to contact him on his recent return to Britain, to congratulate him on his most wonderful success in 'Phantom', but had no luck. What a fantastically talented man!

Another superstar from the stage was Peter Wyngarde, whom I met at another of Frank Allen's bashes. My brother John, his partner Tommy Trevatt and Les were with me that night as Jason King was in full flight – how he loved a pose. My pal Les, who loved his clothes and also had them all made at Major's, tried to find out where Peter had his 'whistles' done, but Peter was having none of it. We became great friends from there on, with Peter once coming to a house-warming party of mine at my first home in Sispara Gardens, Southfields, SW18. That evening he was late and called to say that his 'Morgan' – there were only six in the world – had broken down. (I said, 'Is that why they only made six?') A friend, Peter Shepherd, said tell him to wait there and I'll shoot down and pick him up. On his arrival, it was like royalty entering the house as Wyngarde – or King, I'm not sure – approached the bar area with the biggest bunch of flowers you've ever seen. Handing them over to my missus, he was a sight to be seen. At this precise moment, my little mate Tony Davis turned to him, gin and tonic in hand, and said, 'Let's get one thing straight, Jason. There's only two kings in this house, and you're not one of them.' That broke the ice, and Peter went on to steal the show as usual with his charming wit and bonhomie. Nice one, TD.

Talking of ice, we were at the Palladium another time to see Frank with the Searchers, and standing in the bar were just Les, Peter and I, with a few other people mingling around. Peter went off somewhere for a minute or so, and came back screaming at everyone in sight that somebody had been tampering with his drink. You see, Wyngarde drank just straight vodka, and the barmaid had put enough ice in there to sink two Titanics. The ice had melted, and Peter thought some clown had been watering it down. He was a drinkers' drinker and a genuine talent. He never did tell us where he bought his suits.

I did not meet Dennis Waterman until after I had left Arsenal. It was at a luncheon one day in Park Lane, and we were at the same table. I was an out-of-work footballer, again, and he was getting knocked out on my TV set a couple of times a week (and always blaming his 'guvnor', John Thaw) in *The Sweeney*. On this particular day, my mate Mick Carter and I were to leave the luncheon with him and go on to terrorise a downstairs cellar bar just off Berkeley Square. It was as if I had known this bloke my entire life. I remember wishing he could have played in our seventies side, such was the passion he had not only for the Blues but the game itself. Believe me, he would have fitted in perfectly with the off-field activities. I have played football several times with Den, and can always say that I have one over him. He will never know if I can act, but I know he can't play – although he did score a magnificent goal in Tony Currie's testimonial a few years ago.

After our first meeting he would come to Stamford Bridge at every opportunity and visit our box, which was sponsored by Christine Matthews, Chelsea's long-serving secretary before Bates arrived. She asked me to look after it for her for the season to entertain a few guests, which is where I got my experience of introducing people to each other, making them welcome to the club and offering them all the best food and drink at Stamford Bridge. Our head waiter Massimo would come around and see if Bobby Moore was OK – and on the odd occasion we would have some lesser mortals in. All in all, these were wonderful times at the club and Christine must take a lot of the credit for looking after the players so well. I could go to her with any problem in the world and in a jiffy it was a problem solved. She did a magnificent job over the years, one, I think, only appreciated by the players. This is where Dennis and I became great friends. I can only say that I do not see enough of the old rascal, and that I look forward to the launch of this book to see that smiling face which has been bashed-in so many times on *Minder* and *The Sweeney*.

One of my all-time favourite groups, whom I rank right up there in the Premier League of music, were Supertramp, now sadly broken up, with their wonderful range of songs from 'Breakfast in America' to 'The Logical Song' and 'Take The Long Way Home' to 'Bloody Well Right'. Then there were their instrumental albums, the only music of that kind I could listen to. It was a treat for the whole of Seattle when they came to play in our Downtown Coliseum within a few months of my arrival. Harry Redknapp, Bobby Howe, Gabby, Tony Davis and I were there to see a fantastic exhibition of sheer brilliance which had the entire audience entranced throughout. Backstage afterwards, they were delighted to see some friendly footballers from back home, and we became bigger fans from then on. This went down as one of the highlights of that season, with even Gabby tapping those old feet that had rapped so many famous shins in their time.

I was to come across the boys again about three years later, when they were playing at the Albert Hall and I was in Alexandres with a friend of mine, Eddie Petros. While finishing our meal, we heard that they were partying in The Pheasantry, which to my delight was on the next block. It was where Tommy Baldwin and Charlie Cooke closed up at night. Obviously, we joined their party and reminded them of the welcome we had given them in Seattle; and needless to say, the greeting was returned. Dougie Thompson once told me in Seattle that if the *Breakfast in America* album was unsuccessful, they would all have to go their separate ways being labelled a failure. I'm delighted to say that it was one of the best-sellers of all time and kept them together, to the delight of millions of music lovers. I am proud to rank them along with the greats of their and all the other fields that I have had the pleasure to meet.

Other legends of their sport that I have come across include the 'King and I, two of the greatest cricketers to ever grace the field for their respective countries. Both are great football lovers, with Ian Botham having played for Scunthorpe while Viv Richards represented his country at both football and cricket, in which he was, to my mind, the 'boss'. As a kid, I never thought I'd ever see another like Gary Sobers, but the Man up there keeps coming up with these kind of geniuses. To watch Viv, and the ease and grace with which he hits bowlers to every part of the ground, is another testimony to 'The Working Man's Ballet'. I would say that when these two were at the wicket, and in form, playing for Somerset, it was the most impossible situation for any bowler. Talk about nowhere to hide! I had the pleasure to meet both men and found them like most other genuine superstars I come across, simply delightful. The first time I met the great Vivian it was as if we had met before, such is the way he puts people at ease. He epitomises greatness and shows that life is not about 'what you are' but 'who you are'. It really was a fantastic thrill to be in such a wonderful man's company. And I can tell you, I am not easily impressed.

I was once travelling through Germany after doing a coaching clinic in my Arsenal days, when a journalist pulled me aside at the airport and invited me across to meet a band of golfers, which included Seve Ballesteros. I found him quite charming, and although I am not a golfing fan, I have followed his career ever since and was absolutely thrilled when he reached those tremendous heights a decade ago. While in Puerto Banos one year with my pal George

Byatt, I bumped into the great racing driver Stirling Moss, and once again found that some people who can handle such stardom are a delight. We had a few glasses of wine and once more it seemed as if it was just two old friends bumping into each other along the way.

Over the years there have been numerous stars who have passed through the corridors of Stamford Bridge, which in my day was the Long Bar at the back of the East Stand. The names at that time were my good friends Rodney Bewes, Richard O'Sullivan and his old mucker George Leyton, who still stomachs Barnet on a Saturday afternoon. You could walk through and see John Cleese, John Alderton, Lance Percival, my goalkeeping team-mate and ageless Jess Conrad who still defies time with his super good looks; and my good friend, although an Arsenal man at heart, Peter Murray. The first superstar I was to see there, at the tender age of fourteen, was Sean Connery, in his early James Bond days. Connery, or Bond if you like, was very influential on the way I dressed as a youngster, and I can still be impressed with his beautifully-tailored grey suit. This was when I decided to go to Major's; powder-blue shirt, dark tie and handkerchief, which for me was class. With the help of mum and dad, I was to start my wardrobe.

I must also mention the influence going into Fleet Street at an early age had on me, for ever since I was a kid I had always wanted to be a writer if I could not make the grade at my one love. Hence my work today with *Action Replay*, the magazine that will surely become a 'cult', the *Sporting Life* and – where it all started – the *Evening Sentinel*.

The people from whom I have learned my trade over these past few years have been the incomparable Brian Madley of the *Sunday People*, a friend and drinking companion since my exit from Australia; Ken Montgomery, the only man from the 'Street' to witness a Hudson prefab party with all the great names from Chelsea featured in this book; and Jeff Powell, who was my introduction to the media through our friendship with the agent Ken Adam, to whom I owe a great deal for his help in getting this book on the shelves.

I must also mention Hugh McIlvanney who, like Charlie Cooke, was very unpredictable, not only with the pen but with the bottle. In the early days he would drool over the silky skills of Charlie – a little biased because of their Scottish upbringing, but who isn't? Lastly, the most avid 'Blue' to come out of this part of the city, Nigel Clarke, and his photographic side-kick Kent Gavin. I did a shoot for the Chelsea–Manchester United Cup Final with these two, and driving down the King's Road was like going back through a time tunnel, only to find that all our favourite 'joints' had disappeared. A quick mention must go to the 'little people', who never get heard of in the big cities, and a man who is as talented as all his peers, Peter Hewitt, whom I met at my first press conference on arriving at Stoke-on-Trent station back in 1974. The likes of 'Percy', to his office pals, will carry their flag and go unnoticed in this very vast industry.

We must not forget the Editors, and I have to say that if all my managers had been like the three I know best, I might have had quite a different story to tell. My first memory of Neville Holden was when he threw Terry Neill out of his office after the fracas in Australia – TN thought he was in his office with one of his players. Nev's been a pal ever since. Then we have my two current bosses: first, Mr Sean Dooley of Stoke's *Evening Sentinel*, who I've been with for about six years now. I have such great respect for the way he runs that terrific paper, and for the way he has overcome his medical problems and still finds time to buy me lunch. I finish with the incomparable Tom Clarke. He is a man I have known distantly for many years, yet I have never known anyone to be held in such high esteem by all his co-workers. That, I think, is a testament not only to his work but, more important, to his ability to relate and get on with people.

The reason I mention all these different people, from so many varying industries, is because I believe that life is very much like a kiddies' jigsaw puzzle, and these are the pieces in my puzzle so far. I have laughed with most of the names mentioned – which is more important than being a big star – and can testify that it really is rewarding, and sometimes astonishing, that the bigger and greater the person, the nicer they are. And there is no in-between, for stardom either goes one way or the other, to your heart or to your head. I'm one of the lucky ones – I was never any good with my head!

Greatness, in my eyes, cannot be judged simply from a person's ability on the football field, cricket pitch, movie screen, race track, or up there on the big stage. It is how they carry that ability into the real world that is the key. That is why I have taken time to write this chapter, for my life is, and always will be, in the entertainment business. I can assure you that the names I have mentioned are just like the man on the street, and to me *that* is what makes a star!

23

And Now the End is Near

The Final Chapter
In the back of my mind, it was obvious I could not stay away from
this game for too long; the reason being that it left a gaping hole in
my life, and that while there were so many mugs in it, why
shouldn't I? I could not accept this. Frank Sinatra and Alan
Hudson

'In me you see A Man Alone' – one of the all-time great Sinatra
songs, which shows the 'other' side of the great life people see you
have – Frank himself very much included. As I finish this book,
Francis Albert Sinatra is critically ill at the age of eighty-one. What
an absolutely incredible life 'Ol' Blue Eyes' has endured. I said in
my introduction that he was inspirational to everything I tried to
achieve, and I will cherish his songs and music, like millions of
others do, for the rest of my days. You always know greatness when
it carries on into younger generations, and his music stands even
now with the kids of today. Just like that old 'gunslinger' Frank
Worthington carries the torch for Elvis Presley, so I am hooked on
Sinatra, and one thing is for sure: just like Worthington himself,

they both had style in abundance.

It was 1989 and I was now back doing what I loved most, but I had lost my best friend and my father, and was about to lose the man who was responsible for the title of this book. I was at Tony Waddington's bedside on the day of his death and, as we all are when we lose our loved ones, was devastated. He took with him the most wonderful memories of his remarkable life as a husband, father, scout, coach, manager, businessman and friend to anybody who cared to be one, from an audience with the Pope to the man on the Boothen End. I can honestly say that I do not think there was anybody closer to him than I was, and I say that with such pride it almost seems like bragging. It is fitting that you mention the loved ones you lost when you come to the end of your life story – in football, that is – to remind people that they were of such importance to you, and a big part of other people's lives. I still fly the flag for them, for maybe it is not all over yet!

The project was about two years in planning. From the moment I heard that the States would be holding the 1994 World Cup, I felt sure that somebody somewhere was missing something, and that with a little experience 'over the other side' – which is where I came in – it could be done. Although I had been out of the game for three years, my love for it was still there, and I went to matches all over the Midlands every Saturday. One week Wolves, the next West Brom, but my favourite was Derby County, where they seemed to really appreciate their football. We would always get the best treatment there because they were more in touch with what was happening in the higher leagues, having been the most successful team in the region not long before. Stuart Webb, the secretary, would always make a point of coming over for a chat about the good old days of Cloughie.

Stuart was the one who was first in to the dressing-room that dreaded evening when Rioch broke my leg. (I actually walked off the field with a broken leg while Charlie George was stretchered off with the same thing, only it was his arm.) I just sat there, knowing only that something was not right – if you've never had a broken leg before, you don't know, do you? – when Stuart entered the room.

'Are you OK Alan?'

'I think I've broken it, mate.'

'Do you want something, maybe a brandy?'

He must have been watching too many Westerns, I thought, but who am I to argue? He returned with a massive 'Amos' in a lovely big tumbler and placed it right next to me on the bench. At that precise moment, our club doctor popped his head around the door. He had gone out in the afternoon – as they always did before the match – and had a few.

'Are you OK, son?'

'No, I think I've broken it.'

'Try standing up, putting all your weight on your leg, sitting down and standing up again.'

After doing this twice I could not do it any more.

'It's not broken,' he announced, immediately picking up the brandy and emptying the glass in one fell swoop, leaving me sitting there on my own with an empty glass. My pal Micky Carter was the next one in, and when I told him the story he went to find Stuart to get a refill (and one for himself, obviously). Stuart, having heard of me, must have thought I was a bit partial to the stuff.

That evening I went to a nightclub called Maxim's. It was after midnight and I was plotted at the bar when Messrs Waddington and the doctor appeared, totally out of their jurisdiction. 'We have come to see how you are and what you're doing here,' they said, to which I replied that if they could not be bothered to send me straight to hospital, why should I bother about Saturday – after all, I wouldn't be playing with a broken leg, would I? 'You'll be playing at Villa Park on Saturday, mark my words,' said our doctor. The following day, he held up the X-rays at the North Staffs Royal Infirmary and said, 'I thought so, you've broken your fibula.' Thanks but no thanks!

If it wasn't bad enough walking off the field, the only thing I didn't do that night was dance. Carter and I proceeded to the Noah's Ark, right bang opposite the gates of the hospital, where we sat having a livener – which the doc needed more than us – before calling a cab home. That summer, the heat-wave of 1976, was to become the most gruelling of my career but I won the battle, running the back lanes of lovely Barlaston in heats of over ninety degrees, with my old mucker riding my wife's bike next to me.

That, and the match at the Baseball Ground a year earlier, the Saturday after my England debut, were my two memories of the place, and it hit me every time on returning there. I found the people of the area a delight.

This was also the place where I first met Graham Taylor and made a proposal to him about our 'Pre-World Cup Tournament'. I found him very warm and approachable, and must say that although I did not agree with what he did as England manager, he did nothing very different from Robson or Venners. The big advantages Terry had over him were obvious: his upbringing under Docherty, his superb playing career, his charismatic style, his holding the players' utmost respect from word go, and his ability to handle the media. The last, of course, was Taylor's biggest flaw of the lot. We all know he did not deserve the 'turnip head' bit, but he only got that for trying to fight the media, thinking he knew more than them. Well, that is one match that will always be an away win.

Taylor did a truly magnificent job at the Villa, knowing that you had to have great players to get you through – and in Paul McGrath he had the finest all-round centre-half I have seen in my days of being involved with the game. I always say it is between him and Jimmy Hill's mate Alan Hansen, who was a colossus of a footballing centre-half. But the Irish international proved himself all over the world with different teams, including being outstanding in World Cups and European Championships for his country. I would hate to have to choose between the two, but if I could have them both they would be worth a lot more than Shearer and Ferdinand today. Centre-halves have always panicked over the years, kicking the ball out at every given opportunity. With these two it would be like having two 'Fonzes' at the heart of your defence, in an era when it is more important than ever to keep possession. Sky TV even monitors the time of the 'Ball in Play'.

So the outcome with Taylor was that we invited the England team to take part in our tournament. Taylor was very straightforward, explaining that in the FA's wisdom – I thought he was talking about Norman taking over – they were touring Australia. 'How do you prepare for a World Cup in America by going to Australia?' I asked. He had already mentioned Norman Wisdom. I thanked him for his time, while he said he thought it was a great idea, with great insight on my part, and wished me luck with my venture.

Our team putting this all together was Terry Bate, a businessman from Stoke-on-Trent; Trevor Cotton, our Alan Sugar, only he was a gentleman; and Paul McCormack, who is more well-known in the world of horse racing. Living down in the lovely area of Lambourn, how can you not be? Our plan was quite simple, really. All it needed was the contacts at both ends, and I had them – or so I thought. Terry and I did most of the leg-work, meaning we spent most of the time over in Tampa. It all seems very glamorous and you're dead right, it was! We booked into the Holiday Inn on Fowler Avenue, just off the 275 going north, for a while, then moved into a suite at the downtown Riverside Hotel for the best part of nine months. This would be, as my pal Johnny Westwood would say, our HQ.

Our first quest was to get the Tampa Bay Stadium for the tournament. There, Micky Farrell was as easy to work with as Jimmy Greenhoff, and Terry and I jumped that hurdle very sweetly. Everyone seemed impressed; they wanted soccer back on its feet again in the area, following those magic days of the late seventies and early eighties when the crowds were forty thousand, the kids were going in droves and the future of American soccer looked truly exciting. We felt that if we got this right, on a local scale, we would be involved in helping Tampa host their corner of the world in 1994.

Having got the agreement from the stadium, our next step was for Paul and Trevor to sell the idea to the British clubs we wanted to participate. We flew back for a week to finalise the deals and confirm that we had been over to the venue to organise the training facilities, hotels, health clubs etc. You name it, we did it – but the one thing we did not cater for was Rodney Marsh, who was then general manager of Tampa Bay Rowdies. It had only been fifteen years earlier that Rodney and I used to meet in the Markham Arms, talking about how great it was that two local players could make such an impact at clubs like Chelsea, Fulham and Queen's Park Rangers, with England to follow. Now, out of all the people we had come across, he was our stumbling block! We had met with Attorneys, Accountants, Schoolteachers, School Boards, Travel

Boards, the Tourist Board (who were the most interested), the Stadium, Race Relations, Public Relations, Immigration (which was the toughest) – and the only problem we had encountered was this local lad who I used to drink with.

From the moment we put our feet on the runway tarmac, Marsh was letting people around town know that he would do anything in his power to prevent such an event taking place. The president of his club, a Mrs Cornelia Corbett, was rather taken with Marsh, with his golden-haired good looks and charm. Now I know where they got the saying 'Snake Charmer'. (The only 'Charmer' I had ever come across was Chelsea and Tottenham's Tommy Harmer.) It seemed that the president of the club – by all accounts, from a very powerful and wealthy family – had been given the red light by Marsh where we were concerned. Every question was questioned, and every answer too. It appeared that these two were clearly put out that we were coming into town.

The question – and it is always the first in the USA – of finance was the order of the day. Corbett said she had had enough of foreign teams coming over to Tampa, playing matches and leaving town with her club holding the baby, so to speak – meaning they had not paid outstanding 'incidentals' in their hotels, for phone calls, drinks, snacks and so on. We heard a different story from the clubs concerned.

We had it all under control: the stadium, the four teams, who were Nottingham Forest under Clough, Sheffield Wednesday with 'Big Ron', Manchester City whilst in the big time with Reidy, and Billy McNeill's Glasgow Celtic. This was the perfect opportunity for the USA to promote the 1994 World Cup, and for Tampa in particular to put itself ahead of Orlando in the race to be one of those precious venues in the state of Florida. We had organised training sessions, with the local schools coming over to watch and learn from players who they'd only ever read about in magazines. A kiddies' dream, and the Yanks would pay for this. We had the public relations side fixed up – players to spend time each day with the kids, special deals lined up with companies like McDonald's for the kids to come in free of charge – and biggest of all, at the last meeting we had been talking in terms of seven figures for sponsorship. We had even flown Mr Bob Hall, of Midlands TV

Sport, out for a week to organise the television side of it. There was a buzz everywhere we went in the city, except in the English quarter where there would be some jealous remarks. What's new with the people who want to be American in our company and English in theirs?

At our first meeting, while Corbett was on about not paying bills and all the rest of it, we could not have been any fairer. We said in front of the whole office, about twelve people, that they should give us a 'cut-off' date, of maybe six weeks before the tournament, and that if everything wasn't paid then, we would call the whole thing off. That scared Corbett, because now she knew we were serious. She knew that people around town were talking about this great event, and asking why it wasn't being done from inside the community. It would have been so much simpler to organise, it would have put them in a strong position for the World Cup, and more importantly it would have been a feather-in-the-cap for the Rowdies and for her and Marsh. But they were too busy – or did they just not have the insight? – to see into the future. As far as they were concerned they had no competition, which made them think they could just cruise around town as the ones who owned the biggest soccer club in it.

In our meetings – and boy, did we have some – the question most asked of Terry and I was, 'What's in it for us?' We quickly learned this and got in first, just to let them know that we knew what was coming next. I stormed out of one particular meeting after being treated as if I had just come to Tampa – I had had a home there for six or seven years – as a tourist and was trying to jump on some kind of Rodney Marsh bandwagon. I can assure you now, I only get involved with winners. I may get beat from time to time, but that is because I don't cling on to people to provide for me. Anyway, there's nothing wrong in defeat, as long as it is all in the human race – but this quite clearly was not. It was a case of, 'If this goes ahead, Cornelia, we will be left rowing down the railway into the sunset with no coal on the fire.'

We were now into negotiations with the North American Soccer Federation, who we found suddenly had objections to this competition but would not say what it was they were objecting to. We paid deposits to secure the sanction and blessing of the State of

Florida, who were delighted to sponsor it (another word for giving their blessing). 'Real English football coming over for the first time ever' was how almost the whole of Tampa Bay saw it. On top of that, for the clubs involved it would have been a fantastic promotional exercise, with the American kids now being able to relate to their own club in England, sending away for football strips and all the merchandise that goes with it. It was a dream come true for merchandisers. Anheiser Bush, Budweiser's representatives, were as excited as everyone else at the prospect of 'football coming home', not only for this competition but for the 'big one' to follow. Can you imagine the amount Budweiser would sell in a month of football throughout the entire World Cup in Tampa?

It was at about this time that I was paid a visit by my great friends Tommy and Irene Nicholson. For those of you who don't know the City of London, they had the Cartoonist pub; those of you who do will know them. Tommy is Liverpool's representative in London and runs his pubs the same way Shankly used to run his teams, 'keeping it simple'. He is always available for a sing-song at the Horse and Groom these days. Tommy was one of the original Merseybeats and still plays their music in his pub, along with that of every other artist who ever came down the M6 – and from Scouseland there is always one artist or another. He arrived at the famous Bay Harbour Hotel on the causeway leading over to Clearwater, having come to help Terry and me celebrate our great achievement. Sitting by the pool that day I had just left a meeting with Anheiser Bush, so to say I was delighted to see the pair of them could just be spot-on. I was explaining that a million dollars had been mentioned, and the way they reacted made me think I might have gone in too low. But what the heck, we said, and continued to enjoy the beauty of this marvellous hotel. Tommy had come with me the year before in the early stages of setting things up, and was very enthusiastic and excited about the whole event. Mind you, he should have been – he would have been working in the stadium for two weeks, running the bars.

One of the reasons Corbett was trying to stop the event was because she said it coincided with a Rowdies match – they were playing in the College at this time, in front of about 700 people – so we said we could move the dates to suit her, and also pay her for any inconvenience. It was now becoming crunch time, and although Terry and I were still confident about the whole thing going ahead, we had that element of doubt that Marsh and Corbett might have something up their sleeve (probably both wearing it at the same time). We had covered everything there was to be covered – or were we underestimating them? We went to our promotional and marketing offices, where they put in a call to the representatives of the American FA and spoke to a certain Sunil Galatti. For a moment he was a little distant, but then gave us the official sanction we wanted, saying we would receive it in writing the following day. The telephone speakers were open for all to hear, and it was like a scene from a movie as the president is elected. After all the handshakes, Terry and I were out the door to find a place to celebrate. We were on Kennedy Avenue, so we were stuck for places to go. Should it be The Doll House, Terry's second home, Whiskey Joe's, The Conch Club, The Proud Lion, Chillis, who are getting so popular here now, Castaway's, or the Admiral Benbow right next to the office? We really were stuck! Or should we cross over the causeway into Reddington and hit Divino, our little Chicago-Sicilian Crown Royal drinking buddy from way back, who tended a bar in Caddy's on the Waterfront?

We needed to be with a barman we knew, to share not only the joy but the relief this telephone call had brought, not only to us but to all our friends and families involved back in the UK. We were on our way once again, yet another high in the up-and-down world of yours truly. There could be no problems now. I could not go over on my ankle like at West Brom, be hacked from the back by Bruce Rioch, hunted by Terry Neill and Dave Sexton, questioned by Revie and Ramsey, or have my intelligence insulted by Lawrie Calloway and Tony Lacey. I now felt for those last two people who, though they would be in the game all their lives, would leave it with nothing but the joy of aggravating others whom they didn't like to see getting on in life. You see, one of the great things in my life is that when things really go well or take off, I find it is the time to share it. I am a great believer that there is always enough for everybody in this world, and that those who want everything for themselves deserve to be unhappy, and not to see all the wonderful places – bars in our case – around this world of ours. They can sit in their counting-houses for ever and a day, but to go out and achieve what Terry and I did was something more than doing a deal with, as my favourite comedian Les Dawson would say, 'Cheque Book and Pen'.

We never did get that sanction in writing. Only the news, at the other end of a telephone, that a change of decision had been made: 'No'. So Corbett and Marsh had won the battle, but not the war. Devastated though we were – what's new in one's life? – we had had a truly marvellous time putting this together. The last grab at the straw was a visit to the top lawyer and immigration official in Tampa Bay, a certain Mr Richard Maney, one of Florida's most respected and a backer of all great sporting events in the area. I sat in front of Richard as his words made my heart pump faster and faster, using that most wonderful word, 'if'. He explained to me that he was in complete shock about the decision not to sanction this event, but 'if' only we had gone to him in the very beginning there would have been absolutely no problems at all. Telling me that Rodney Marsh would not dare cross him, because he dealt with all immigration matters in the area and had been responsible for sanctioning Marsh's some years ago – and as for Corbett, he knew which way the wind blew with her. This was the opposite of 'music to my ears'. I would rather have had him say that you 'messed up', you did this wrong and that wrong, you abused this and did not do your homework there; but he didn't. He was just so disappointed that Tampa Bay were being represented by two people who were terrified of the shadows that got off the aeroplanes from London.

I do not know where this ranks in the list of disappointments throughout my life; because life, in my case, is all about avoiding them. It is about facing one challenge after the other, and getting over things that look like going in the right direction and then swiftly change. The most hurtful and painful thing is that through all my time in football, I can honestly say I have only come across a mere handful of people who could have done what Marsh did. I can understand people who are notorious for being 'cowboys' or 'conmen' and things like that, but when certain people mix in the same circles as we have over the years and make out to be so-called 'mavericks' it just really makes me so sad. I knew I would overcome this latest and greatest set-back – probably costing our company millions and bankrupting the lot of us in the meantime – because of the investments we made over the years in the States. All because of a fellow Londoner, all those miles away, who you thought might just have said, 'How can we help you succeed?' so that we all could. But no, we all lost including Tampa Bay, which incredibly lost out to Orlando in their quest to stage World Cup matches in 1994.

In fact, after the phone call, Terry and I quickly tried to divert the whole shebang down Interstate 4 and into the home of Disney, and almost succeeded. But that was a different ball-game. We had a couple of people there who loved the idea and tried their damnedest to squeeze it in, but time had beaten us according to Mr John Higgins, who was the man in the Orlando organization, having at one time played with Ferguson at Aberdeen. Had he been in Tampa, we would have found ourselves, as James Cagney said, 'On Top of the World, Ma'. Higgins also told me some time later that the preparation and package that Tampa put forward for the World Cup had not been helped by the refusal to give us the go-ahead. My closing line to John Higgins was: 'There is a Mickey Mouse in both Orlando and Tampa – and thank God you have the right one.' Looking back, this was the last opportunity I had to get back into the game big-time. I have not had much (if any) help from anyone in the game – but having said that, I never really did!

So I finished where I started, with absolutely nothing, but can at least say that I gave more to the game than it gave to me – because everything I got, I had to fight for. OK, you may say 'You didn't help yourself with the way you conducted yourself ', but I see it differently. I was brought up in an age when players were all 'Rebels', 'Rascals' or 'Mavericks', call them what you want, but there was something else about us: we were honest in what we did in our profession, and that is all anyone can ask for. I have met Pele three times, and on each occasion he had a drink in his hand, including the first time when I was an impressionable eighteen-year-old. Bogicevic, my favourite midfield player, was the same. Look at Maradona, Jim Baxter, Jimmy Greaves, Gary Sobers, Viv Richards, Ian Botham, Frank Sinatra and his rat-pack, George Best, Richard Burton – to name just some of the hell-raisers who have given more pleasure to the entire universe than all the conformists, creeps and crawlers, backstabbers, yes-men, do-gooders, and men from Lilleshall who even need a coaching badge. Don't make me laugh; did Sinatra need one?

Today's game is bringing a little sanity back after the helter-skelter football of the mid eighties, when the game was run by the Lilleshall mafia. The likes of Ruud Gullit realised that the man paying extortionate money to watch a match was being not only cheated but brainwashed. As I finish these last few pages, the news of Kevin Keegan walking out on Newcastle has broken. My first reaction was that it was a good job he never had the kind of experiences in his career that I have told you about. He has been spoon-fed in this game of ours since leaving Scunthorpe, and was fortunate enough to be a part of that magnificent castle Bill Shankly built. Keegan has built a castle himself, but his is one of sand. It has no depth or heart and soul which will stand the test of time. For the last two or three years there have always been rumblings within, and as we all come to learn, the trouble stems from the top. It is the man at the helm who steadies the ship, or in this case rocks it constantly. He should have remembered all the attributes which Shankly brought to Liverpool, the biggest being continuity and team-work. By buying the Colombian Asprilla, Keegan broke all the golden rules that Shanks made at Anfield. He disrupted a team which was moving along quite smoothly. What do they say? 'If it isn't broken, don't try to fix it.' My ex-England team-mate has had to carry this on his back, and finally it has become too heavy a burden to carry any longer. He must have looked at this signing every morning and dreaded going home to his bed. Newcastle will survive, but they will never be a Liverpool or Manchester United, for the simple reason that you cannot build a club like that with a cheque book. It comes, as we all know, from the grass roots. Keegan seemed to have a problem with his judgement of a player and, after purchasing him, finding the best way to play him. That to me suggests that he does not have what it takes to become a great 'traditional' manager. When I signed for Tony Waddington, he made it quite clear, both to me and the rest of his players, where and how he wanted me to play; so everybody knew what they were doing. In Keegan's case it was the opposite, which is really the end of his story and one he will not recover from, because he has left not only the game but Newcastle United with a reputation like Old Mother Hubbard.

It makes me wonder, and reminds me, how such managers have the authority to make or break people, which coincides with my bumping into a player from my youth team days just recently. Frank Conboy, a full back who could easily hack it in the premiership, along with Johnny Wilson, Harry Wingrove, Roger Wasahlo, Dave Bibby, Alan Cox, Alan Lochead, Kenny Halliday and Ian Frewin were the unlucky ones who were not dealt the right cards. Football, like life, can be tragic and heartbreaking if you don't get a second bite of the cherry. It's like going to war where some don't return and some get left behind. I have very happy memories of my youth team days and the boys mentioned above; it was a shame that so many did get left behind.

I hope you have enjoyed reading this book, and will finish up by saying that it is not all about Alan Hudson, it is all about the Alan Hudsons of this world – only I have taken time (and I have plenty of that, thanks to certain individuals) to sit and put my thoughts and feelings on to paper, for two reasons. First, because I feel so strongly about the wrongdoers in the game; and lastly, because of how very proud I was to be a part of 'The Working Man's Ballet'.

Matthew Harding
A Tribute

At the beginning of this book I wrote of this story being a sad one and in waiting for publication we have just witnessed another tragedy. Matthew Harding, the man who went through every kick, header and tackle with us has tragically been taken away from his friends and loved ones in a horrific helicopter disaster. It was just before midnight on Tuesday 22 October 1996, on his way back from his beloved Chelsea's Coca-Cola Cup match at Bolton when we lost possibly the most famous and inspirational Chelsea fan of all time. I met Matthew only a couple of years ago and it was he who said, 'Yes of course I know Huddy, I've known him for years'. I just stood back and realised that he really meant it, such was his passion for all those players wore the 'blue' of his team.

These are my last words to be written in my first ever book, and they are fittingly going out to Matthew. He belongs in *The Working Man's Ballet* along with the Bill Hudsons, Tony Waddingtons, Peter Housemans and Leslie Mays of our football world because, like all the others, Matthew started from scratch and ended up being such a success in our tiny little world revolving around the game of football. He was heading towards a reputation that would have seen him become one of the most important and influential characters ever to set foot inside a football club.

I left a very sad Matthew Harding just 12 days before this tragic crash, he was disillusioned and disappointed that he was not getting there quickly enough, not getting Chelsea to where HE wanted them to be. He was being held back by powers that were out of his control, for the only thing Matthew ever wanted was Chelsea Football Club and he was prepared to sacrifice almost anything to get it. He did not want it for himself though, he wanted to get it and give it to the fans, but, before he gave it to them, he wanted to finish what he started. He wanted to hand them a club they could be proud of just like the one he started watching in the early 1960s.

Matthew Harding had my utmost respect for what he was about to achieve and we will never know of all the great things he had in store for us. He was a man of fantastic insight, a man who should have been given the opportunity to carry on and 'go with it' instead of being ignored and at times demoralised and insulted by others at the Bridge. The time last season when he was 'barred' from certain parts of the ground was nothing short of ignorance and barbarism, to treat a man who was aiming his club at the stars in this manner was totally unacceptable to the likes of myself who admire men who stand up and show their passion and wear their hearts on their sleeves.

I will never know what Matthew Harding thought of my book for he was due to let me know the day after he left us. So this book finishes the way it started with a feeling of ghostliness hanging over Stamford Bridge. Matthew has gone to the Board Meeting in the sky along with other great names mentioned in this book. He will be sadly missed, not only by those at Stamford Bridge but by everybody who had the great fortune to meet him and be touched by him.

My dedication to Matthew Harding I feel should be the last part of this book. This tribute could go on for ever so I will clsoe by saying that 'Blue Really Is The Colour'.

Backword
by Tommy Docherty

Having come to me at the age of thirteen, Alan was immediately noted as a player who would go far in the game. We had some brilliantly gifted youngsters in those days at Stamford Bridge and he was no exception. From those Tuesday and Thursday evening sessions I had him noted as the successor to Terry Venables in a side that was brimming with young talent. I signed him in England's finest hour when winning the 1966 World Cup and had no doubt that he would become one of Chelsea's all-time great footballers. I was proved right!

I left the club, and sadly Alan, behind while he was nursing a knee injury which threatened his career at such an early age. He emerged three years later and took the country by storm and I was quite proud to be a part of his growing into such a player. I had him in the first team squad at the age of fifteen years of age and was tempted to play him then, but this mystery knee injury stopped me from doing so. I only wish I could have taken him with me to Manchester United to captain that terrific young side there.

Years and incredibly two international caps later, he is still a great friend and as passionate about the game as the day I left Stamford bridge. I was proud to have been his boss – which he still calls me – and could never understand how he never became one too. His knowledge, as you've seen from this book, is second to none. Alan Hudson is journalism's gain while it is football's loss. He would have been one of the new breed of real football coaches and managers who could pass all that vast experience on to those coming through, something in this country we have lacked for so very long. Alan would have been a revelation as a manager but once again it is a case of 'Not what you know, but who you know'. *The Working Man's Ballet* is yet another reminder of his charm, humour, talent and overall personality. My only regret was that he was not Scottish, for when I was manager alongside Baxter and Law we would have seen a real international footballer. It is my privilege to be asked to do a piece to finish this book and wish him as much luck with it as he had while playing our great game so brilliantly.

Afterthoughts

Nureyev of the King's Road by Tom Tranter

In 1959 at the age of 19 I left home in Shropshire to begin my life in London. I was born in Iron Bridge – as was William Ambrose Wright, my boyhood hero. Captain of Wolves and England, he lived down the road from my parents.

I wanted to become a physical education teacher and I looked at the list of colleges I could attend and then I saw the one for me – the College of St Mark and St John, King's Road, Chelsea, London SW10. I was unaware at the time of the real significance that the King's Road would have for me in the years to come.

I searched on a map of London for the position of the college. It lay between the King's Road and the Fulham Road and was directly across from Stamford Bridge! My decision was made and it was SW10 for me.

In May 1965, after teaching in Notting Hill Gate for two years at Isaac Newton School, I was offered the job as Head of Physical Education at Kingsley School, Glebe Place, Chelsea. Kingsley was an old Victorian building with classrooms situated around a central hall. I soon learnt that the boys who attended this school came from the World's End, Lots Road and the area around Fulham Broadway. They were all Chelsea or Fulham football fans and all

286

characters in their own way.

A colleague of mine, John Harvey, told me there was an outstanding young footballer at Kingsley School by the name of Alan Hudson. Alan became my pupil and I his teacher, and I look back with great pleasure to our relationship at this time. Alan and his dear friend Orville (Bill) Boyce, an outstanding cricketer and athlete, were my assistants, rustling up boys to play for school teams, checking out the kit and making sure the young 12-year-olds knew how to get to Hammersmith and on to a number 72 bus to get to the Barn Elms playing fields on Saturday mornings.

Kingsley School soon gained a reputation in all sports. With only a small number of pupils compared to other schools in West London we won many trophies in the mid 1960s. Alan was a leading light in this success and he inspired the younger pupils with his enthusiasm and love of sport. He was talented, modest and reliable, and he represented the school with distinction in Association Football, Cricket and Athletics. He was an outstanding leader who could easily have developed into a young man only interested in his own importance as a future professional footballer with Chelsea Football Club. Instead, he encouraged those of his own age and was a hero figure to the younger boys.

I met Bill and Barbara Hudson on many occasions and they were great supporters of Kingsley School and West London Schools football, not to say Chelsea Old Boys. Alan was a model pupil, punctual, always smart in his school uniform (soon to be exchanged for fashionable clothes bought in the King's Road) and extremely co-operative as far as his teachers were concerned.

I talked to Alan's dad about his future. Chelsea had first refusal as his brother John had already signed for them, but Wilf Chitty desperately wanted Alan to sign for West Ham. We all know the outcome. Whatever was to happen in the future, I knew that the very special talents of Alan Hudson would make its mark on professional football in this country during the 1960s and 70s.

I have one vivid and lasting memory of the Hudson skill. You have heard of the Cruyff turn, the Zico turn and Littbanski turn, but the Hudson 'drag-back' was equal to any of these. Alan would take the ball up to an opponent and tempt the tackle before dragging the ball back and forward and past the defender. I can verify to the fact that this move was almost impossible to stop without conceding a free kick.

It is a real pleasure for me to make this small contribution to the book. Alan, I have followed your career with great interest and I wish you all the success you deserve with the book and for the future.

By Sean Dooley, Editor, Stoke *Evening Sentinel*

As any football manager will testify, having Alan Hudson on the books is not unlike playing basketball with a hand grenade – the exhilaration of getting the missile through the hoop is only exceeded by the relief of catching it before it hits the floor and paralyses everyone within a ten-mile radius.

Alan is one of those infuriating people who have a natural ability to do many of the things we'd like to do ourselves but never quite manage because hard work isn't a complete substitute for flair. And that goes just as much for his talent to survive life's colourful moments as for his legendary skills on the pitch.

For me he is a gift. The facility to combine knowledge and outrageous irreverence with the discipline to file his copy on time is a hallmark of a born columnist. It probably also explains why he manages to stay original, controversial and essential reading.

What it doesn't always explain is how he manages to stay alive! There is hardly a manager or player of note who hasn't had a red card from Hudson. He enrages fans, exasperates administrators and loves nothing more than to fly in the face of current football wisdom.

Survive he does though – on passion, unquestionable insight into the game and having a reputation of being a genius on the field. And in the Potteries, where they understand these things, that counts for almost everything.

By Tom Clarke, Editor, *The Sporting Life*

Alan Hudson is different, very different, perhaps too different for his own good.

As a footballer, he was blessed with extraordinary talent and imagination, and he was cursed with being a determined non-conformist. He could read a game and pass the ball as well as anybody of his time, but, such was the perception of him, he played only twice for England.

As a football columnist, he has a wisdom, sharpness and clarity that are matched by few writers; he has, too, an unrelenting dislike of those whose views don't match his own.

Huddy won't compromise. He has a vision of his working-man's ballet: it's not just a game of passion and patterns on the field, it's also the game which provides extra pleasures for people, like the dream of winning the pools or having a few pounds with the bookies.

He's complex and controversial and, above all, he knows what he's talking about. That's why *The Sporting Life* likes him and his work.